INVOLUNTARY CLIENTS
IN SOCIAL WORK PRACTICE

MODERN APPLICATIONS OF SOCIAL WORK

An Aldine de Gruyter Series of Texts and Monographs

SERIES EDITOR

James K. Whittaker

INVOLUNTARY CLIENTS IN SOCIAL WORK PRACTICE

A Research-Based Approach

André Ivanoff, Betty J. Blythe, and
Tony Tripodi

ALDINE DE GRUYTER
New York

About the Authors

André Ivanoff is Associate Professor of Social Work at Columbia University School of Social Work where she teaches clinical practice. Dr. Ivanoff conducts assessment and intervention research on mental health issues in criminal justice populations.

Betty J. Blythe is Professor of Social Work at Florida International University and directs the School's MSW Program. Dr. Blythe is Principal Investigator of a large experimental study to evaluate the effectiveness of family preservation services in the state of Michigan.

Tony Tripodi is Associate Director, Ph.D Program Coordinator, and Professor of Social Work, Florida International University.

Copyright © 1994 Walter de Gruyter, Inc., New York

ALDINE DE GRUYTER
A division of Walter de Gruyter, Inc.
200 Saw Mill River Road
Hawthorne, New York 10532

This publication is printed on acid-free paper ∞

Library of Congress Cataloging-in-Publication Data
Ivanoff, André Marie.
    Involuntary clients in social work practice : a research-based
approach / André Ivanoff, Betty J. Blythe, and Tony Tripodi.
        p.   cm. — (Modern applications of social work)
    Includes bibliographical references and index.
    ISBN 0-202-36087-3 (cloth : alk. paper). — ISBN 0-202-36088-1
(pbk. : alk. paper)
    1. Social service—Research—Methodology.   2. Social service.
I. Blythe, Betty J.   II. Tripodi, Tony.   III. Title.   IV. Series.
HV11.I93   1994
361.3'2—dc20   93-36647
                                                                  CIP

Manufactured in the United States of America

10 9 8 7 6 5 4 3 2 1

To Alexander and Andy, With Our Love
To Stephen and David

Contents

Foreword

While not setting out to write a book about social policy, Ivanoff, Blythe and Tripodi, seasoned and well-known contributors to the spirited debate on the proper relationship of research and practice methods in direct services, have, nonetheless, delivered much useful commentary on *how* those direct services resources ought best be deployed. How refreshing, in a period in social work sometimes awash in the euphoria for "prevention," to hear a clear call for commitment of skilled professional resources for those citizens whose serious and often multiple problems have already deeply involved them in public sector services. How welcome the strong and unqualified plea for more systematic and sympathetic attention to those whose initial encounter with a social worker is often not of their choosing: this, alone, a welcome counterpoint to the oft-heard (and only sometimes justified) caricature of social work "clinical practice" as co-terminus with the private, voluntary, fee-for-service variety.

These authors, clinical researchers and practice scholars, do indeed have a "policy" perspective. It is that direct social work services, properly designed, implemented and continuously evaluated, have a critical role to play in the lives of those who are afflicted with chronic mental illness, or who are detained in the criminal justice system, or who, like characters in some unpublished novel by Kafka, are caught up in the bewildering labyrinth of the child protective service system. It is also that "involuntary" clients, who are all too frequently poor and who come from communities lacking in basic services, are no less deserving of the respect accorded by the provision of up to date, systematic and well crafted social services delivered by knowledgeable professionals who care about their clientele.

Ivanoff, Blythe and Tripodi go beyond the offering of a simple prescription for involuntary clients in social services. Indeed, they begin by helping us think through the gradations of "involuntariness" in ways that are helpful in assessing the client in situ. Moreover, their pragmatic (and undogmatic) approach to using the products and processes of research to guide practice activity helps ensure that practitioners will not only offer the "right medicine" but will titrate the dosage relative to each client's unique situation to ensure maximum effectiveness. I find much that is empowering for clients and workers alike in a strategy of practice that systematically seeks out alternative remedies, assays their relative merits and, once chosen, carefully evaluates their effectiveness. Following the many useful guidelines offered in this richly detailed practice text will help workers make the shift from a passive-reactive to a more proactive, critical, and inquiring practice stance. Similarly, clients will be helped to become more critical consumers of services through a more active partnership at all points in the helping encounter.

One hopes that the data generated by these front line practitioners cum "personal scientists" and the citizen-clients they serve will provide a major knowledge source for the next generation of service policy experiments and serve in significant ways as a reality check on the voguish social science theory and moral presumptions of culpability that often stimulate such efforts. This current volume, rich in its implications for both practice and research, helps ensure that this will happen.

James K. Whittaker
The University of Washington

Acknowledgments

The material in this text is drawn from our collective research and years of teaching and practice. To our students, clients, and colleagues who have participated in these endeavors, we are grateful. We are indebted to Pressley Ridge Schools and the Families First Program of Michigan, and to the New York State Office of Mental Health Bureau of Forensic Services for permission to reprint clinical forms. We would also like to thank Karl Gohlke, Stuart Kirk, Susan McNeill, and Martha Tjhin for their helpful comments on chapter drafts, and Faye Jacob for research and library assistance. We would also like to express our appreciation to Ned Walsh, Dolores Ogle, Marcia Piel and Virginia Rhodes for typing and administrative assistance. Special thanks are due to Arlene Perazzini, for support in our labors.

Chapter 1

Introduction

PURPOSE OF THE BOOK

This book describes social work practice with a challenging client population: those clients who do not voluntarily seek help from social workers. Three basic aims are emphasized. First, concepts, principles, and techniques for effectively working with involuntary clients are presented and exemplified in the following settings: child protective services, mental health, and criminal justice agencies. Viewing settings along a continuum of client restrictiveness, that is, the degree to which personal freedoms are limited, ranging from low restrictiveness to high restrictiveness (Hawkins, Almeida, Fabry, and Reitz, 1992), we offer practice guidelines for working with clients at varying levels of restrictiveness. The second objective is to describe research-based practice from the viewpoint of the practitioner and to illustrate its application in work with involuntary clients. Research-based practice actively seeks and uses research products to inform the content and process of intervention. It emphasizes the use of systematic methods of assessment, implementation, and evaluation. Practice is the organizing principle, and all research concepts, tools, and procedures are embedded within the context of practice. The third goal is to present guidelines within a phase model of practice, emphasizing key decisions that social workers make in each practice phase. The model we employ is a problem-solving one, which consists of interrelated phases: assessment, planning interventions, implementing interventions, and termination and follow-up (Blythe & Tripodi, 1989). Accordingly, research-based practice is discussed within the framework of the phase model of practice.

This book is written for graduate students, practitioners in human service agencies, and practice theoreticians and researchers. For students, we offer a model of research-based practice in working with difficult client populations. We believe that practice can be research

1

based, and we illustrate how research concepts and tools can be incorporated into everyday practice. Practitioners and their supervisors are provided with a number of clinical examples of effective practice with involuntary clients. Moreover, special attention is devoted to strategies for making and maintaining working relationships to achieve practice objectives with these clients. Practice theoreticians and researchers can consider the relative advantages and disadvantages of incorporating research methods and substantive knowledge obtained from research studies into practice. Most importantly, attention is given to the notion of differential modes of practice in relation to different degrees of restrictiveness found in the various settings where involuntary clients are served. Theoreticians and researchers can consider the extent to which some treatment methods are applicable, irrespective of degree of client restrictiveness, whether some methods should only be used for high degrees of restrictiveness, and whether some methods should be employed primarily for low degrees of restrictiveness. That is, an implicit objective is to stimulate theoreticians to expand their theories of practice to allow for differential uses of techniques as a function of degrees of client restrictiveness and the voluntary-involuntary nature of their clientele. It is hoped that clinical researchers will be stimulated to test the relative efficacy of different approaches for both voluntary and involuntary clients.

THE NEED FOR THIS BOOK

Although Cingolani (1984, p. 442) has called for the social work profession to improve concepts and strategies in work with involuntary clients, little attention has been paid to developing innovations in working with this group of clients in recent years. These clients are found in agencies serving children and their families, schools, criminal justice, and health and mental health settings. It is believed that involuntary clients may number in the millions; yet there is no precise estimate of their number and location (Epstein, 1985). Garvin and Seabury (1984) mention involuntary clients as one category of potential clients. Gitterman (1991) offers preview chapters describing social work practice with "vulnerable populations", voluntary and involuntary. Various authors discuss clients in the three target settings selected for this book: child protective services, mental health services, and criminal justice services. Stein (1981), for instance, discusses working with at-risk families, following a phase model, but does not consider some of the less restrictive services. More recently, Kinney, Haapala, and Booth (1991) describe a specific approach to working with families referred by protective services or mental health services. Similarly, Dixon (1987) outlines a crisis intervention model for working with clients who are potentially suicidal or homicidal. Both of these models represent specific points on a continuum of restrictiveness in child protective services and mental health services. Grodd and Simon (1991) and Netherland (1987) present selected chapters that describe social work practice within correctional services, but they do not focus exclusively on involuntary clients. Rooney (1992) recently has written a book that is devoted in its entirety to involuntary clients. However, it is not written within a framework of research-based practice.

While no other book systematically integrates the themes of involuntary clients, the phase model, and research-based practice, there are some contributions that discuss certain aspects of these themes. As indicated above, there has been very little theoretical and practice research activity geared to involuntary clients. The phase model of social work practice, however, has been addressed several times. Compton and Galaway (1989) provide a basic introduction to the phase model. Garvin and Seabury (1984) also describe the phase model, but do not address follow-up issues in detail. More recently, Whittaker and Tracy (1989) delineate phases of direct social work practice, and Blythe and Tripodi (1989) extend the phase model of direct practice in research-based practice.

Social work education continues to place emphasis on training direct practice students in research and measurement concepts and on evaluating their practice. This book advances Whittaker and Tracy's (1989) call for empirically based practice, as seen in their delineation of the relationship between mission-oriented research and social work practice. Several books have considered the integration of research into social work practice, although only a few examine this from the perspective of the practitioner rather than from that of the researcher. An early contribution came from Fischer (1978), who discussed eclectic social work practice and devoted a chapter to the discussion of one aspect of social work research, single-subject methods, as applied to social work practice. Gambrill (1983) described the use of observational data in social work practice, although not strictly within a phase model. Blythe and Tripodi (1989) articulated a phase model of practice and integrated research concepts of measurement, data gathering, evaluation, and data analysis. This book begins where their work ended, extending and applying the model to social work practice with involuntary clients. It is to be noted that none of the publications mentioned above that have attempted to integrate practice with research has focused on work with involuntary clients.

INVOLUNTARY CLIENTS

Bruce T. is a 22-year-old white male who worked part-time in a sporting goods store until his recent arrest on charges of sale of controlled substances. Along with the general manager of the store, Bruce was arrested selling a kilogram of cocaine to undercover police officers. Because it was his first conviction, Bruce was offered an alternative to the standard sentence of 2+ years in a state correctional facility. His alternative sentence consisted of electronic monitoring, house arrest, community service, and weekly supervision. Bruce is an involuntary client in the criminal justice system.

Langley O. is a 24-year-old mulatto woman of South African descent who came to the United States to attend graduate school at a prestigious university. Following a difficult first year of marginal academic performance, lack of close friendships, and increasing worry about her family's safety at home, Langley appeared to withdraw into delusions of persecution. Fellow students and instructors became quite concerned. Langley was involuntarily admitted to the psychiatric unit of the university hospital after a classmate found a note in a textbook outlining her plans for revenge against those who were tormenting her and for her eventual suicide. Langley is an involuntary client in the mental health system.

Maygar and Nikolai R. are 36-year-old Russian immigrants who belong to an extremely conservative orthodox Jewish sect. They have three children, ages 10, 7, and 4. Reports of suspected child abuse were independently filed by two of the children's public school teachers, who observed bruises on the children's thighs and legs. When investigated, the parents displayed fear and anger, denying any knowledge or occurrence of inappropriately rough punishment. The two children involved immediately stopped attending public school and were enrolled by their parents in a school run by sect leaders. Maygar and Nikolai indicated they had no use for public social services. The child welfare worker investigating the case recommended they be offered family preservation services prior to initiating removal and foster placement procedures. These parents, their children, and even supervising sect leaders became involuntary clients of the child welfare system.

Involuntary clients are persons who receive social and psychological services from human service agencies, but do not actively seek them. Typically they are not motivated to engage in relationships with social work practitioners for the purpose of achieving goals for themselves, their families, and/or other important persons in their environment. According to Epstein, "Involuntary clients tend to be individuals or families who have come to public attention because they are part of a social problem that is currently of official public concern" (1985, p. 250). Hence, the adult felon who is on parole, the chronic schizophrenic who lives in a group home, and the parent who is reported as abusive to his or her child are also examples of involuntary clients. Cingolani (1984) believes that these clients resist involvement with practitioners particularly when their basic reason for contact with human service agencies is the fact that they are defined as deviant or their behavior is viewed as troublesome by others. And, as indicated by Murdach, "(involuntary) clients, despite their wishes to the contrary, are forced by those around them, such as parents, spouses, neighbors, and police, to seek assistance from social workers and other official helpers" (1980, p. 458).

Social work theoreticians (Cingolani, 1984; Epstein, 1985; Rooney, 1992) believe that clients range along a continuum from voluntary to involuntary. At the extreme end of the continuum of voluntary clients are those clients who believe in the value and efficacy of social services such as counseling and who actively seek help in solving their problems and in achieving their personal goals. For example, spouses may voluntarily seek marital counseling from family service agencies; parents may ask for assistance in dealing with tensions to avoid abusing their children; and substance abusers may voluntarily participate in counseling to reduce the frequency of their undesirable behaviors. In contrast to voluntary clients are those involuntary clients who are legally mandated to receive services. These include prisoners and other institutionalized clients in correctional and mental health settings as well as those clients who are mandated by the courts to receive services. Other examples of involuntary services are counseling for alcoholics involved in automobile accidents, group therapy for wife batterers, and parenting skill training for neglectful parents. In the middle ranges of the continuum of voluntary to involuntary clients are those clients who are pressured by important persons in their environment to seek assistance, as in the instance of an employer urging an employee to seek help for a drinking problem or a person pleading with a spouse to participate in marital counseling (Cingolani, 1984).

Following Rooney (1992) we distinguish between legally mandated and non–legally mandated involuntary clients. Unlike Rooney (1992), we do not use the term *nonvoluntary* as a subtype of involuntary client. This is due to the fact that the terms *nonvoluntary* and *involuntary* are difficult to distinguish conceptually. For example, Murdach (1980) uses the term *nonvoluntary* in a way that appears to be identical to the term *involuntary*. Moreover, a dictionary definition of *involuntary* seems to convey the same meaning as *nonvoluntary* (which is not in that dictionary):

1: done contrary to or without choice   2: compulsory   3: not subject to
control of the will. (Merriam Webster Inc., Webster's Ninth New Collegiate Dictionary, 1990, p. 637)

We prefer to use the term *nonmandated involuntary* client instead of
nonvoluntary client to refer to those involuntary clients who are not
legally mandated to receive services but still are pressured or forced to
receive those services. The notion of formal, official, or legal mandates
as opposed to informal pressures from significant others is an important
distinction that we endorse (Cingolani, 1984; Epstein, 1985; Rooney,
1992).

Whether a client is voluntary or involuntary may vary according to
whether the client views the services as desirable or undesirable. As
Epstein (1985) points out, the completely voluntary client does not appear frequently in social work counseling. The client who seeks help for
a given problem, such as assistance in controlling the impulsive behaviors of her child, can became an involuntary client. This is particularly
true when the social worker redefines the problem and offers services
only in the context of this newly defined problem. For example, that
client may be advised to seek individual counseling as well as parent-
child counseling. The client may be reluctant to receive individual counseling but may do so if it is perceived as a condition that must be met
before help can be obtained with her child's behavior problems. On the
contrary, legally mandated involuntary clients, such as involuntary psychiatric patients who are required to receive treatment, may truly act as
if they are voluntary clients.

The degree to which clients are voluntary or involuntary may also
vary in relation to the conception of the client unit as well as the dimen-
sion of time. The client unit may be an individual, dyad, family, or
group. When there are two or more individuals in the client unit, one
may be mandated to receive services or may be receiving services involuntarily while the others may not. Whether or not the other persons are
involuntary clients depends on the degree to which they wish to participate in services provided by the social worker. For example, the
family of an institutionalized mentally ill person, who is an involuntary
client, may voluntarily ask for help in understanding their family member's mental health problem. Or, the social worker may be planning the
institutionalized person's return to the community, and the participation of family members may be required. The degree to which the family
members are reluctant to participate and/or are hostile to the social
worker may be indicants of the involuntary nature of the practitioner-
client relationship.

Over time, the status of a client may change from legally mandated to
nonmandated and vice versa. Thus, those clients who have satisfied the

requirements of their institutionalization (served their time; completed the mandatory counseling with observable changes in behavior; attained an age that is no longer subject to the authorities of the schools and of juvenile court; and so forth) or are no longer perceived as socially deviant, may change their status from involuntary to ex-clients or voluntary clients. And, in contrast, voluntary clients may change their status to involuntary clients. For example, a mother who as a voluntary client is receiving counseling for depression may become an involuntary client if she abuses her children, or if the practitioner learns that she has committed a felony, or if she becomes psychotic and exhibits symptoms that are dangerous to herself or to others.

RESTRICTIVENESS OF SETTING

Social work practitioners work with involuntary clients in a variety of different settings ranging from hospitals and institutions such as prisons, jails, and detention facilities to group homes and temporary shelters to clients' own homes. Hawkins and his colleagues have developed a scale for rating the restrictiveness of living environments and in so doing have developed a definition of restrictive environments for children and youth, which is as follows:

A living environment can be made restrictive by: (A) the *physical facility*, including its appearance (size, institutional look, etc.), its internal structure and equipment (locks, privacy of bathing, kinds of kitchen facilities, etc.), and the physical layout; (B) the *rules and requirements* that affect free movement, activity or other choice; and (C) the *voluntariness with which the children/youths enter or leave* that setting permanently. A setting is restrictive to the extent that one or more of these three factors do the following: (1) limit the frequency, variety, or quality of interpersonal *family relationships* involving the child as a permanent, integral member of a family; (2) limit the opportunities to engage in normal *personal and family responsibilities*, such as cleaning, cooking, managing own allowance, caring for the yard, helping repair things, etc.; (3) limit *personal choices* such as the type of food to eat, when to eat, the temperature of the room, the decor of his/her room, personal clothing, privacy, etc.; (4) limit the child's free choice of *involvement in recreational activities*, such as watching his/her choice of television programs, listening to his/her preferred music, reading books, playing outdoor games, bicycling, etc.; (5) limit the child's *independence of movement* within the setting's rooms and buildings (e.g., via locks, prohibitions), on the property, or in the community; (6) limit *contacts with other environments*, such as shopping, church, schooling outside the agency, homes of friends or relatives, etc.; (7) limit the frequency, variety, or quality of *social relations outside the family*, with normal peers, adults, or

Table 1.1.   High, Moderate, and Low Degrees of Restrictive Settings.

Degrees of Restrictiveness	Type of Services		
	Child Protective Services	Criminal Justice Services	Mental Health Services
High	Child residential treatment facilities Jail (for parents)	Prison and youth training schools Jail	Inpatient Psychiatric facilities and hospitalization
Moderate	Shelters Group homes	Detention facilities Group homes	Group homes Day treatment
Low	Home-based services	Probation or parole services Home-based services	Outpatient clinics Home-based services

younger children; or (8) *identify the child as different* (stigmatize) because neighbors or peers know that the child is in some kind of special care. (1992, p. 55)

Hawkins and his colleagues (1992) also referred to the work of Ransohoff, Zachary, Gaynor, and Hargreaves (1982), who studied the restrictiveness of treatment in psychiatric settings. They conceived of restrictiveness in psychiatric settings as being comprised of limitations on the following dimensions: movements and activity, legal constraints, time, independent use of finances and living arrangements, dosage of medication, and use of physical treatments.

Both of these conceptions of restrictiveness essentially include legal constraints and other restrictions imposed upon clients. The clients who have legal constraints regarding their activities, choices, and responsibilities are, by definition, mandated involuntary clients. These clients, however, can receive services in different settings along a continuum of restrictiveness. Involuntary clients may have limitations imposed on their freedom to choose settings, to move in the settings and outside the settings in the community, to use time in the settings to engage in activities, and/or to choose the types and amounts of services and treatments offered. We employ these notions to refer to a continuum of restrictiveness in settings where social work practitioners work with involuntary clients. In this manner, examples of high, moderate, and low degrees of restrictiveness for clients in child protective, mental health, and correctional services can be depicted as shown in Table 1.1. Within any of those settings, clients may have legal mandates to work with social work practitioners. For example, clients might receive services in a setting with a low degree of restrictiveness, such as their own home, but there may be a court mandate to work with a social worker, as in the case of a client receiving probation services in the community. In contrast, in a highly restrictive setting, clients may be institutionalized, spending required amounts of time in jail, correctional facilities, or psychiatric hospitals.

PHASE MODEL OF PRACTICE

A phase model of practice delineates different stages or phases of practice with social work clients. It specifies activities of the social work practitioner who is practicing from a problem-solving perspective. Hence, it includes decisions, tasks, and activities of the social work practitioner from the first contact with a client unit (individual, family, or group) to the termination of social work contacts. Although the phases depicted in most textbooks on social work practice follow sequentially from the beginning of direct practice with clients to the end, there are variations among various authors with respect to the naming of phases and to the relative emphasis placed on specific activities such as engagement and follow-up (Blythe & Tripodi, 1989; Compton & Galaway, 1989; Garvin & Seabury, 1984; Stein, 1981; and Whittaker & Tracy, 1989). Stein (1981), in discussing social work practice with child welfare clients, emphasizes the beginning phase of assessment of the client's problems at intake, followed by an investigation in a home visit. This, in turn, leads to case planning in which intervention is provided, followed by case termination and follow-up of client's progress. In comparison, Compton and Galaway (1989) emphasize three phases of social work practice, specifying the process of engaging clients but placing less emphasis on follow-up of clients after termination. Compton and Galaway refer to the practitioner's activities in these phases as:

I. *Contact (or Engagement) Phase*
   Engagement and Problem Definition
   Definition of the Problem for Work
   Goal Identification
   Negotiation of Preliminary Contact
   Explanation, Investigation, Data Collection
II. *Contract Phase*
   Assessment and Evaluation
   Formulation of an Action Plan
   Prognosis
III. *Action Phase*
   Carrying Out Plan
   Termination
   Evaluation (1989, pp. 244–245)

Garvin and Seabury (1984) specify activities in their phase model that are similar to those of Compton and Galaway (1989), but suggest that monitoring and evaluation plans should occur at the initial stage of practice. Another distinction is that Garvin and Seabury discuss maintaining client gains and engaging clients in new services during the termination stage. Correspondingly, Whittaker and Tracy (1989) identify sequential but interrelated activities in phases of social treatment. Similar to Stein (1981), Whittaker and Tracy (1989) treat engagement of clients as an activity involved in but not separate from assessment, and they emphasize services for their clientele after termination.

The phase model that we employ in this book is similar to these models. We emphasize a problem-solving framework for practice because it provides a basis for the integration of research into practice. Indeed, many social work authors in the past 30 years have shown similarities between research and practice activities from a problem-solving perspective (Siegel, 1984; Tripodi, 1974). Moreover, it has been demonstrated that social research concepts and tools could easily be incorporated into various stages of practice to help practitioners gather information and make inferences of practice effectiveness that, in turn, are helpful for making decisions within practice phases (Blythe & Tripodi, 1989).

Our phase model is a heuristic device to specify decisions and activities of social work practitioners. As is true in all of the various descriptions of phases in social work practice, there are two main considerations to bear in mind. First, the various phase models of practice are very similar, following a basic problem-solving model from determining client problems and goals, to developing interventions to solve them, to determining whether or not further interventions are required once the problems are solved. The second consideration to bear in mind is that the specified phases (or stages) are interrelated and may exhibit a great degree of overlap when treatment is short-term because the phases are compressed. In contrast, the phases are more likely to be distinct in longer term treatments such as residential treatment for delinquent youth.

The phase model we employ in this book consists of these four sequential and interrelated phases: assessment, planning interventions, implementing interventions, and termination and follow-up. *Assessment* is that phase in which the social worker discerns the nature and extent of problems and issues confronting the client. The practitioner decides on the severity of problems and the necessity for intervention, and also obtains information to determine the parameters of the client system. Is the family the primary client as opposed to a parent or a child, relatives, and/or significant others? Moreover, the practitioner must consider the extent to which the client is voluntary or involuntary, and whether services and interventions are legally mandated or not. Working within the confines of a social agency, the practitioner needs to decide whether the interventions and services available from the agency are appropriate for the clients' problems. The worker also needs to determine whether or not the client is eligible to receive the agency's services. If the client is ineligible, the practitioner seeks to refer the client for more appropriate services elsewhere, For those clients eligible for or mandated to receive services, the practitioner answers questions such as these:

- What are the most important problems, if any, for the client?
- Are the problems sufficiently serious so that intervention is justified?
- Do the problems involve prevention, maintenance, or change of behaviors?
- If the problems require change, what is the desired level of change?

To answer these questions and to make decisions about offering interventions to achieve goals for solving problems, it is necessary for the practitioner to accomplish several important things. The practitioner needs to establish rapport with the client and significant others to facilitate gathering information for making judgments about the clients' problem(s). In addition, in this initial phase of direct practice, it is important to begin to engage the clients in a working relationship. The practitioner explains the types of services and interventions that can be provided, and indicates those activities in which the clients and worker might be involved.

Closely related to and overlapping with the assessment phase is the second phase of direct practice—planning interventions. In this phase, the practitioner specifies more precisely the persons who are to be involved in the intervention and seeks to determine the extent to which the client is willing to participate in the intervention process. Continually seeking to engage the client and significant others in an effective working relationship, the practitioner delineates the treatment goals with respect to the client's problems. Goals may be simple or complex, short-term or long-term. The goals are specified in terms of specific expectations as a result of social work interventions. Thus, they may range from immediate objectives such as getting a significant other to administer psychotropic medication to a partner at scheduled intervals or having a delinquent report at prescribed times to his probation officer (who may be the social worker), to longer range goals, such as reducing instances of verbal child abuse by a child's family or preventing delinquent activities by young people in a low-income community.

Practitioners need to choose those interventions that are most suitable for their particular clients and that are most likely to result in achieving treatment goals. Effective interventions may be identified by reviewing the literature, reviewing the findings of others, and/or examining one's own previous results with clients having similar problems. And, following the selection of one or more interventions, practitioners plan how they will monitor the degree to which each interventions is implemented and specify the predicted changes (or lack of change for prevention and maintenance goals).

The third phase of this phase model is *implementing interventions*, in which the practitioner tests specific interventions in practice. First of all, the practitioner needs to indicate, as precisely as possible, what procedures and activities must be employed in work with the clients targeted for interventions. This task of specifying interventions is known as *proceduralization*. It begins in the second practice phase, planning interventions, and is completed in this phase (Thomas, 1984). Having specified interventions, the practitioner gathers information to make the following determinations: Is the intervention implemented as planned? If not, what modifications can be made to facilitate the intervention? Should a different intervention be introduced if it is not possible to implement the planned intervention? If the intervention is adequately implemented, to what extent is progress being made in achieving the practice goals? If no progress is being made, should the practitioner continue to implement the intervention? If the goals are attained, should the practitioner continue to administer the intervention?

In this phase, the practitioner continues to be alert to the potential discovery of other problems confronting the client and family members. Depending on the severity of these problems, their priority, and their relationship to the problems identified in the assessment phase, the practitioner may decide to continue the intervention, modify it, or introduce other interventions. For example, a practice goal with an adolescent boy may be to increase his frequency of doing homework for the purpose of improving his grades in school. Over time, it might be discovered that it is impossible for him to do his homework due to the chaos in the family. This would necessitate assessing the boy's living situation and examining whether the parents or older siblings are distracting and/or preventing the boy from attending to his homework, and determining how to address the environmental conditions.

The fourth phase is *termination and follow-up*. Termination of clients ideally occurs when all of the practice goals have been attained and there are no serious problems confronting the client; it is the cessation of social work activity with the client. A special type of termination might occur even when the practitioner is continuing to work with the client. This happens in the event that there are multiple goals for a client, and the practitioner chooses to work on only one or a few of them, but not all. If the goals that the worker and client focus on are attained, it can be said that the practitioner terminates work on these goals (but not work with the client) and then begins new work to achieve the other goals (Blythe & Tripodi, 1989, p. 18). The practitioners and clients, however, may terminate their work with each other, for less desirable reasons. The practitioner may determine that an intervention cannot be fully or appropriately implemented or that no progress has been made in a reasonable amount of time. Hence, the practitioner might terminate (cease using) the intervention and choose another, or may terminate all work with the client, preferably referring the client to other workers or other agencies. Or, clients who are legally mandated to receive services might cease working with the practitioner once the legal requirements are waived. More subtly, involuntary clients may disengage from the working relationship, going through the motions of participating in the intervention, but not really incorporating any of the ideas in their daily lives.

Follow-up is contact with the client after an intervention has been terminated to determine whether the gains from the intervention are maintained and whether new problems and issues have arisen for the client. In a sense it involves a reassessment of the client's situations. Follow-up can occur in a planned fashion by arranging with the client one or more contacts (by phone, in person, or by mail) to check on progress and to give the client the opportunity to become reinvolved with social work services. With mandated clients, there may be legally prescribed follow-up in the sense of aftercare. Examples of prescribed follow-up are parole for persons released early from prison and aftercare services for those released from psychiatric institutions. Follow-up contacts also can be made with other professionals who are currently working with the client.

The practitioner continues to gather information regarding the client's progress, and uses those data to make decisions about termination, referral, and reinvolvement in social work services. Ever mindful of the practice goals, the practitioner is alert to information about the client's progress and, simultaneously, is continually focused on engaging and reengaging the client in an effective working relationship. Because this is especially important in work with involuntary clients, we discuss various strategies for engagement and reengagement of clients in subsequent chapters.

RESEARCH-BASED PRACTICE

Empirically based practice has been criticized recently by Witkin as follows: "Because the use of empirically validated interventions and the empirical validation of practice methods are, in practice, based not on empirical data, but on practitioner judgment, the ECP [Empirical Clinical Practice] model does not meet its own criteria of superiority" (1991, p. 159) Essentially, he argues that practice decisions are ultimately based on practitioner judgments, which may or may not be based on "empirical" data. This argument fails to include the notion that the purpose of data and of rules of inference are to provide information for making judgments.

The meaning of *empirical*, according to *Webster's Ninth New Collegiate Dictionary* is as follows:

> **1:** relying on experience or observation alone often without due regard for system and theory   **2:** originating in or based on observation or experience (data)   **3:** capable of being verified or disproved by observation or experiment (laws). (Merriam Webster Inc., 1990, p. 408)

It is obvious from this definition that the books on practice to which we have referred previously in our discussion of the phase model are empirically based! This is due to the fact that practitioners make judgments based on their observations, such as in assessment, and on their experiences with the client, as well as on their other experiences and observations developed from working with other clients. When problem-solving models of practice are employed, these models are empirically based, irrespective of whether or not research methods are employed. That is to say that the application of social research methods is only one way to provide empirical knowledge; a practitioner's use of observations, case notes, process and summary recordings is another way; and still another mode is the use of rules of evidence, as in a court of law.

We use the term *research-based practice* here to avoid the semantic difficulties, confusions, and misuse of the word *empirical*. Research-based practice is defined as direct practice that incorporates research knowledge to provide information for making decisions about practice; it is a subset of empirically based practice. Direct practice is defined as the use of social work interventions with individuals, couples, families, and groups to enhance their intra- and interpersonal functioning, and research knowledge is conceived as being comprised of conceptual, substantive, and methodological knowledge (Tripodi, Fellin, & Meyer, 1983).

We regard conceptual and substantive knowledge as results of previous research about phenomena pertinent to working with clients. This knowledge is in the form of concepts, hypotheses, descriptions, and explanations. For example, knowledge about ways to assess problems for clients from different cultures may be described with concepts such as culture, cultural sensitivity, and cultural relativism. Descriptive knowledge may concern the distributions of demographic characteristics for populations of involuntary clients and explanatory knowledge may refer to client changes brought about as a function of interventions. These types of knowledge can be employed to help social workers make judgments about using assessment tools, choosing interventions to use with their clients, and selecting checklists and other available devices for determining the extent to which interventions are being implemented.

Methodological knowledge refers to the concepts, procedures, and strategies from social research that are employed to gather information and to make inferences about the effectiveness of interventions. Hence, this type of knowledge may include concepts such as reliability, validity, and representativeness; tools such as questionnaires and rating scales; principles for constructing forms and other information-gathering devices; and judgments about effectiveness.

Research-based practice, as we conceive it, begins with practice issues and problems. It employs findings, concepts, and methods to provide information that can be used for making decisions in each phase of practice from assessment to termination and follow-up. Building on our previous work, we believe variables can be identified and used for descriptive or comparative purposes in each phase of practice (Blythe & Tripodi, 1989) and that research procedures can facilitate the development and use of information to inform practitioners when making decisions about implementing, continuing, and discontinuing interventions in work with their clientele (Ivanoff, Blythe, & Briar, 1987; Ivanoff, Robinson, & Blythe, 1987).

We do not offer here a narrow conception of research-based practice as requiring the rigorous application of single-subject design methods. Under certain conditions, it can be useful to employ these designs as mechanisms for making causal inferences. All practice decisions, however, do not need to be based on causal knowledge. Many decisions are based on simple descriptions from quantitative or qualitative data. Moreover, some interventions are based on previous studies and experiences attesting to their effectiveness. In addition, associational knowledge about an intervention and desired client changes, although not causal, can provide information that practice goals have been accomplished.

The spirit of research-based practice is that research knowledge and methods are used as a part of practice. Often empirically based practice is criticized because it has not demonstrated that the use of research procedures in practice will lead to more effective practice (Witkin, 1991). This is not the pertinent question in our way of thinking about research-based practice. The question should be: Can research methods produce information that practitioners can use to facilitate their judgments about practice? The answer is clearly yes! Just to note a few examples, it is obvious from a review of standard practice and research texts in a wide variety of fields that instruments such as questionnaires, interviews, and observations are effective in gathering and summarizing large amounts of information; that operationalizing and specifying concepts leads to greater consistency in their use; that graphic displays and analyses can portray client trends over time in a way that is easy to analyze and understand; that samples of specified populations of people, interviews, interview segments, and the like can be chosen in such a way that they are representative of the populations from which they are drawn; that simple statistical procedures can be employed to show the extent to which practice goals have been attained; and that there are concepts and procedures for considering the extent to which generalizations about practice can be made.

We do not believe in a rigid application of research such that the same protocols and procedures should be used for all clients. Nor do we ascribe to the notion that gathering data should be an end in and of itself. In this book, we offer strategies and suggestions for using research methods that are relevant for important questions that practitioners must answer to assess client problems and implement and evaluate interventions selected to solve those problems.

Due to observed difficulties in working with involuntary clients, practitioners should be knowledgeable about different strategies and procedures for engaging these clients in effective working relationships and for eliciting their cooperation in implementing interventions designed to be relevant to their problems and to the level of restrictiveness of the setting in which the interventions are applied. This, and the fact that there is not a great deal of published knowledge for working with involuntary clients, is a primary reason for this book. But, another basic motivation is that we believe that practitioners should use research methods to help assist in formulating and developing their own knowledge in their work with involuntary clients. This is especially the case when little is known about the client population. Research-based practice can provide basic information that is useful in practice with involuntary clients.

Several books have considered the integration of research into social work practice, although only a few examine this theme from the perspective of the practitioner rather than the researcher. An early contribution came from Fischer (1978), who discussed eclectic social work practice and devoted a chapter to one aspect of social research, single-subject methods, as applied to social work practice. Although not strictly within a phase model, Gambrill (1983) described the use of observational data and data-gathering procedures in social work practice. Blythe and Tripodi (1989) discuss how research concepts can be used in a phase model of practice, in any type of social work practice. However, none of these books focuses on involuntary clients.

FORMAT OF THE BOOK

Chapters 2 through 4 describe in detail phases of research-based practice with involuntary clients. Chapter 2 describes the process of engagement with involuntary clients and the assessment phase, including the identification of variables and measurement tools as well as procedures for increasing the reliability of assessment information. Chapter 3 describes the processes and tasks involved in the next two phases of work with involuntary clients: planning interventions and implementing interventions. Procedures are presented for successfully implementing interventions with involuntary clients and for monitoring their progress in achieving practice goals. Chapter 4 focuses on termination and follow-up with involuntary clients. Mandated and nonmandated terminations are distinguished, and methods for securing participation of involuntary clients in follow-up activities are discussed.

The final three chapters of the book represent the application of our notions of research-based practice with involuntary clients to three types of social services. Chapter 5 describes the application of the phases of research-based practice with involuntary clients in criminal justice services. Examples from various criminal justice settings are presented, and, as in Chapters 6 and 7, attention is given to ways in which to engage clients as well as collaterals in the process of service provision. Chapter 6 describes the application of the phases of research-based practice with involuntary clients in child protective services. Two different practice settings—family preservation services and treatment foster care—are used as case examples. Each setting represents a different level of restrictiveness. Chapter 7 describes research-based practice with involuntary clients in mental health settings. The range of service settings from highly restrictive to less restrictive is explored. Examples from various mental health settings are used to illustrate concepts for engaging clients, assessing problems, developing goals and contracts, selecting research-based interventions, implementing interventions, evaluating client progress, and making judgments about termination and follow-up.

Chapter 2

Engagement and Assessment

Robert S. is a 26-year-old man of mixed Latino and African-American descent, and a parolee who served a sentence of two years for armed robbery. His two children live with his wife, from whom he is separated. Every week Robert meets with his parole officer and drops off a urine sample for drug testing. Robert also participates at a local church with other former offenders in a weekly group that focuses on such life problems as finding a job and staying off drugs. Although one of the individuals in the group sees a clinical practitioner for help in solving life problems, each person in the group receives help from other persons. One attends an Alcoholics Anonymous or Narcotics Anonymous meeting every day. One attends a daily job training program run by the state department of vocational rehabilitation. Another confides in his minister. Finally, the last sees a spiritualist.

Many people find help with problems as a result of participating in some form of treatment intervention. Many people obtain similar, if not better, assistance as a result of interactions with other types of helpers such as self-help group leaders, clergy, and friends. The quality of the relationship between the client and the helping person is extremely important and should not be underestimated. Every major approach to psychosocial intervention emphasizes the importance of the relationship between client and practitioner. This relationship underlies and provides the foundation for client and practitioner interactions. The more positive the relationship between the client and practitioner, the more likely the client is to disclose and explore difficult and personal problems, as well as listen to and act on change efforts or advice offered by the practitioner. This has been demonstrated across fields outside social work, such as education and medicine, as well as in laboratory studies.

By identifying and examining the procedures, events, or circumstances that characterize successful engagement and helping relationships, we can facilitate the development of effective working relationships with involuntary clients. Although it is difficult to develop trust and rapport with clients who do not believe you want or know how to help them, we believe that it is possible with almost all clients. Our approach is a positive one, emphasizing what can realistically be done within the constraints of a formal involuntary helping relationship to maximize the likelihood that the relationship will enhance productive work and change.

CLIENTS AND ENGAGEMENT

The term *client* generally refers to *recipients* of service or treatment, individuals who *come for help* to an agency or practitioner, and who *expect to benefit* from that help. Clients also accept a *contract* to receive service (Garvin & Seabury, 1984). To be a client, the individual must be eligible for service, be socialized into the client role, and enter into the contract (Alcabes & Jones, 1985). In involuntary treatment settings, the recipients of direct service do not ask or apply for service, may not willingly accept service, and may not see the need for or any possible gain from service. Yet, those recipients must be regarded as clients. They possess identified problems, and by virtue of contacts with the practitioners, demonstrate minimal acceptance and compliance with the activities of treatment.

In direct practice, client engagement is comprised of two activities: (1) establishing a beginning relationship of trust between the client and the practitioner; and (2) establishing the client in the role of "client," willing to mutually identify and work on the identified target problem. Establishing rapport and creating a "helping alliance" (Luborsky, 1984) are terms that also describe what we refer to as engagement.

Voluntary clients usually approach a practitioner or agency with mixed feelings. In work with voluntary clients, the variables of concern in engagement are often discussed under the topic of "relationship enhancement." This assumes a neutral, if not positive, start. Specific techniques for developing relationships with clients, known as relationship enhancers, include client structuring, imitation, and conformity; helper expertness, credibility, empathy, warmth, and self-disclosure; helper-client matching, physical closeness and posture, and negotiation of meaning; and overcoming helper-client cultural differences (cf. Goldstein & Higginbotham, 1991). Psychotherapy research with voluntary clients suggests the quality of the practitioner-client relationship improves as the quantity and quality of these enhancers increase. These individual relationship enhancers group together to create the three qualities most often attributed to effective practitioners: interpersonal attraction, perceived expertness, and trustworthiness (Beutler, 1979;

Weary, 1987; Beutler & Clarkin, 1990). These qualities are based on research studying interpersonal influence in persuasive relationships and have been widely applied to psychological interventions. The relationship between practitioner and the voluntary client is heavily influenced in a positive manner by preexisting attitudes about treatment the client brings to the relationship, the client's interactions with specific practitioners, and the client's initially positive global attributions about treatment. In contrast, an involuntary client's preconceptions about treatment and the practitioner are initially negatively weighted. This means the practitioner–involuntary client relationship cannot depend on the same positive persuasive factors that can facilitate relationship enhancement with voluntary clients.

The small but significant body of data available on engagement with involuntary clients is slightly at odds with, and in some cases is even contrary to, the research on engagement with voluntary clients. As we begin to understand more about the influence of involuntary status on the worker-client relationship, data suggest that the same variables that enhance effective relationships with voluntary clients may be irrelevant or even have a negative influence on relationships with other types of clients. For example, practitioner empathy and genuineness are widely described and accepted as key characteristics of successful practice. Research over the past two decades, however, suggests that among some groups of juvenile delinquents, an empathic, genuine helping relationship may overwhelm the client, particularly in the early stages of treatment (Edelman & Goldstein, 1984; Goldstein, Heller, & Sechrest, 1966). This is consistent with data on clients suffering from some major mental disorders and antisocial personality disorder (Strasburger, 1986). Clinical findings concur with these studies across numerous client subgroups (Munjack & Oziel, 1978). DeVoge & Beck (1978), for example, describe hostile clients or those who "prefer noncompliance or resistance" toward a practitioner as those for whom the closeness, submissiveness, and warmth of the ideal clinical relationship could be highly aversive.

Obstacles to Engagement With Involuntary Clients

Because engaging involuntary clients often requires special considerations and actions by the social worker, it is helpful to examine obstacles that may need to be addressed. There are four major sets of obstacles to successful engagement with involuntary clients:

1. Practitioner-centered obstacles including problem orientation and worldview, professional expectations, and inadequate training.

2. Client-centered obstacles including reluctance, unwillingness, and noncompliant behavior; overagreeable or compliant behavior.
3. Environmentally centered obstacles including the sociopolitical bases of mandated treatment and the agency and setting demands.
4. Client-environment centered obstacles such as malingering and deception.

Practitioner-Centered Obstacles

Problem orientation and worldview.   Problem orientation is a set of responses an individual typically makes when reacting to problem situations. Orienting responses include one's sensitivity to problems and a set of general and relatively stable beliefs, assumptions, appraisals, values, and expectations concerning life's problems and one's own general problem-solving ability. Depending on the specific nature of these cognitive variables, a particular problem orientation may have either a facilitative or disruptive effect on subsequent problem-solving. For example, if a female practitioner believes she has major difficulty establishing relationships with particular types of male clients, then it is likely that she will tend to avoid active attempts at problem-solving that might enable her to establish relationships with these types of clients. Several orientation variables relevant to clinical situations cut across theoretical orientations. These mainly involve attitudes and values about social dysfunction or deviance and mental health. For example, most practitioners, regardless of orientation, view clinical intervention as a viable means for people to deal with their psychosocial difficulties. The practitioner's worldview also affects problem orientation. Worldviews are cohesive philosophical frameworks within which people attempt to understand how the world works (Pepper, 1942). For social workers, the major concern regarding a worldview revolves around the way people function. This worldview provides a perspective that helps in understanding, predicting, and explaining human behavior and psychopathology.

The practitioner's problem orientation and worldview, as well as that of the client, affect assessment and treatment in powerful ways. Research indicates that what the worker and client think, feel, and assume about each other may be at least as important as the intervention techniques per se (Lorion, 1974; Lorion & Parron, 1985). Problem orientation and worldview variables may decrease a practitioner's ability to engage involuntary clients. The problem orientation and worldview a practitioner brings to work with an involuntary client reflect an accumulation of experience and reinforced learning over time. Bias and stereotypes about certain groups of people unfortunately create some of these expectations.

The perceived effects of malingering and deception, discussed more under client-environment obstacles to engagement, are also commonly tied to the worker's problem orientation and worldview. "The pride of a doctor who has caught a malingerer is akin to that of a fisherman who has landed an enormous fish" (Asher, 1972, p. 145). The sense of pleasure found in identifying a malingerer results from the insult taken from the deceit and also from the misperception that the sole purpose of such behavior is purely external and conscious (Menninger, 1935). Fortunately, as workers' assessment and diagnostic skills improve in this area, many learn to avoid personalizing the "apparent personal effrontery" of deceptive patients (Rogers, 1988, p. 14).

Studies of practitioners working with lower socioeconomic status (SES) clients demonstrate that practitioners possess common misconceptions of the lives of economically disadvantaged people (Lorion & Felner, 1986). For a variety of reasons, largely environmental, involuntary clients are more likely to come from lower SES backgrounds. Common stereotypes about lower SES clients include homogeneity across all people, and assumptions of a bleak, joyless life (Lorion & Parron, 1985). Long-standing misconceptions are also held about the unreliability and impulsivity of low-income individuals (Turner & Armstrong, 1981). These can have potentially damaging effects on the practitioner's attitude toward working with economically disadvantaged clients. To counteract these misconceptions, carefully defining pejorative terms is a useful exercise. Is an unreliable individual one who is occasionally late to appointments due to reliance on an erratic public transportation system? Is impulsivity buying a toy for a child immediately after cashing a public assistance check? Is not having money left at midmonth indicative of impulsive spending or a reality of economic hardship?

While it is true that some involuntary and voluntary clients do have problems with reliability and with impulsivity, the practitioner should not assume that *all* clients of involuntary status possess these negative characteristics associated with social dysfunction. Moreover, the practitioner should carefully examine assumptions based on such client characteristics as ethnicity, gender, sexual orientation, or economic status that may affect work with clients.

Professional expectations. Beginning practitioners often interpret silence, hostility, or other indications of unwillingness on the part of the client as meaning that the client devalues them or that they (practitioners) lack certain skills. Even experienced practitioners can fall prey to this type of cognitive trap. The thinking attached to these interpretations includes thoughts such as, I'm not a good practitioner; My client isn't cooperating because I'm doing something wrong; My client doesn't like me; I'm doing everything I can to establish rapport and it's not working!

These errors in thinking can be caused by (1) the practitioner's failure to acknowledge the reasonableness of the client's unwilling position, and (2) the practitioner's expectations of a good client. When these expectations go unmet, the worker experiences feelings of disappointment. A practitioner who is unable or unwilling to accept the client as involuntary experiences frustration, impatience, and feelings of failure. A practitioner who fails to respond appropriately to a client's unwillingness, and avoids the mention of involuntary status may communicate irritation and prevent positive relationship development.

Inadequate training.   A final practitioner-centered obstacle is the lack of appropriate training for working with involuntary clients. Few practitioners are taught to deal effectively with negatively charged emotional material, reluctance, or noncompliant behavior. There are few didactics, standard role play exercises, or internship opportunities that prepare practitioners to work with these clients. Even in settings that offer opportunities for work with involuntary clients, trainees may be protected from the experience by only being given easy cases, or by doing follow-up after the client has been engaged and served. Thus, workers often meet with frustration when they cannot successfully engage involuntary clients and, ultimately, may experience job stress or burnout.

Client-Centered Obstacles

Reluctance, unwillingness, and noncompliant behavior.   Why are involuntary clients unwilling? Don't they understand that practitioners could help them fix their lives if they would only listen and learn? While this is intended as flippant, even the best workers sometimes have these thoughts as they work with involuntary clients. It is important to understand the sources of uncooperative behavior, even if not all of them can be meaningfully overcome. Vriend and Dyer (1973) suggest several broad causal categories. One category involves basic acknowledgment of the problem. When confronted by a helpful practitioner asking, "How can I help you?" or "What is your problem?" clients are forced to admit to another person, and to themselves, that they are experiencing difficulties in some aspect of their lives. Giving in or acquiescing to the situation by acknowledging a problem may be regarded as admitting to failure. Simply avoiding this unpleasant experience by *not admitting* a problem can help maintain a more stable self-image. This is a logical and entirely reasonable response because coping with life is easier when one's sense of self, no matter how distorted, is stable.

As discussed earlier, most involuntary clients do not arrive at treatment of their own volition, but are mandated to receive treatment by a third party. Cooperating with the worker or agency in this situation may be an admission that the referring party is right and that a problem exists. Moreover, it implies that the referring agent knows more about the client than the client does. Why should any client fully submit to the implications of a diagnosis or value judgment by a court, mental health practitioner, or child welfare authority? Indicating disagreement or reluctance to agree with the purpose and method for the mandate may disprove the notion that the referral source was correct in the first place, or at least offer the hope that the alleged problem will be disproved.

Some involuntary clients have fought long, hard battles against "the system" with varying success. Some have witnessed friends and family receive little help and perhaps even harm from other helpers supposedly in a position to provide assistance. For a variety of reasons, a client may learn to act against the system, taking on a role as rebel or class advocate, often as a way of accomplishing personal goals. In searching out the causes of reluctant behavior, the practitioner should remember that the act of being nonconformist or uncooperative is an avenue for acceptance in some circles. The acting-out inmate, overly strict parent, or aggressive inpatient dealing with staff can frequently gain the attention and approval of his peers. Similarly, aggressive delinquents who stake out certain street territories may gain dominance, acceptance and a higher status in the neighborhood pecking order.

The too-agreeable client. Client-centered obstacles to change may take many forms. Open reluctance, noncompliance, and uncooperative behavior are obvious examples. Extremely cooperative, compliant, or agreeable behavior, however, may also indicate a lack of successful engagement and contribute to later difficulties in treatment. Early in contact this agreeability may have the effect of distracting the practitioner from important problem exploration and, later, intervention. Some clinicians suggest that these seemingly positive responses may reflect a more complex, problematic, creative, or subtle type of client obstacle (Cingolani, 1984; Vriend & Dyer, 1973).

Environmentally Centered Obstacles

The sociopolitical bases of mandated treatment. The influence of the broader social and political environment in involuntary treatment should not be underestimated. Through social definitions of morality, safety, and personal rights, decisions are made to mandate treatment for subgroups who act in socially maladaptive ways according to these definitions. Involuntary treatment may be regarded as a political process that involves the socially sanctioned use of power in a context of conflicting interests between the client and some part of the social environment (Cingolani, 1984) or as moral interference in the life of the client (Szasz, 1974). Taking this perspective to an extreme, enforced treatment relationships are a false construction. They constitute dehumanizing

dominant-submissive acts that distort or misrepresent their true purpose to the supposed beneficiaries. These actions are societally justified
on the basis that individuals do not have the right to harm or endanger
themselves or others.

The sociopolitical context of practice also includes professional values.
One of the major values of the social work profession is client self-
determination: The ability of clients to make decisions about their lives,
their involvement in service or treatment, and the degree to which they
comply or participate in recommended intervention activities. Involuntary clients by definition do not possess the primary criterion for self-
determination: they have, to one extent or another, lost the ability to
freely choose treatment.

Agency and setting demands. Agencies that provide services for involuntary clients are under public mandate or contract to carry out a current
sociopolitical agenda. Agencies demand that practitioners effectively
and efficiently implement their missions and goals. Involuntary clients
served by these agencies perceive the rules and goals of agencies as
taking precedence over their personal problems, needs, and struggles,
as well as their strengths. This quickly translates into several real obstacles to engagement: limited or absent confidentiality, perceived lack of
empathy, and a primary focus, often on the parts of both worker and
client, on simply meeting the minimum standards of compliance required to avoid sanction. The physical proximity of the agency to the
clients it serves, the arrangement of service structure (i.e., accessibility
and availability), and the physical structure of the agency itself may
create yet further obstacles to engagement (Hepworth & Larsen, 1993).
For instance, professional staff at a residential treatment center for adolescents located on a beautiful campus in a middle-class suburb with no
public transportation may have difficulty engaging and working with
the parents of their adolescent children.

Client-Environment-Centered Obstacles

Malingering and deception. Malingering and deception figure prominently in practitioner engagement and assessment concerns with all
involuntary clients, but particularly with those who have engaged in
criminal or antisocial behavior. Malingering is the voluntary production
of false or grossly exaggerated physical or psychological symptoms.
These symptoms are produced in pursuit of a goal that is easily recognizable within an understanding of the individual's current circumstances
rather than of his or her individual psychology. Such goals may include
avoiding work, obtaining financial compensation, evading criminal
prosecution, obtaining drugs, or getting moved to a more desirable living situation (APA, 1987). Our preference is to regard malingering as a

problem-solving strategy the client uses as a method of coping with adverse circumstances. Why do individuals persist in trying to malinger again and again, even after they've been detected? For the simple reason that, from time to time (more often if they're good at it), malingering works and the environment changes. This is extremely reinforcing and increases the likelihood the client will again use this method of problem-solving in the future.

Although practitioners often state that determining whether a client is truly malingering can be a difficult assessment problem, there is little written about how to reliably assess malingering in a clinical setting. The best that practitioners may be able to do is to identify certain indicators of malingering. Rogers (1987) has organized the results of interview-based clinical findings on malingering into attitudinal characteristics and clinical indicators; his summary is reprinted in Table 2.1.

Other clinical indicators to look for in assessing malingering include inconsistency between diagnosis and self-reported symptoms, or a clear overendorsement of obvious symptoms. The client should first be presented with the incongruities and asked for an explanation. If they persist, corroborative data from reliable records, collateral interviews, or psychometric tests should always be sought prior to assigning a diagnosis of malingering.

Factitious disorders, often confused with and closely related diagnostically to malingering, are less likely found in involuntary or highly restrictive settings. The essential feature of factitious disorders is the voluntary production of physical or psychological symptoms with the apparent goal of assuming the role of patient. This goal, however, must not be otherwise understandable in light of the individual's environmental circumstances (APA, 1987).

Strategies for Enhancing Engagement

To date, there is no empirically identified set of relationship enhancers for involuntary clients as there is for voluntary clients. There are, however, factors linked to successful and unsuccessful treatment outcome with voluntary and involuntary clients in the social work literature suggesting relationship enhancers that might be targeted in work with involuntary clients. We first summarize these principles and then offer guidelines for engaging involuntary clients prior to and during initial client contact. In the next chapter we discuss implementation of several of these enhancement principles during intervention planning and implementation.

Prior to Client Contact

Problem orientation and worldview check. Practitioners should attempt to identify, acknowledge, and examine their problem orientations and

Table 2.1. Traditional Interviews and Malingering: A Summary of
    Clinical Findings [a]

A. Overplayed and dramatic presentation
    1. Clownish or fantastic quality (Davidson, 1949)
    2. Theatrical presentation (Ossipov, 1944)
    3. Eagerness to discuss symptoms (Ritson & Forrest, 1970)
    4. Extreme severity (Resnick, 1984)
    5. Indiscriminate endorsement of symptoms (Rogers, 1984b)
B. Deliberateness and carefulness
    1. Repeat questions (Resnick, 1984)
    2. Slower rate of speech (Kasl & Mahl, 1965; Rosenfeld, 1966)
    3. More hesitations (Harrison, Hwalek, Raney, & Fritz, 1978)
    4. Extensive use of qualifiers (Resnick, 1984)
    5. Vague nonspecific responses (Knapp, Hart, & Dennis, 1974)
C. Inconsistent with psychiatric diagnosis
    1. Rapid onset and resolution (Davidson, 1949; Ossipov, 1944; Sadow &
        Suslick, 1961)
    2. Rarity of symptoms (Resnick, 1984; Rogers, 1986a)
    3. Unusual combinations of symptoms (Rogers, 1987)
D. Consistency of self-report
    1. Contradictory symptoms (Rogers, 1984a, 1986a)
    2. Disparities between reported and observed symptoms (Ossipov, 1944;
        Wachskress, Berenberg, & Jacobson, 1953)
E. Endorsement of obvious symptoms
    1. More positive than negative symptoms (Rogers, 1986a)
    2. More impaired content than process (Resnick, 1984; Sherman, Tres, &
        Stafkin, 1975)
    3. More blatant than subtle symptoms (Rogers, 1984b)

Note. Adapted from R. Rogers, "The Assessment of Malingering Within a Forensic Context," pp. 216–219 in Law and Psychiatry: International Perspectives, Vol. 3, edited by D. N.
Weisstaub, New York: Plenum (1987).
[a] The term Clinical findings is employed since many of the indicators have little or no
empirical basis. References in table appear in original article.

worldviews since these provide a framework for interpreting client
interaction and assessment information. Unacknowledged negative
biases and assumptions about clients can be dangerous and compro-
mise effective practice. Examining one's beliefs, assumptions, values,
and expectations about clients and client problems is the first step: How
do clients wind up in these circumstances? Who is responsible for the
client's problem? What is the real problem? Sometimes this is usefully
done with a supervisor, colleague, or friend who will help clarify beliefs
by asking probing questions: The practitioner may find it helpful to ask
a question like, Does this perspective prevent me from following
through with the full range of problem-solving options in working with
this client? Based on values, personal beliefs, and assumptions I have
made about this individual, have I made decisions to eliminate
intervention options?

Developing realistic expectations for practice. Most training programs prepare practitioners to work with ideal, but not *real* clients, resulting in disappointment with clients and oneself for not eliciting better responses from the client. Given little previous opportunity to observe or learn alternative (and more compatible) sets of expectations, practitioners may develop views that clients and/or practitioners are inadequate. If they do exist, it is important to change views about bad clients and bad practitioners. The following set of practitioner self-statements can be helpful in beginning work with involuntary clients. They should be kept where the practitioner will see and read them frequently.

1. It is reasonable that involuntary clients resent being forced to participate in treatment.
2. Because they are forced to participate in treatment, hostility, silence, and noncompliance are common responses by involuntary clients and do not reflect my skill as a practitioner.
3. Due to the barriers created by the practice situation, clients have little opportunity to discover if they like me.
4. Lack of client cooperation is due to the practice situation, not to my specific actions and activities.

During Initial Contacts With the Client

General guidelines. Before considering specific techniques for engaging involuntary clients, it is helpful to think about a general stance workers should adopt as they begin to engage involuntary clients. Obviously, this should be a nondefensive stance. We offer two recommendations for practitioners. The first is to be clear, honest, and direct. The second is to acknowledge the involuntary nature of the arrangement. This means that the worker who is responsible for explaining the structure and content of treatment to the client should clarify these aspects of intervention:

1. The role of practitioner, and the expected role of client.
2. The activity necessary to achieve mandated compliance.
3. The structure and format of contacts.
4. Reporting and monitoring procedures.
5. How the practitioner can be expected to respond to noncompliance, reluctance, and/or unwillingness on the part of the client.
6. The possibilities or options for rewards, incentives, early discharge, or termination of mandated treatment.

Although the above information acknowledges this, it is also recommended that the worker initiate separate, direct discussion with the client about the involuntary nature of their interactions where possible. This can be accomplished in several ways.

After directly reviewing the involuntary nature of the treatment relationship, the practitioner might want to suggest that this relationship may present certain obstacles that they will need to address. The worker also should invite the client to describe obstacles he or she believes are present or likely to be present. Based on information about the client and the involuntary nature of the interaction, the practitioner should note potential difficulties in developing a working relationship. Finally, if the client was previously in voluntary treatment, the practitioner may want to discuss the differences between voluntary and involuntary treatment.

Motivational congruence between client and practitioner. Described by Reid and Hanrahan (1982) as a fit between the client's motivation and what the practitioner attempts to provide, a lack of motivational congruence was first noted as a factor in the poor outcomes of casework effectiveness research reviewed by Wood (1978). Later reviews (Reid & Hanrahan, 1982; Videka-Sherman, 1985) suggest such congruence is a factor in positive outcomes and may explain similar outcomes between voluntary and involuntary clients. The literature on voluntary and involuntary clients suggests that enhancing motivational congruence may be carried out in several ways: (1) preparing clients to assume their role, that is, socialization to the expectations of the client role; (2) facilitating client commitment and participation in the design and selection of intervention activities to promote treatment adherence; (3) behavioral contracting; and (4) emphasizing client choices and self-control.

Role preparation involving information about the course of treatment and expected client behavior in mental health settings has been linked to increased treatment benefits as well as less premature termination from treatment (Heitler, 1973, 1976; Videka-Sherman, 1985). Work with men in domestic violence programs suggests advantages from role preparation may fade over time and are most important in beginning treatment (Tolman & Bhosely, 1991). Client adherence to treatment activities, also called compliance, is a large problem in voluntary populations presenting for help with physical as well as psychological problems. Rates of substance abuse relapse range from 50 to 75% during the first year following treatment. Rates of adherence among involuntary clients can be expected to be at least as low. Extrapolating from research with voluntary clients, in Chapter 3, we describe specific factors identified to increase treatment adherence.

Behavioral contracting, admittedly difficult with involuntary clients, refers to an agreement between client and practitioner that stipulates the purpose, process, and procedures of their interaction. Among voluntary and involuntary clients, client commitment is associated with positive treatment outcomes (Stein, Gambrill, & Wiltse, 1978, 1979; Reid & Hanrahan, 1982; Rubin, 1985). Contracting is discussed in Chapter 3.

Emphasizing client choices and sense of control over participation in treatment can begin early. The practitioner, however, must clearly separate real choices from illusory choices and avoid suggesting the client may exert control where none is possible. Must the involuntary client participate in treatment? What is the alternative choice? There may be no alternative, or it may be return to prison or jail, or loss of child custody. Beyond participation, is there any choice in the *type* of treatment the client receives? In correctional programs, residential or nonresidential alternatives may be available with varying levels of supervision. In programs for drinking drivers, program format and location may involve concern for client interest such as employment schedules. Even the intensity, format, and the time of day or evening the intervention is conducted may be factors amenable to enhancing client choice.

Conversational responses. Wolberg (1967) identified conversational responses to avoid and responses he recommends in the beginning stages of building a client-practitioner relationship. The following are examples derived from these lists that illustrate conversational themes that commonly arise with involuntary clients. A typical client statement is followed by possible practitioner responses, some of which are judged to be unsuitable and some of which are seen as more suitable.

Avoid Expressions of Overconcern

    Client: I often feel as if I'm going to die.

Unsuitable Responses

  Practitioner: That's awful! How do you stand it?
                 Well, we'll start work on that right away!
                 Why, you poor thing! I'm sure I can help you.

Suitable Responses

  Practitioner: That must be upsetting to you.
                 Do you think any specific events might have led to this feeling?
                 What brings on this feeling most commonly?

Avoid Moralistic Judgments

    Client: I get an uncontrollable impulse to hit someone.

Unsuitable Responses

Practitioner: That's what got you here in the first place!
                Control is all in your mind.
                That's very bad.

Suitable Responses

Practitioner: Do you have any idea of what's behind this impulse?
                How far back does this impulse go?
                How does that make you feel?

Avoid Criticizing the Client

Client: I just refuse to pay child support.

Unsuitable Responses

Practitioner: You just don't care about anyone else, do you?
                You're a real man, aren't you? Shows them all, doesn't it?
                Are you aware you can be put in jail for that?

Suitable Response

Practitioner: It sounds as if you have strong feelings about that. Can you tell
                me what led to these feelings?
                If you did pay child support, what would that mean for you?
                What does that feel like?

Avoid Making False Promises

Client: Do you think I'll ever be normal?

Unsuitable Responses

Practitioner: If you work hard, there's no question about that.
                In a short while, you're going to see a difference.
                I see no reason why not.

Suitable Responses

Practitioner: A good deal will depend on how well we work together.
                You seem to have some doubts about that.
                Let's talk about what normal means to you.

Avoid Displays of Impatience

Client: I slipped again; I feel helpless and think I ought to end it all.

Unsuitable Responses

Practitioner: You'd better snap out of it soon.
                If you're feeling suicidal, we'd better try to hospitalize you.
                You won't be able to continue treatment here if you're using
                drugs.

Suitable Responses

Practitioner: I wonder what is behind this feeling.
Rather than focusing on what you did wrong, I'd like to talk about the fact that you stopped yourself before you slid back to where you were three months ago.
You sound as if you're at the end of your rope.

Avoid Ridiculing the Client

Client: There isn't much I can't do, once I set my mind on it.

Unsuitable Responses

Practitioner: You don't think much of yourself, do you?
Maybe you exaggerate your abilities.
Right. Did you learn that on the street or in prison?

Suitable Responses

Practitioner: I would wonder if that puts kind of a strain on you.
It's good to feel confident, but I hope you also realize it's okay to make mistakes or to struggle when you are tackling a big problem.
You must feel pretty confident once your mind is made up.

Avoid Blaming the Client for His or Her Failures

Client: I again forgot to bring my doctor's report with me.

Unsuitable Responses

Practitioner: You are irresponsible about your treatment!
There you go again. You'll never change.
When I tell you I need something, you'd best listen.

Suitable Responses

Practitioner: We still need to have it. Can you remember what it said?
Let's see how we can be sure you bring it next time. Do you have any ideas?
I wonder if you don't want to bring it.

Avoid Dogmatic Utterances

Client: I feel cold and detached in the presence of women.

Unsuitable Responses

Practitioner: That's because you're afraid of women.
You must want to detach yourself.
You want to destroy women and have to protect yourself.

Suitable Responses

Practitioner: That's interesting. Why do you think you feel this way?
                How far back does this go?
                What feelings do you have when you're with men?

**Respect the Right of the Client to Express Different Values and
Preferences From Yours**

Client: I don't like the pictures on your walls.

Unsuitable Responses

Practitioner: Well, that's just too bad.
                They are considered excellent pictures by those who know.
                That's strange. Most of my clients like them.

Suitable Responses

Practitioner: What don't you like about them?
                What type of pictures do you like?
                What do you think of me for having such pictures on the walls?

Evaluating Engagement and Relationship
With Involuntary Clients

Evaluating a practitioner-client relationship is a difficult task to accomplish reliably and validly. Not surprisingly, few practitioners attempt to examine their relationships with clients independent from the client's progress toward intervention goals. We consider it a worthwhile activity with involuntary clients for two basic reasons. First, the client-practitioner relationship provides the foundation for assessment and intervention; the helping process between the practitioner and an involuntary client most frequently breaks down in the beginning stages of treatment (Cingolani, 1984). If sources of difficulty can be identified early, the practitioner can develop plans to address them. Second, due to the special conditions of work with involuntary clients, the inherently coercive nature of the relationship with the involuntary client should be monitored and mediated whenever possible.

To estimate the extent to which the practitioner has engaged the client in a working relationship, the practitioner may evaluate such variables as client satisfaction with treatment, therapeutic alliance, and communication effectiveness. Client satisfaction, for example, can be measured through the use of a paper and pencil questionnaire such as the Reid-Grundlach Social Service Satisfaction Questionnaire or the Client Satisfaction Questionnaire, both found in *Measures for Clinical Practice: A Sourcebook* (Corcoran & Fischer, 1987). Another good resource is Luborsky's (1984) Helping Relationship Questionnaire (see Figure 2.1). To better suit an individual client, these instruments can be easily adapted or shortened.

Most clients have a natural tendency to respond in a socially desirable manner when it is easy to do so when it is at low or no personal cost or inconvenience, and when it may have positive social consequences. There is no evidence, however, that involuntary clients are more likely to provide unreliable information on surveys or psychological measures (Von Cleve, Jemelka, & Trupin, 1991). We recommend several ways to decrease reactivity when monitoring relationship variables:

1. Explain to the client well before administering the instrument that he or she will be asked to complete information about the practitioner and the services received.
2. Explain to the client that the answers will have no impact on the rules or conditions of treatment and continue to reinforce this periodically.
3. If possible, have another staff or agency clerical staff administer and collect the survey or interview questions.
4. Have the client complete the survey at home or somewhere other than in the presence of the worker and return to an administrator or someone other than the practitioner at the agency.

ASSESSMENT

The purpose of assessment is to identify and locate the nature and extent of client problems. Assessment provides the framework for making the major decisions of practice: What are the problems to be addressed during intervention? Is the client complying with the requirements of mandated contact or treatment? Should the client be referred elsewhere for other services? Is the service provided addressing the problem of referral or mandate or other problems identified during the assessment phase?

The amount of time devoted to assessment varies widely depending on the type and function of the agency, the nature of the problem(s), and specific services delivered. In emergency service units, such as those in child protection, acute psychiatric settings, or correctional detention, initial intervention decisions must be made quickly. The role of assessment in these circumstances is to ascertain the need for service and the level of restrictiveness required. In nonemergent work with

Below are listed a variety of ways that one person may feel or behave in relation to another person. Please consider each statement with reference to your present relationship with your therapist.

Mark each statement according to how strongly you feel that is true, or not true, in this relationship. Please mark every one. Write in +3, +2, +1 or −1, −2, −3, to stand for the following answers:

+3. Yes, I strongly feel that it is true
+2. Yes, I feel it is true
+1. Yes, I feel that it is probably true, or more true than untrue

−1. No, I feel that it is probably untrue, or more untrue than true
−2. No, I feel it is not true
−3. No, I strongly feel that it is not true

_____ 1. I believe that my therapist is helping me.
_____ 2. I believe that the treatment is helping me.
_____ 3. I have obtained some new understanding.
_____ 4. I have been feeling better recently.
_____ 5. I can already see that I will eventually work out the problems I came to treatment for.
_____ 6. I feel I can depend upon the therapist.
_____ 7. I feel the therapist understands me.
_____ 8. I feel the therapist wants me to achieve my goals.
_____ 9. I feel I am working together with the therapist in a joint effort.
_____ 10. I believe we have similar ideas about the nature of my problems.
_____ 11. I feel now that I can understand myself and deal with myself on my own (that is, even if the therapist and I were no longer meeting for treatment appointments).

Kinds of Change:
I feel improved in the following ways: _____

_____

_____

I feel worse in the following ways: _____

_____

_____

Estimate of Improvement so Far:

1	2	3	4	5
Not at All	Slightly	Moderately	Much	Very Much

Figure 2.1. The helping relationship questionnaire.
Source: Luborsky, L. (1984). *Principles of psychoanalytic psychotherapy: A manual for supportive-expressive treatment.* New York: Basic Books. Reprinted with permission.

involuntary clients, the practitioner usually has information about the nature and severity of the client's problem prior to contact. Generally, others have identified the problem as illegal, immoral, or both, and it is judged to seriously endanger the well-being of the client or others. Our approach is to assume there is sufficient time to conduct assessment. Because an involuntary client's rights and freedoms, as well as access to treatment, may depend on the practitioner's assessment, accurate facts and careful inferences are crucial.

Assessment begins by making an inventory of potential client problems, answering the question, What brings the client here? With involuntary clients, the referral or mandated problem is regarded as one, but not the only problem for attention. As noted above, effective engagement requires that the practitioner elicit what the client sees as problems as well as laying the foundation for a mutual understanding of the problems for work. Along with this problem inventory, and equally important, the worker and the client jointly (1) identify the strengths, weaknesses, and resources the client possesses, answering, In what client context do these problems exist? (2) determine the client's behavior, cognitions (thinking), and feelings in response to the problems; and (3) specify the context and the conditions under which the problem occurs, framing the question, How did we arrive here?

Problem-Focused Assessment

We encourage the use of a problem-solving *formulation* of practice (Nezu & Nezu, 1989) in addition to the use of specific problem-solving models with clients. In problem-solving formulations of practice, the activities of practice are themselves regarded as a problem-solving enterprise, i.e., treatment is a problem-solving process. Each time a practitioner is scheduled to see a client, a problem faces the practitioner. The problem is how to provide optimally effective treatment to an individual possessing a unique set of life circumstances, symptoms, complaints, developmental history, and biological makeup. Solving this problem entails both identifying and implementing an intervention plan.

It is important to start by considering this term *problem*. We use the term broadly here to refer to situations or events the client, worker, agency, and/or public identify as troubling, whether to the client, agency or public. *Problem* in this sense incorporates the notion of basic human needs. Solving the problem may require change in the problem itself, in the attitudes and feelings of the client or others about the problem, or in the conditions under which the problem occurs. As an example, in the instance of drug use by a parolee, the problem is identified as breaking the law, regardless of whether or not the parolee views it as a problem. Or, the problem may be identified as the parolee's inability to see that drug use is a serious problem warranting public concern.

Initially, involuntary clients are less likely to define problems for themselves in most treatment situations. In the criminal justice system, protective services, and psychiatric settings, service is most often initiated in response to problems defined by some segment of the community. In contrast, clients in less restrictive, voluntary service settings usually initiate treatment with an initial working definition of their own problems. During the assessment phase of practice, client problems are explored and evaluated from the perspectives of all involved agents: client, practitioner, significant others, and agency or community. In contrast to voluntary clients, involuntary clients' perceptions of their problems may be markedly different from the definition of the problem specified in the mandate for service. In addition, they may deny that they have a problem, or they may be so angry about the involuntary nature of their contact that even acknowledging problems becomes a major task.

What Information Do You Need for Assessment?

In research-based practice, workers should emphasize clear and specific descriptions, focus on relevant data-gathering, and use, to the extent possible, multiple information sources. Individual assessment models vary according to the practitioner's theoretical orientation and the treatment setting. Conceptually however, all assessments contain four major types of information (Blythe & Tripodi, 1989):

Type I: Characteristics of the client observable by others.
Type II: Client moods, feelings, attitudes, and beliefs.
Type III: Client ability, knowledge, and achievement.
Type IV: Behavior of the client.

Type I: Characteristics observable by others.   The specific contents of this information depend on the nature of the client problem, the agency function, and the practitioner's theoretical orientation. Type I information includes basic client identifying information, such as age, sex, education, and socioeconomic variables, psychiatric diagnosis or other categorical labeling, and environmental information such as family and social support structure. An example of Type I information about a client is as follows:

A 21-year-African-American female with two children aged three years and six months was referred for service following an initial investigative call by the child welfare authority. The client is currently living in a one-room apartment in East Harlem with no safe source of electricity or heat. The apartment is infested with vermin. She receives no services or entitlements. She is unemployed, but reports previously working as a data entry operator in Detroit. The young woman moved to New York two years ago with her husband who left the family shortly afterward. She has one aunt living in a suburb about 20 miles away, but no other relatives or close friends in the area. She reports she was in drug treatment before her first child was born and was told by the doctor then that she was "depressed."

Many agencies and organizations classify clients according to their problem characteristics. The best known psychiatric classification system, the DSM-IIIR (APA, 1987), is used by mental health practitioners in all disciplines to diagnose mental disorders. Diagnosis is a medical term that refers to a specific type of assessment that assumes a problem resides primarily within the individual, that is, a disease is identified by its symptoms. The DSM-IIIR manual contains information organized around five axes: clinical syndromes; personality and developmental disorders; physical disorders and conditions; severity of psychosocial stressors; and highest level of adaptive functioning in the past year. Practitioners in involuntary mental health settings are frequently called on to make DSM-IIIR diagnoses for clients. Moreover, acute treatment, length of restrictive treatment option, and medications often are based on these diagnoses. In correctional settings, clients may be classified as possessing a personality or developmental disorder. Using the DSM-IIIR, this might be a pervasive and long-term Axis II diagnosis, without a clinical syndrome, or an Axis I diagnosis. Axes I, II, and III are the most commonly used. Diagnoses on Axes IV and V are rarely used except by social workers who find the focus on psychosocial stress level and premorbid functioning useful in assessment.

DSM-IIIR can be used to help a client receive service or obtain treatment for specific problems. A misdiagnosis, however, may harm a client by preventing appropriate service and discouraging practitioners and other care providers. A serious problem with the DSM-IIIR is that despite its status as the most widely used diagnostic system in the world, supporting reliability and validity data are scant and exist only for very broad categories, rather than for individual diagnoses (Kirk & Kutchins, 1992).

To provide information about a client's environment, the ecomap is often used to identify sources of informal and formal social support and the status of relationships with important others and agencies. As illustrated by Hartman (1982), different types of lines can be used to distinguish between strong, tenuous, lost, or conflictual relationships connecting the client to other parts of the environment. Examples of completed ecomaps are provided later in this chapter and in Chapter 4.

Type II: Client moods, feelings, attitudes, and beliefs. Information about client moods, feelings, attitudes, and beliefs can be obtained through standardized scales or rating inventories, or through self-anchored ratings or scales. The most commonly used standardized scale is the Beck Depression Inventory (BDI; Beck, Ward, Mendelson, Mock, & Erbaugh, 1961). Another example of one of these instruments is the Linehan Reasons for Living Inventory (RFL). This standardized scale asks respondents to identify how important particular beliefs would be in mitigating suicidal thoughts and behaviors. The RFL has successfully discriminated suicidal from nonsuicidal individuals in psychiatric inpatient, delinquent, college student, and prison inmate samples. The Brief Reasons for Living Inventory (Ivanoff, Jang, Smyth, & Linehan, in press) is reprinted in Figure 2.2.

Some authors have prepared collections of standardized instruments. For example, Corcoran and Fischer (1987) include standardized scales, problem inventories, and paper-and-pencil instruments that address client problems ranging from anxiety and stress to suicidal thinking and family conflict. While not all measures present reliability and validity information, a good number in this collection do. Information about appropriate clients, administration, scoring, and a primary reference is provided for each instrument.

Self-anchored scales measure a specific problem in a specific individual. *Self-anchored* means that each client defines the anchor or referent points on the scale, with the assistance of the practitioner, rather than using those determined by the author of the test. For example, a practitioner and client can design a self-anchored scale to measure feelings of anger. Using a 7-point scale specific to this client, a 1 rating could indicate no feelings of anger and a state of rest or peacefulness, while a 7 is the most angry the client has ever been. Self-anchored scales can be extremely valid and useful in describing personal feelings and thoughts. Figure 2.3 gives three examples of client self-anchored scales.

Type III: Client ability, knowledge, and achievement. This information can be gathered from standardized instruments and informal tests and measures. Standardized tests and measures contain prescribed administration and scoring methods and generally possess normative data, and reliability and validity information based on numerous previous administrations. *The Eleventh Mental Measurement Yearbook* (Kramer & Conoley, 1992) is the classic reference for psychological tests.

Informal tests of knowledge and ability frequently are developed by practitioners to assess whether clients have necessary knowledge or skills or if they might benefit from a psychoeducational intervention. For

Figure 2.2 Brief Reasons for Living Inventory.

Many people have thought of suicide at least once. Others have never considered it. Whether you have considered it or not, we are interested in the
reasons you would have for *not* committing suicide if the thought were to occur
to you or if someone were to suggest it to you. We would like to know how
important each of these possible reasons would be to you at this time in your life
as a reason to NOT kill yourself.

Each reason can be rated from 1 (Not At All Important) to 4 (Extremely
Important).

1. Not at all Important (as a reason for not killing myself, or, does not apply
   to me, I don't believe this at all).
2. Not very important.
3. Important.
4. Extremely important (as a reason for not killing myself, I believe this very
   much and it is very important).

If you never have or firmly believe you never would seriously consider killing
yourself, it is still important that you rate each reason on the basis of why killing
yourself is not or would never be an alternative for you.

1. I believe I can find a purpose in life, a reason to live.
2. My family depends upon me and needs me.
3. The effect on my children could be harmful.
4. I am afraid of the actual "act" of killing myself (the pain, blood, violence).
5. I would not want people to think I did not have control over my life.
6. My religious beliefs forbid it.
7. I do not want to die.
8. I love and enjoy my family too much and could not leave them.
9. I want to watch my children as they grow.
10. I am afraid of death.
11. I am concerned about what others would think of me.
12. I consider it morally wrong.

example, parents identified by protective services might be asked to
describe how they would handle various child management problems.
This test could screen for possible members in a parent skills training
group, and might suggest group topics. After the training group is implemented, the test could be administered again to determine the effectiveness of the group.

Type IV: Behavior of the clients.   Client behavior can be observed by the
client, by other staff or professionals, or by the practitioner. There are
many examples of this type of measurement in the literature, and the
procedures and the forms developed for monitoring behaviors may have
been developed either for an individual client's behavior or for monitoring many clients' behaviors. Behavioral observation forms range from

a) Jayneen's *anger* at her child

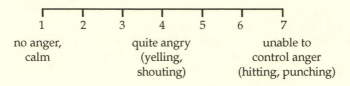

a) Anthony's *urges* to "get high" (e.g., smoke crack, inject or snort heroin)

a) Hector's *satisfaction* with his work performance (rated daily)

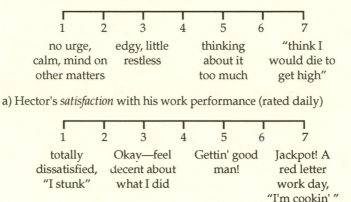

Figure 2.3.   Examples of client 7-point scales.

simple to complex data collection systems. As an example of a simple observational form, if staff on a psychiatric inpatient unit are concerned about the withdrawal and limited social interaction of a depressed schizophrenic male, they may decide to monitor the number of times the patient goes to his room during the day. This can be done simply by attaching a small piece of paper to the front of the unit log, which is usually kept at the front desk. Each time the patient passes by the front desk on his way to his room, a hatch mark could be made on the paper. At the end of the shift, the marks could be tallied and the sum entered into the patient's chart.

Some overt behaviors can only be reliably observed by clients themselves because observers are not present in all situations where the behavior occurs. These can include such behaviors as asking others for help, swearing at others, or masturbating in public. Covert behavior such as feelings and thoughts must be assessed by clients themselves, because they cannot be directly observed by others. The importance of operationally defining the feelings and thoughts for assessment cannot be overstated. In addition to more common feelings of anger, depression, and anxiety, more troubling thoughts and feelings that are given clear operational definitions also may be monitored. Examples of such thoughts and feelings include depersonalization, urges to take drugs, impulses to strike a child, hallucinations, flashbacks regarding a sexual assault, and suicidal ideation. An example of an individualized client self-monitoring plan for self-critical thoughts is described by Berlin (1978). A similar form, depicted in Figure 2.4, allows the client to monitor types of self-criticism throughout the day by checking the appropriate time category if the self-criticism has occurred.

There are multiple factors that warrant consideration when deciding what kind of information to gather. The purpose of the assessment is paramount, but in social work practice the realities of what can *feasibly* be collected raise important considerations. Is information already available and, if so, can this information be used with confidence? How much time is available for assessment? In this agency, what are the assessment priorities and eligibility requirements for service? If other practitioners, staff, or agencies have gathered assessment data previously, the practitioner needs to question the accuracy and verify this information before using it.

The purpose of assessment varies with agency or setting purpose. The assessment may provide information for other staff who are working with the client and/or it may provide a basis for the client and practitio-

Criticism Category	6–9 am	9–12	12–3 pm	3–5	5–7	7 and later
Stupidity	✓	✓✓		✓✓		
Appearance	✓✓✓✓					
Forethought					✓	
Inconsideration			✓			
Self-blame		✓				

Figure 2.4. Self-Criticism Log.

ner to select problems to address in treatment. Assessment may determine the suitability of a particular client for a specific program or placement, or it may prescribe the intensity or length of treatment. It also may explicate patterns of behavior that led to the current problematic life situation, which would inform the selection of a treatment plan.

Previously gathered information can be extremely useful in assessment. Since the problem orientation of an involuntary client may differ from that of the referral source or mandate, the practitioner often meets the client for the first time equipped with records, rap sheets, court orders, and the like. Previous agency files, discharge or treatment summaries, and adjunct referrals also may be available. In using this information, a worker must exercise caution. For example, the worker should consider the source of information. A DSM-IIIR diagnosis of Antisocial Personality Disorder (formerly called Sociopathic Personality) applied to the parent of an abused child by a harried psychiatric resident in a chaotic hospital emergency room may not be an accurate indication of the parent's mental functioning. Alternatively, the same diagnosis applied to an inmate at entry to the state prison system by a practitioner who regularly works with inmates may provide useful information pertinent to identifying security, vocational, and treatment program options for that individual.

Reducing Bias in Assessment

Bias is introduced into assessment in three general ways. The first is through the worldview and problem orientation the worker brings to the client and the client's problem situation. This was discussed earlier under practitioner obstacles to engagement. In assessment, this perspective may influence what information is gathered and how that information is interpreted and used.

Two other sources of bias, more overtly related to measurement, include the methods used to gather information, and the context of assessment. The methods used to gather information refer to the actual types of measures and how the measurement is conducted. Measurement instruments should be examined for reliability and validity. Reliability refers to the consistency of measurement on repeated applications of a measuring instrument, while validity attests to the accuracy and predictability of measurement. (See Blythe & Tripodi, 1989, for a more detailed discussion of these concepts.) In cases where more than one measure of a client problem is used, it is important to examine and compare all the information gathered at one time. Does each instrument or measurement source define the problem the same way? Are there inconsistencies across measures? For instance, do self-reported medication compliance, observations of medication intake by group home staff, and monitored blood levels all provide consistent information about the client's compliance with a psychotropic medication regimen?

The environment in which information is gathered includes the setting, available time and assistance, and agency auspice and mission. To minimize bias in agency contexts, the practitioner should attempt to do the following whenever possible:

1. Stay nonjudgmental when gathering and synthesizing information.
2. Gather information from more than one source, hopefully representing different viewpoints in the assessment.
3. Examine information with the concepts of reliability and validity in mind.
4. Consider any environmentally predisposing factors that may have biased assessment.

The assessment environment may have a great deal to do with the type and quality of information gathered. Language barriers, illiteracy, anxiety, anger at involuntarily detention, side effects of substances, and lack of appropriate medication can all produce significant variations in how a client may respond to an assessment instrument. As much as possible, the practitioner must make the environment more conducive to eliciting unbiased information from clients. For example, attention and care are taken in providing a suitable assessment environment for a suicidal risk screening program for people newly admitted to local jails (Cox, Landsberg, & Paravati, 1989). Jail staff administer the questionnaire in a quiet, private setting. The staff are carefully trained to thoughtfully, emphatically, and slowly ask each question, and to be alert to clients' nonverbal communication, not understanding questions, and possible interference from substance use or thought disorder.

Choosing the Best Measure of Client Problems: Existence, Magnitude, Duration, or Frequency

Client problems are measurable to the extent that they can be operationalized into discrete variables. Some problems, such as child abuse, unemployment, or drug use lend themselves well to specification using discrete variables in many situations. Other problems are more complex and may require more than one variable for adequate representation, such as difficulty controlling anger, or poor self-esteem. These more complex problems may require further examination to identify the salient variables. Upon closer inspection, poor self-esteem may involve

making negative self-references in conversation, having trouble expressing one's wishes in important relationships, and a depressed mood.
Likewise, anger control problems may involve holding unreasonable
expectations for others, inconsistent application of discipline, and depression.

The practitioner's job is to learn how to operationalize these variables,
that is, to break down client problems into meaningful measurable
units. The key to identifying problems that can be measured is to operationally define variables that can register change or the absence of
change. The change can be registered in one of four ways: The change
can reduce or resolve (end) the problem, prevent the problem from
occurring, or provide intervention to maintain or to change a client's
situations. In each of these events, the operationally defined variables
specific to the client's problem provide the yardstick (benchmark) practitioners can use in evaluating the results of their work.

After operationalizing a problem, there are four primary conceptual
means used to measure client problems: existence, frequency, magnitude, and duration. Each of these can be used to indicate change or lack
of change in a problem over time.

Problem existence indicates the presence or absence of a problem, that
is, Is it *there*? Based on a nominal scale, it is the simplest form of problem
measurement possible, a dichotomous measure. This means that the
problem is either present (yes) or absent (no). Problem existence can be
used as a measure of change *only* after an operationally clear definition
of the problem has taken place. Of greatest importance in using this
kind of measure is *knowing what does and does not constitute the problem*.
For example, child abuse may be defined as an act of overt physical
violence toward a child that leaves marks or causes other bodily injury.
A drug screen that tests for the presence of illegal drugs in the urine is
an example of a dichotomous measure of problem existence. The illegal
substance is either present or not present in the urine of the client being
tested.

Problem frequency refers to the number of times a problem occurs
within an identified time period, that is, How often does it happen?
Frequency is recorded on a ratio scale, beginning at 0. Once you have
defined a problem such that its presence or absence can be noted, the
number of times the problem occurs can be counted. To count the frequency of a problem, however, an observer must be able to reliably
report the problem. This can be difficult in cases of illegal and/or private
behaviors such as drug use or child abuse. The child abuser and the
child may be the only ones present when the a child is abused; the child
is usually too frightened to report; and the abuser is unlikely to report
reliably. Counting the frequency of less direct measures that may be
observed by others, such as bruises, or in cases of drug use, rapid

behavior or mood changes associated with use, may be a more appropriate measure. Using frequency as a problem measure works best with problems that occur repeatedly. While this may appear self-evident, trying to count a problem that does not occur with some regularity can be frustrating and can delay intervention needlessly. For example, if the child abuse does not occur more than once per week, it may be important to identify and count angry, out-of-control thought patterns that lead to abusive behavior rather than the actual abuse incident itself.

Problem magnitude refers to the intensity, severity, or strength of a problem. Using an ordinal scale, the problem is rated by the client, practitioner, or others. The scale includes two or more points, although some have as many as 7–10 points. The scale is also calibrated so that it is appropriate for the problem being assessed. As an example, a 1 to 5 scale with values ranging from 1 = no problem to 5 = very severe problem could be used by a client to measure feelings of anger. Scales that range from 1 to 10 or from 1 to 100 are often used to measure anxiety. A rating of 1 on this scale indicates no discernible anxiety at all, while a 10 or a 100 indicates the most extreme level of anxiety possible. The number of points used in constructing a scale for measuring problem magnitude is determined by the number of points the client can meaningfully understand and discriminate. Children for example, can often grasp the meaning of a 3-point scale of problem magnitude, particularly if represented by visual analog. A 100-point anxiety scale can be quite useful for adults measuring affective states such as anger and anxiety because smaller changes in feeling level can be distinguished. The number of points or steps on a scale should be sufficient to distinguish reliably between different degrees of the problem, but not so numerous that the client cannot make the distinction between two adjacent points. Most widely used scales contain between 3 and 11 points.

The more specific the scale steps are to an individual client's problem, the more reliable and valid a measure the scale will be. This process is called *anchoring* the scale. Anchoring involves identifying specific events from the client's past experiences that relate to the points on the scale. Working with a client to identify these individual anchor points usually also yields valuable assessment information. The 7-point scales in Figure 2.3 include anchor points based on feelings and self-statements. The following scale anchors were developed for a client's 10-point anger scale:

1 = lying in bed near sleep, a total lack of anger, feeling pleasant and calm,
3 = a minor irritation, like being interrupted by a co-worker when I'm talking,

5 = feeling anger that will pass, yelling, perhaps being verbally
abusive for up to 15 minutes—like being stuck in traffic,
8 = being quite angry, yelling loudly and feeling the urge to hit or
punch,
9 = blind rage, out-of-control, hitting and punching.

Problem duration refers to the length of time a problem occurs once it
begins. It is registered according to a unit of time, an interval level
measurement, which can be adjusted so that the measure accurately
represents the problem. For example, angry outbursts and negative verbal interactions might be measured in minutes, sleep in hours, absence
from school by class periods or days, and absconding (escape) by both
hours and days. Duration can be measured by the client or others.

Visually Representing Client Problems

There are important reasons to use visual representation for assessment and for monitoring change in client problems. The most important
reason is that visual representation can often convey a broad conceptualization of the problem situation *more readily understood by the client* than
paragraphs of professional words. In this way, visual representation
enhances communication and the relationship between practitioner and
client. If the client can literally point to a specific problem juncture when
describing current conflict using an ecomap or see and plot information
on a graph indicating a change in problem status or maintenance of
positive change, it increases the client's sense of participation and self-
management in treatment. This is a simple example of *empowerment*.
Empowerment is important with all clients, but particularly with involuntary clients who by virtue of social or economic status, illiteracy, age,
sex, or their involuntary status have not had input into previous services
or treatment.

Graphs can be used to depict variables representing client problems at
one or more points in time. Figure 2.5 illustrates how graphs are constructed and used. Although there are a couple of new terms to learn,
using graphs is a simple form of visual data representation. The X-axis,
the horizontal line, represents time; the time segments are equally di-
vided so that they represent equal periods of time. Days and weeks are
the time segments most often used in measuring client progress. The
Y-axis, the vertical line extending upward from the bottom left of the
X-axis, measures problem existence, frequency, duration, or magnitude.
Problem existence is graphed as either 0 (absence) or 1 (presence). The
client for this example is a hospitalized, depressed man for whom the
treatment goal is to increase social interactions (speaking to other patients or staff on the inpatient unit). Graphing the occurrence of his

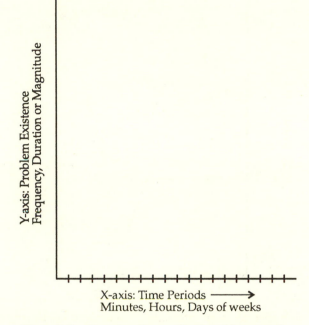

Y-axis: Problem Existence
Frequency, Duration or Magnitude

X-axis: Time Periods ───────→
Minutes, Hours, Days of weeks

Figure 2.5.   Constructing a client problem graph.

social interactions on a daily basis would look like Figure 2.6. The client or staff person simply notes or reports whether the client spoke with anyone at any time during the day; this is graphed by plotting a 0 or 1 for each day of the week. The points are then connected to form a graph. Figure 2.6 indicates that the client spoke to others Sunday through Wednesday, but beginning on Thursday, did not engage in any verbal social interactions.

Graphs that represent simple frequency, magnitude, and duration are all constructed in the same way. To graph the frequency of our depressed client's verbal interactions, the Y-axis entry would be the number of times the client speaks to others on each given day (see Figure 2.7). By collecting this information, we may learn that our client spoke to others 3 times on Sunday, 8 on Monday, 15 on Tuesday, and 4 on Wednesday. A graph could also be used to plot the duration of this verbal interaction, most likely in seconds or minutes. The Y-axis looks like that found in Figure 2.7 and measures minutes of verbal interaction. With staff assistance, the client's observable level of engagement (intensity of verbal interactions in this example) could also be monitored and later plotted on this form of simple graph.

General guidelines in constructing graphs follow. These apply to most graphs a practitioner might use.

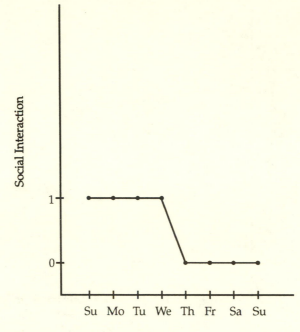

Figure 2.6. Presence of social interaction, example of problem/goal existence
graph.

1. Time is always measured along the horizontal X-axis.
2. Problem level is always measured along the Y-axis.
3. The length of the X- and Y-axes should be similar to avoid distortion.
4. Points used to represent time and problem level should always be equidistant from each other.
5. Points representing problem level should be meaningful in portraying this client's specific problem.

Graphs can usually be easily drawn by the practitioner, often while in session with the client. In some cases, however, data collection is more complex. Information may be obtained on several problem variables or problems at once, as well as for many clients simultaneously such as in residential treatment centers. In some agencies, computer-assisted graphing programs are available that enable the practitioner to complete these tasks more efficiently. At least three types of software are available for graphing. Programs specifically designed for graphing, such as Chart, are one option. Spreadsheet programs such as Lotus 1–2–3 or Excel also make graphs with the added advantages of data management and mathematical functions. Some of the graphs in this text were orig-

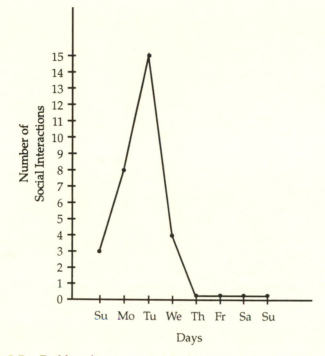

Figure 2.7. Problem frequency graph, frequency of social interaction.

inally drawn with Excel. Lotus 1–2-3, for example, can be used to graph client data and to perform routine statistical tests to analyze the degree of client change (Bronson & Blythe, 1987). Each time new data are available, this information can be added to the client's computer file and a new, updated graph can be generated.

Practitioners have used graphic aids to assessment since the 1970s. These include the Social Network Support Map (Cheers, 1987), and the ecomap (Hartman, 1982) and genograms (McGoldrick, 1985). Support exists for increasingly sophisticated types of graphic assessment. While several recent efforts represent excellent approaches to organizing complex contextual assessment information, most are not yet available for research-based practice. The primary reason limiting the use of these graphic assessment and treatment monitoring aids is that they cannot be used repeatedly over time and then meaningfully compared. One notable exception is Mattaini's (1993) computerized ecomap based on non-linear hypermedia technology, which shows great promise for concurrently dealing with contextual, multivariate data in graphic and quantitative ways. This program makes it possible to enter data on a case at multiple points in time and watch the graphic change dynamically on the screen (see Figure 2.8).

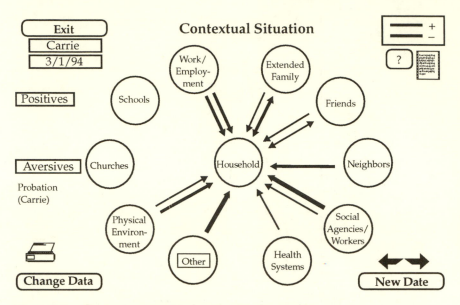

Figure 2.8.   Computer generated ecomap.

From: Mattaini, M. A. (1993). *More than a thousand words: Graphics for clinical practice.*
Washington, D.C.: NASW Press. Reprinted with permission.

Some computer-assisted rating scales also have graphing capabilities. Specific to social work assessment is Hudson's Clinical Assessment System (Hudson, 1982; Hudson, Nurius, & Reisman, 1988; Nurius & Hudson, 1988), a set of 20 standardized summated ordinal scales covering a wide variety of presenting problems such as depression, self-esteem, and parent-child relationships. The scales, which demonstrate good to excellent validity and reliability, can be used individually or in combination and can be completed by the client either at a computer or with paper and pencil. The program stores the scale information and can generate a graph depicting all of the client's scores on a particular scale.

Baseline: Measuring the Problem Prior to Intervention

Measuring the problem before intervention is helpful in at least two ways. First, it enables the practitioner to select the correct method and appropriate level of intervention. Particularly in cases where restrictive interventions may take place, such as abridging client freedom or parental rights, accurate measurement is an ethical responsibility to both the client and public. Second, measurement of the problem before intervention is necessary to determine changes in the problem during and after intervention. The baseline helps the practitioner tell whether the intervention has made a difference.

Baselines are most typically represented by graphs, ideally with at least three data points so that the trend of the data pattern can be determined. The more data points available, the easier it is to interpret the baseline data. Baseline data can be gathered using any measure or data-gathering device; they can be gathered in four different ways:

1. Observing the problem during assessment prior to any intervention.
2. Reconstructing problem data based on available records.
3. Retrospectively assessing the problem by means of interview or questionnaire with the client or significant others.
4. Observing one problem while intervention is being carried out to address a different problem than the one being baselined.

From a measurement perspective, the first choice is the best. It requires sufficient time to observe the problem, however, and it requires that the problem is not so severe that delaying intervention could cause serious harm. Ideally, data should be collected until there are clear trends in the graph indicating increase, decrease, or stability. If observations can be made daily, a baseline of 1 to 2 weeks is usually adequate. In institutional settings, longer baselines are sometimes feasible.

Reconstructed baseline data have been previously gathered and are available for the practitioner's use. These data may have been gathered by a previous practitioner or institution, or even by legal authorities. The practitioner must be clear about the operational definition employed and should assess the validity of the data, not using it if there is reason to suspect it is invalid. An example of a retrospective baseline consists of data that were gathered from a local emergency room hospital chart where a client presented herself repeatedly after making razor cuts on her arms. From the nursing notes in this chart, it was possible to compile 18 months of systematic information on the frequency of visits, the severity of the injury, the client's emotional state during the visits, and the resolution of the visits. Records of previous criminal behavior and even attendance at previous treatment programs may also be used in reconstructing baseline data.

Retrospectively gathered data are the least reliable type of data used for baselines. Using questionnaires or interviews, the client or significant other is asked to recall past occurrences of the problem. As such, this baseline is only as reliable as the memory of the person reporting and should not be used if the practitioner suspects it may not be valid. Or, the practitioner should only reconstruct data back in time as long as the client appears able to make reliable reports. Verification of reconstructed data is sometimes possible, as in the case of the bipolar disordered client whose family was able to corroborate his recall of manic episodes during the year.

Collecting baseline information on a problem not currently undergoing intervention can be useful when working with multiproblem clients who, for example, have concurrent problems with child discipline and depression. Collecting data in this manner also allows the practitioner to assess the relationship between the two problems. For example, as the client gains an improved sense of control over her life by learning new ways of responding to her child, does her depression also improve? In some instances, the variables in question are so significant that they can be reliably recalled.

The seeming urgency of client problems and our own wishes to begin *doing something* can result in the rationalization that gathering baseline data is not in the best interests of the client. In crisis or emergency cases, it is not always possible to collect baseline data for a week or so and crisis intervention should proceed.Once the immediate crisis is resolved, however, it is often the case that many other client problems have been going on for long periods of time and require more thorough assessment. In any case, it is important to understand the trade-off in beginning intervention without baseline data. Without baseline data of some type, a practitioner cannot reliably examine the changes that occur following intervention nor demonstrate that changes are the result of intervention.

Baseline data can be used to determine four things in assessment: (1) whether the problem is in fact a problem; (2) the extent of the problem; (3) the persistence of the problem; and (4) when intervention should be started. If the problem to be baselined is cocaine use and the three-times-weekly urine screens all come back negative for cocaine, for clinical purposes drug use is not a problem at this time. If a practitioner is concerned about suicidal thinking in a client who has had periodic thoughts of suicide in the past, but baseline data indicate no suicidal thinking over a two- or three-week period, suicidal thinking is not a problem for intervention at this time. Periodic observations, however, should be made in the future. The extent and persistence of the problem are evaluated by the magnitude, frequency, or duration of the problem and by whether the problem continues unabated forward into time. If a problem dissipates over time through natural helping resources or of its own accord, the practitioner may shift attention to more important problems. Using practitioner time and effort effectively is important in providing efficient treatment.

Whether or not to implement intervention also depends on the severity of the problem and is largely dependent on applying clinical judgment to interpret the baseline data. While one incident of hitting a child

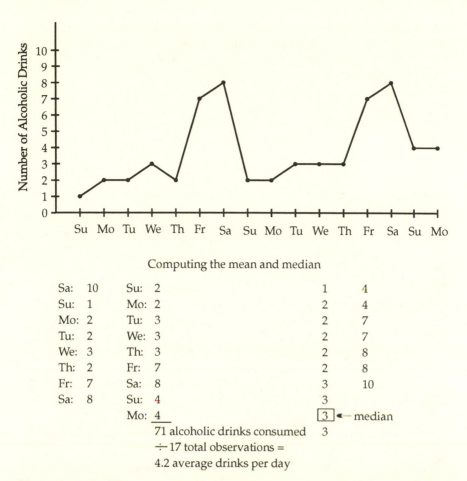

Computing the mean and median

Sa:	10	Su:	2		1	4
Su:	1	Mo:	2		2	4
Mo:	2	Tu:	3		2	7
Tu:	2	We:	3		2	7
We:	3	Th:	3		2	8
Th:	2	Fr:	7		2	8
Fr:	7	Sa:	8		3	10
Sa:	8	Su:	4		3	
		Mo:	4		3	← median
			71 alcoholic drinks consumed		3	
			÷ 17 total observations =			
			4.2 average drinks per day			

Figure 2.9. Problem seventy baseline: daily drinking for C, an 18-year-old woman.

may warrant intervention, does having two glasses of wine daily also warrant intervention? Referring to the ordinate numbers (problem level) on a graph, a practitioner can assess the severity of the problem for this particular client (see Figure 2.9).

The graphic patterns observed at baseline are used as a benchmark against which to measure possible changes during the intervention phase. In addition to visually representing the graphic pattern, it may be helpful to present some simple descriptive statistics that describe average observations at baseline. The two statistics most commonly used are the mean and the median. The mean or average is computed by summing the problem level observations and dividing by the number of total observations. The median is the point in a set of data above and below which 50% of the observations lie. This is determined by listing all observations in rank order and specifying the midpoint in the observations. That midpoint is the median. Figure 2.9 also illustrates a baseline mean and median.

CONCLUSION

In a phase model of practice, engagement and assessment provide the critical foundation for intervention planning and implementation. Ineffective engagement and inaccurate assessment prevent successful intervention planning and implementation. Obstacles to engagement include those centered in the practitioner, client, environment, and client-environment. Strategies for addressing these obstacles and enhancing engagement may be implemented by the practitioner prior to client contact, as well as during initial contacts during this phase. Several methods are recommended for evaluating engagement and relationship between the client and practitioner.

Problem-focused assessment is described in terms of the types of information needed. Multiple types and sources of information are extremely important in helping reduce assessment bias. Identifying the best method of problem measurement is followed by visually presenting the information so that it most clearly represents the client's problem over time. New and innovative ways have been developed to convey more complex client problems; these can be used independently or in conjunction with more traditional graphs and charts. Collecting baseline data about the problem prior to intervention is the best method for increasing assessment specificity, intervention focus and accuracy, and targeted monitoring of client progress. Taken together, the methods and procedures described in this chapter help ensure that practitioners gather systematic and reliable research-based assessment information to inform intervention.

Chapter 3

Planning and Implementing Research-Based Practice

In the preceding chapter we reviewed studies suggesting factors that are associated with positive outcomes and reducing treatment dropout. These factors include client involvement, motivational congruence, and role socialization. They suggest that problem selection should be a mutual process between client and practitioner, a perspective reinforced by the social work practice literature. Typically, a problem hierarchy is mutually generated by the practitioner and the client (Blythe & Tripodi, 1989; Compton & Galaway, 1989; Gambrill, 1983), and some models of practice argue that the client's expressed, considered wishes should be given precedence over other problems defined by the agency, practitioner, or others (Reid, 1978). However, this is usually not possible with mandated involuntary clients. A major focus of treatment has already been identified by a legal source outside the practitioner-client in work with mandated involuntary clients; this focus is the primary purpose for service and for the degree of restrictiveness judged necessary. The purpose, for example, may be to reduce the potential for further child abuse, suicide attempts, or criminal behavior. As such, it demands attention from an ethical as well as a mandated perspective. In work with nonmandated involuntary clients, the client's expressed wishes may be given higher precedence.

Honest and straightforward explanation of the service and mandated requirements, along with the contingencies for allowances and the consequences of not meeting these requirements, is the best policy in working with involuntary clients. While there is a distinction between the problem of referral and other mutually chosen intervention problems, this distinction is not usefully highlighted. It is most important that both client and practitioner understand the priority of the mandated referral problem. Furthermore, the models used in voluntary practice must be adapted to suit the involuntary practice situation; as in the areas of assessment and engagement, there is scant empirical information about effective intervention planning and implementation with involuntary clients.

Consistent with social work values of client self-determination and worth, we hold two premises about intervention with involuntary clients:

1. The client has a right to understand the theoretical premises that guide the practitioner's choice of intervention to the extent possible.
2. Client problems are the result of combinations of deficits and excesses in learning, biological, and social factors. While client problems may not respond 100% to intervention, most problem situations can be somewhat improved through the appropriate use of interventions based in methods that address these learning, social, environmental, and biological factors.

These premises are as important in work with involuntary clients as with voluntary clients, perhaps even more so. Clients should understand why a practitioner judges a particular intervention as appropriate and effective. This would include some understanding of the practitioner's theoretical bases and problem conceptualization, how information about individual circumstances affects this assessment, and the likely intervention options. In moving an involuntary client toward the fullest possible participation in all phases of treatment (assessment, intervention planning, and implementation), such understanding may be critical for treatment progress. Deciphering the multiple causes and maintaining factors of client problems and designing intervention plans that address these are hallmarks of social work practice. Irrespective of individual theoretical orientation, intervention plans should include appropriate action or referral to address learning, environmental, social, and biological factors.

Profound emotional learning deficits may be labeled as characterological or as personality disorders. Involuntary clients, particularly those who commit crimes against others, are often labeled as psychopathic or diagnosed with Antisocial Personality disorder (DSM-IIIR; APA, 1987). They are also generally regarded as particularly manipulative and unresponsive to treatment. While not the focus of this text, readers are encouraged to explore the reliability of DSM-IIIR diagnoses as covered in Kirk and Kutchins (1992) and the problems associated specifically with psychopathy and antisocial personality disorder researched by Hare and colleagues (e.g., Hare, Hart, & Harpur, 1991).

A basic objective of problem identification with involuntary clients is to acknowledge the parameters of the mandated problem before moving to other mutually identified problems that might be simultaneously addressed. Involuntary clients often possess a different view of the mandated problem or precipitating situation than the referring agency (Rooney, 1988). Direct confrontations about problem responsibility during this phase of practice are rarely productive and usually result in defensiveness on the client's part. The skillful practitioner begins by soliciting the client's perspective of the nature of the mandated problem. A few clients will steadfastly insist they played no role whatsoever in the development of the problem. These external attributions on the client's part, e.g., "Lots of people do worse things than I did and don't get *this*!" "I was framed," or "It's that bitch of an ex-wife of mine who set me up, isn't it?" can be extremely frustrating to the practitioner. Verbally acknowledging complete and total responsibility for present life circumstances however, gains little for the involuntary client, unless the practitioner knowingly or unknowingly communicates that this may be necessary to receive desirable services. If such acknowledgment is forced or coerced from the client because the practitioner believes it useful, it can later backfire and negatively affect intervention progress.

Although most clients do not acknowledge sole responsibility for the problem, they will admit to some share of the responsibility when the problem can be appropriately reframed. For example, parents mandated for treatment for child abuse often feel personally blamed and publicly labeled as bad. However, few practitioners would argue that child abuse has a single cause, instead viewing it as a complex failure of social, family, and personal learning. Reframing child abuse more broadly as a family problem may be a less alienating starting point for work with involuntary clients.

SELECTING PROBLEMS FOR WORK

During assessment, a practitioner typically uncovers multiple problems and needs that would benefit from intervention. Beyond the mandated problem, the practitioner must identify other problems for work and the order in which they should be addressed. Whenever possible, the practitioner should demonstrate respect for client self-determination by addressing client concerns that are not a part of the mandated problem (Hutchinson, 1987). In many involuntary cases, there are problems related to meeting required demands of the treatment setting that may require attention first. As examples, some patients admitted to inpatient psychiatric settings may require medication for auditory hallucinations or thought disorders before they can productively engage in counseling or problem-solving, and some clients must undergo evaluations of mental capacity before appropriate levels of treatment restrictiveness can be selected. The practitioner should make appropriate referrals to other resources when necessary, depending on the services needed and the capacity of the practitioner's agency to meet the client's needs.

Involuntary clients most often experience multiple, complex problem situations affecting more than one life domain. A single stated referral problem may represent several problems that are not broken down into operational, manageable units. The lack of identified other or surrounding problems in working with an involuntary client may also be the result of inadequate assessment hampered by poor engagement. Rooney (1988) suggests engaging the client in a problem search when faced with reluctance to identify or acknowledge either mandated or other problems. The objective is to demonstrate respect for the client's perspective, while avoiding the opposition that can arise when the practitioner identifies the entire set of problems for work.

Constructing a Problem Hierarchy

The construction of a problem hierarchy (Blythe & Tripodi, 1989; Gambrill, 1983) is a useful way to choose among a number of problems that may require intervention. The first step in constructing a hierarchy is to list all the problems identified by the practitioner and client without reference to priority. For each problem, there is some basic information required. Using means described in the previous chapter, assessment information about the problem's existence, magnitude, frequency, or duration is added. Problem precipitants, antecedents, consequences, and environmental concomitant variables are also described. This provides an initial framework for prioritizing problems and may allow for the reduction of the list. For example, a problem that occurs only under rare conditions or when certain other individuals are present may not require immediate attention if the client is to be placed in a restrictive residential treatment setting. Timing may also assist in problem prioritization, as in the case of the homeless, drug-abusing adolescent sentenced to two years in a juvenile correction facility: Finding a home can be dealt with later while drug treatment should start as soon as possible. Other problems may be in the process of resolving themselves (e.g., placement of a client on a one-week waiting list at a group residence while currently residing in a relatively safe shelter for homeless persons) and may not be of sufficient magnitude relative to other problems to include on the hierarchy.

The size of the treatment hierarchy depends on the extent of assessment and the number of problems the client possesses. It may reflect engagement, participation, or the capacity for either of these by the client or by the practitioner, or the intensity of services. Working on two or more problems at a time makes sense if they are clinically or functionally related. For example, working with an abusive parent may involve working on parenting skills as well as helping structure the parent's and the children's daily activities so that the parent can more readily implement better parenting responses. A young parolee who experiences severe anxiety in evaluative settings such as social agencies, work training, and potential job settings may need to begin work addressing more than one setting at a time.

The determination of the order in which problems should be addressed is based on several factors: (1) the legal or ethical mandate related to the client's setting restrictiveness, that is, the danger posed to self or others; (2) the practitioner's experience and judgment; (3) the agency and environmental resources that can be enlisted; and (4) the client's sense of urgency and motivation to address the problem.

An essential first step in prioritizing a problem hierarchy with any client is to identify whether any of the problems are life-threatening to the client or others. These include many of the problems tied to involuntary status such as violence toward others or toward self, or basic inability to care for self so that life may be endangered. While a parolee may be mandated to attend treatment to reduce the recurrence of criminal behavior, this individual may also be suicidal and suffering from a mental disorder such that basic cognitive orientation and self-care are impaired, increasing the risk of victimization by others.

The practitioner's judgment about the order in which problems should be addressed is based on several issues. The centrality of the problem within the entire complex of problems, the likelihood that the desired outcome can be attained, and the ethical acceptability of the desired outcome to the practitioner are overarching concerns. The accessibility of the problem, the likelihood of quick visible progress, and the positive and negative consequences of problem resolution should also be evaluated prior to agreeing to a hierarchy (Gambrill, 1983, p. 103). The practitioner also needs to determine whether change in another related condition is necessary before addressing the referral or presenting problem. Basic needs such as shelter, food, and adequate clothing fall easily into this category. The social worker aware of the impact that environmental resources have on intrapersonal and interpersonal functioning must address these problems before those related to higher functioning concerns.

Agency purpose and function can directly affect how well a practitioner addresses a problem. The mental health agency that does not also address substance abuse is a standard example. Despite the increasing prevalence of concomitant psychiatric disorders and chemical abuse, called *dual disorders*, some agencies instruct practitioners to refer elsewhere for treatment specific to the chemical or psychiatric disorder. A physically disabled parolee may have special needs that should be met in a medical or rehabilitation setting in addition to receiving clinical services provided by the practitioner. Problems that can be directly addressed at the practitioner's agency are regarded differently than those that must be referred. Although problem priorities should rarely be selected on the basis of what service the agency has to offer rather than on the needs of the client, this often occurs unwittingly. When this happens, it is usually based on the premise that something helps more than nothing. It may also be based on the theoretical orientation of the practitioner, however, and this can pose ethical issues. As an example, some substance abuse treatment models hold that a client must be chemically free before any other problem may be constructively addressed. At least one successful program for drug-abusing parents would argue against these models, however, teaching parents how to manage home and child safety concerns when they expect drugging will occur (Blythe, Jiordano, & Kelly, 1991). Practitioners who work in mental health settings may see their services as most important to restoring maximum functioning, while others argue that lack of adequate housing is clearly a more important issue. If prospective clients can only receive help by being referred to other agencies, then they should be referred.

In Chapter 2 we discussed the importance of client involvement and motivational congruence in supporting treatment adherence and effective treatment outcomes. The client's motivation and urgency about working on a particular problem should be carefully considered. Given that the involuntary client does not have say over the major prescribed focus of treatment, the practitioner should take advantage of every opportunity to increase the client's involvement by working on problems of importance to the client. Client choice in prioritizing problems should be exercised whenever possible. A practitioner may consciously choose to first address a problem important to the client, rather than one the practitioner identifies as more urgent, or to begin work on a client-prioritized problem at the same time as the mandated problem. Both these strategies can be used as a means of enhancing the client's willingness to negotiate a working agreement with the worker that includes meeting the treatment mandate demands.

Contracting With Involuntary Clients

While some practitioners believe that explicit contracts between client and practitioner are necessary, others view explicit contracts as desirable in some situations, not necessary in others, and impossible or even deleterious in a few situations. Seabury (1976) believes that it is possible but very difficult to contract with involuntary clients, noting that workers find contracting more useful with voluntary than with involuntary families. Workers also found voluntary families significantly clearer about case objectives and about intervention tasks, and better at completing intervention tasks than involuntary families (Hosch, 1973).

A contract necessarily requires that the practitioner and client agree on the problem priorities. With voluntary clients, the mutual construction of a problem hierarchy is ideally followed by the mutual development of a contract for work. While not always true, the involuntary client may lack the desire to engage wholeheartedly in identifying problems and goals, and may lack the motivation to work toward change. Criminal justice system clients who wish to remain on furlough from correctional facilities are often required to meet with a worker two or more times weekly and to submit to random urine tests for drug use. Beyond employment issues, many clients are reluctant to use these meetings to identify or work toward other life goals and may respond disinterestedly to the practitioner's suggestion they broaden the scope of their work. Further, the involuntary client may not agree on the immediate prioritization of the problems for work. For example, according to some protective service regulations, mothers seeking to regain custody of their children must successfully complete a drug treatment program, find suitable housing, and attend a parent education course before other actions toward returning the children are initiated. A mother may have difficulty understanding or agreeing with these priorities.

In many cases with involuntary clients, a reasonable objective is to work toward a working agreement, rather than a full-fledged contract. This is completely acceptable with an involuntary client and should not be regarded as a failure on the part of the practitioner. A working agreement specifies the terms of the mandate and the conditions for work. It includes the expected actions of each involved party and the consequences of nonaction. For example, if a client misses a scheduled appointment, the mandating agency or supervisor may be notified; if the practitioner misses a scheduled appointment, the client will not in any way be penalized.

The practitioner's contract or working agreement with the client should be separate from the mandated contract however, whenever possible. This can occur in several ways. In mandated group treatment programs, the practitioner often first makes clear the provisions of the mandated contract (and consequences for nonadherence) and then moves into discussing "rules for *our* group." Later, individual contract provisions may be discussed as "goals for the week," "homework," or just simply as "During the next week, can we all agree to . . . ?" In individual work, this can occur by clearly demarcating the two topics of conversation verbally, such as, "First, we'll go through the requirements for participating in this program and then we'll talk about how we can focus on the problems you think are most important." The practitioner may also indicate the separateness of the mandated agreement from the contract or working agreement by clarifying the contingency between mandated and other goals, that is, practitioner activities toward individual goals may only begin once mandated goals are satisfied.

From the involuntary client's perspective, negotiating a genuine treatment contract may not appear advantageous. Clients are aware that practitioners are under mandate to report the occurrence of illegal behaviors such as drug use or child abuse. Using evidence of minor violations, e.g., a single positive drug test, is sometimes left up to the discretion of the practitioner, increasing the arbitrary nature of the relationship and the sense of uncertainty for the client. Given the reality or perceived possibility of these situations, clients may be reluctant to openly discuss or work on these or other problems.

Other reasons also may preclude the client's ability to contract. There are cases where the client may be unable to fully participate in assessment based on cognitive deficits or other disabilities. Young children may not understand exactly what is meant by contract. Some agencies may take the position that the client does not possess adequate knowledge to meaningfully participate in assessment. Although client input is elicited to increase the practitioner's understanding of the function and context of the problem in the client's life, ultimately it is seen as the practitioner's responsibility to make decisions regarding problem importance and to clearly separate negotiable from nonnegotiable aspects of work together. The worker seeks to engage the client in treatment and to increase motivation so that the client is involved in the intervention process to the fullest extent possible.

IDENTIFYING GOALS FOR PRACTICE

A practice or treatment goal is the long-term outcome desired for the client, while a practice objective (also called a subgoal) may be thought of as more temporally proximal and related directly to work with the practitioner. Identifying practice objectives involves specifying the expected change or lack of change in the client's problem parameters, i.e., a change in frequency, magnitude, existence, and/or duration of the problem. Typical treatment goals with involuntary clients include remaining drug-free; avoiding further child abuse; obtaining employment, education, or training; continuing to take prescribed psychotropic medication; or regularly reporting to monitoring agencies. Note that each of these intervention goals could be broken down into many smaller subgoals or practice objectives. Treatment goals may be targeted toward change, maintenance, or prevention.

Intervention Objectives

Change objectives are those that describe problem resolution as the reduction of problem magnitude, duration, or frequency, or as the total amelioration of the problem. A change objective with a client who has a drug abuse problem might be to decrease the number of times the client uses drugs in a week; with a severely and persistently disordered psychiatric client, to decrease the number of inpatient admissions in a year. With an angry-explosive parent, change objectives might include increasing recognition of cues to high anger and catching oneself earlier, as well as decreasing the length of the explosive outbursts toward the child. While it is important to know whether change occurred in the desired direction, it is only when specific objectives and interventions are tied together that a practitioner can begin to assess the effectiveness of a particular intervention.

By operationalizing the problem and describing it in measurable terms, practice objectives are linked to the treatment process. This operationalization includes describing the type of data to be gathered, e.g., observing indications of ego strength during sessions, attendance verification chits from AA (Alcoholics Anonymous) meetings, and the like. In this way, the practitioner can be more precise in measuring the extent to which the objective is accomplished. A decrease in depressive symptoms as measured by a standardized scale such as the Beck Depression Inventory (BDI; Beck et al., 1961) is one way of measuring a treatment objective related to improving mood or affective state. As noted in Chapter 2, a good source of standardized scales, selected for their relevance to common practice objectives, is *Measures for Clinical Practice: A Sourcebook* (Corcoran and Fischer, 1987). Other sources and descriptions of standardized instruments useful in practice include Levitt and Reid's (1981) article "Rapid Assessment Instruments in Social Work Practice" and Edelson's (1985) article, which reviews standardized assessment instruments for evaluating practice with children and youth.

An intervention or set of interventions may have more than one desired objective. Standard outcome objectives for most individuals nearing discharge from institutional facilities include finding stable housing, obtaining social service entitlements, and getting connected to community-based supports. A practitioner may use the same intervention, such as guided problem-solving, to attain all of these objectives or may select individual intervention plans for each objective.

Specifying an objective further can be done by indicating, when appropriate, the *amount* of change expected in problem frequency or magnitude, *when* the change is expected to occur, and *how long* the change is expected to last. For example, as a result of participating in the state-mandated educational program for convicted drinking drivers, it might be expected that a client's amount of drinking will be significantly reduced after 5 months of intervention, and that the reduced drinking behavior will persist for 1 year after intervention.

Instrumental and Final Objectives

Nelsen (1983) identifies instrumental objectives as those which must be accomplished before proceeding to more remote objectives. The achievement of instrumental objectives is first necessary before progress can be made toward attaining final objectives. For example, an abusive parent may need to learn mood management skills before learning positive parenting skills. When planning for discharge from an institution, a client usually needs to establish a place to live before exploring employment or day treatment options. More immediate in time than final objectives, instrumental objectives serve to reduce longer-term objectives to more manageable levels for both the practitioner and client. Long-range objectives, such as the development of an adaptive social support, network, can be extremely difficult for a former drug user; yet accomplishing smaller, more concrete goals, such as attending several different neighborhood NA (Narcotics Anonymous) meetings or calling a friend or relative likely to provide adaptive social support, may be indicative of progress toward building an adaptive social support network. These instrumental goals are attainable, thereby offering more encouragement to both the client and practitioner about the possibilities for change.

The necessity of identifying *realistic* objectives that are *manageable* and *achievable* for the involuntary client cannot be overstated. Failure, particularly early in the intervention phase, can be an extremely disempowering experience for any client, but especially an involuntary client. Overall progress and success at accomplishing instrumental objectives are important early in the intervention phase. If the client is not making progress, the practitioner should promptly reevaluate the situation. Are the objectives clear to the client? Are the tasks within objectives clear? Do they feel manageable from the client's perspective? Are the steps between tasks too large? What are the possible client, practitioner, environmental, and interactional obstacles to the accomplishment of objectives? Here the practitioner's focal task is to identify manageable and beneficial objectives, while guarding against trivial objectives that may be of little consequence. Chapters 5, 6, and 7 include examples of treatment goals and instrumental or subgoals used in work with criminal justice, protective services, and mental health clients.

Intervention Hypotheses

An intervention hypothesis states the predicted relationship between an intervention and an expected consequence of that intervention. The intervention is the independent variable. It temporally precedes and is presumably causally related to one or more dependent variables—the intervention objectives. Planning an intervention actually involves formulating a hypothesis that specifies independent and dependent variables. For example, one intervention hypothesis is that self-help groups (independent variable) such as AA are a good intervention for people trying to maintain sobriety or, more specifically, alcohol-free days (dependent variable #1) and to increase adaptive social contacts (dependent variable #2). Another commonly held intervention hypothesis is that participation in day treatment (independent variable) benefits persistently mentally ill individuals because it increases monitoring of symptom exacerbation, potentially preventing rehospitalization (dependent variable #1) and because it develops social and life skills (dependent variable #2). Similarly, a well-known general intervention hypothesis is that verbal praise, encouragement, and support, i.e., positive reinforcement, increases the likelihood that newly learned behavior will recur.

There are four activities central to developing intervention hypotheses:

1. Identify the treatment objectives: Is the goal to achieve prevention, maintenance, or change?
2. Specify the dependent variable: What do we want to see change? Operationalize the intervention objectives in terms of problem existence, magnitude, frequency, and/or duration, specifying the type of data needed to measure variables related to the objective.
3. Identify any predicted intervening variables: What else may affect the dependent variables? Intervening variables are causally connected to the dependent and independent variables such that changing the intervening variable creates a change in the dependent variable.
4. Predict the expected effect of the independent variable: Will this intervention directly affect a dependent variable or will it affect an intervening variable, which will then cause change in a dependent variable?

SELECTING RESEARCH-BASED INTERVENTIONS

Interventions are conscious actions that practitioners take to achieve desired treatment objectives. Interventions are used to prevent, reduce, or eliminate problems and to maintain desired states. They may be relatively simple and specific or they may be complex, involving an entire set of attitudes, beliefs, and behaviors. Interventions may precisely prescribe how the practitioner interacts with the client or they may be a list of rudimentary guidelines for interaction. Interventions *do not* include unconscious actions the practitioner is not aware of and cannot describe; they are also not other extraneous or unplanned events, however helpful they may be in reducing the client's problem. There are two broad criteria to consider in choosing interventions: applicability and support.

Applicability is the relevance of the intervention to the particular problem, client, and practitioner in the case. Important in assessing applicability is the specificity of the intervention. Unless there is enough operational information presented to describe the intervention validly and reliably, its true applicability cannot be assessed. *Support* includes the available evidence that the intervention is effective. Does it result in demonstrable changes in the intervention objectives it was intended to address? There are two kinds of support available: clinical support and empirical support. Clinical support usually is based on a clinician's report that the intervention accomplished its objectives. As such, it requires accepting the judgment of the reporter, because there is little or no systematically gathered or replicable information that is offered as support.

In research-based practice, interventions with empirical support are preferred over those without it. Empirical support means that systematically collected data were used to verify the relationships between interventions (independent variables) and desired outcomes (dependent variables). Moreover, the variables described in the clinical studies should be relevant to the current client or client system, and should be valid, reliable, and generalizable to other client situations. The practitioner should ask, Was the intervention effective in previous studies? Will the intervention be effective for the present client?

Although conventional wisdom suggests that outcomes with involuntary clients are not as successful as those with voluntary clients, empirical evidence of the past decade does not support this view. Early, broad-based reviews of social work practice did find casework services ineffective at preventing delinquency (Fischer, 1973; Wood, 1978) as did reviews in the criminal justice literature (Lipton, Martinson, & Wilks, 1975). However, generalizations drawn from the subsequent evidence across social work and psychology outcome research suggest three summative comments: (1) Mandated clients can accomplish as successful results as voluntary clients; (2) Few studies distinguish voluntary from nonvoluntary from involuntary clients; and (3) as noted in Chapter 2, more positive outcomes appear linked to improving practitioner-client interaction, especially motivational congruence (Wood, 1978; Reid & Hanrahan, 1982; Brehm & Smith, 1986; Videka-Sherman, 1985; Rooney, 1992).

It is remarkable that many interventions with clients do *not* have empirical support. This is true for interventions with voluntary as well as involuntary clients. There are examples where good to strong empirical support links a particular intervention to successful problem amelioration in some client groups. A few examples of this include self-help groups to buffer caregiver stress (Toseland, Rossiter, & Labrecque, 1989), cognitive therapy and pharmacotherapy for reducing unipolar depression in adult outpatients (Hollon, Shelton, & Loosen, 1991), and behavioral therapy for anxiety disorders (Thyer, 1987). Empirically supported interventions specifically carried out with involuntary clients include family preservation services for families at risk of having their children placed in substitute care (Wells & Biegle, 1992), and interventions for spouse batterers (Eisikovitz & Edleson, 1989), as well as programmatic level interventions such as intensive case management (Rubin, 1992) and intensive parole supervision. Interestingly, involuntary clients often possess the same problems as voluntary clients, leading the empirically based practitioner to locate support among other client populations that would be most likely to generalize to the involuntary client group. As an example, support was found for a family preservation intervention that used multisystemic therapy to prevent incarceration of serious juvenile offenders (Henggeler, Melton, & Smith, 1992). This same intervention may likely generalize to use with less severely disordered youth and their families.

As with all intervention research, the empirical support for the interventions cited above varies in amount and quality. Practitioners need to critically evaluate the empirical base for the particular interventions they wish to implement. If the empirical support seems limited and there is no alternative intervention with more support, it is important to carefully monitor client response to the intervention. Practitioners have an ethical obligation to familiarize themselves with the range of approaches and intervention models used to treat the problems they most commonly confront with their clients.

We have stated that the research-based practitioner believes that empirically supported methods of treatment are preferable to those without empirical support. But what does this really mean for practitioners faced with their first client mandated to treatment for child abuse? Or a probationer who must attend drug treatment as a condition of avoiding jail? The phase of engagement and assessment with involuntary clients can be addressed in general terms, through a framework outlining the principles, content, and context or process. Selecting intervention methods, however, requires problem-based specificity. Despite encouraging results suggesting that more structured interventions enhance client motivation and control, there is no one intervention method or procedure that can be regarded as generally effective with involuntary clients. With each case, the practitioner must begin with the literature on that specific problem, set of problems, and client population. From this vantage, the empirical evidence supporting each intervention model should be a major deciding factor in intervention choice.

ACCURATELY DESCRIBING INTERVENTIONS

It would be impossible to describe every action and spoken word necessary to accomplish intervention objectives. Outside, unplanned circumstances, such as missed appointments, illness, or crisis, can affect the sequence and timing of intervention implementation. It is also impossible to anticipate and plan for all contingencies. If we want to test interventions, communicate them to other colleagues, train others to implement them, and develop knowledge about when specific interventions are most useful, there needs to be some degree of specificity and common knowledge in our approach to certain types of problems. In work with clients, when we need to change interventions, we need to know what it is that we should change; without building in some degree of specificity there would be no place to start! Most practitioners are aware of the problems caused by vagueness in trying to communicate interventions to others. This demands flexibility on the part of the practitioner if the most effective known methods of treatment will be used (Seligman, 1990). Although audio- and videotape technologies have improved the ability to accurately communicate, most practitioners still rely on verbal or written descriptions of interventions for instructions.

A good place to start describing an intervention is with its relatively stable parameters, e.g., appointment dates, time length of intervention sessions, number of interventions, when and where the interventions should be delivered, who delivers the interventions, and the targets of interventions. Alternatively, one can begin by delineating the content areas to be covered with as much specificity as possible. Content areas include the topics of discussion, the types of worker involvement, and the nature of tasks included in the intervention. Here the practitioner's theoretical orientation (such as ego psychological, cognitive-behavioral, or psychoanalytic) is important to identify because it includes assumptions about the client's behavior and attitudes as well as prescriptions for how the practitioner should act. Within the practitioner's theoretical framework, it is helpful to delineate *what* specific interactions with the client are planned. Examples of specific actions include the use of supportive verbal statements to encourage a young delinquent to try new activities at school, and the exploration and discussion of painful feelings related to loss of a close relationship. With more information about the parameters of intervention, these descriptions could be even more specific.

Detailed examples of group interventions often are easier to locate in the literature on practice outcomes. Before beginning new groups, many agencies require staff to identify the goals of the group, the prescribed activities to accomplish those goals, the roles of leader and any coleaders, and the contents for discussion, exploration, and group exercises. There are many examples of group intervention protocols with varying levels of specificity. These protocols address problems ranging from improving children's problem-solving skills (Camp & Bash, 1981) and providing support for caregivers of the frail elderly (cf. Toseland, Rossiter, & Labrecque, 1989) to reducing self-criticism in women (cf. Berlin, 1985) and reducing recidivism among substance-abusing offenders (Fabiano, Porporino, & Robinson, 1991).

A number of useful operations have been identified by social workers to describe interventions more specifically: attaining procedural descriptiveness, specifying involvement, determining optimal intervention settings, and developing practice prescriptions. *Procedural descriptiveness* is a term used by Thomas and colleagues to describe the specific and complete set of activities carried out (Thomas, Bastien, Stuebe, Bronson, & Jaffe, 1987). Procedures accomplish practice objectives and are described only to the extent that they are *specific* and *complete*. A complete procedure includes (1) the activities that must be carried out to accomplish an objective, (2) who should engage in the activities, (3) the target(s) of the procedure, (4) the conditions under which the activities are carried out, and (5) the goals that will be accomplished through the use of the procedure. A specific procedure denotes the precise details of the activities to be performed. Clarity, unambiguous readability for the user, and reference to the observable characteristics of the activities are also important (Thomas et al., 1987, p. 45).

Specifying involvement refers to the type and extent of participation by client(s), the practitioner, and any others taking an active interventive or monitoring role. A family may be involved with the department of social services, child protective services, schools, primary health care agencies, and mental health agencies. Additionally, parents, grandparents, and siblings who may not be identified clients may also need to become involved. Intervention with a mentally disordered individual may involve the client's regular (3 or more times per week) attendance for at least 2.5 hours at a day treatment program, an individual 45-minute weekly meeting with the practitioner, monthly meetings with public assistance, SSI (Supplemental Security Income), and child welfare agen-

cies. Further, family members of the client may be involved in monthly
2-hour "helping families manage" meetings at the day treatment center
and have periodic meetings as needed with the practitioner and client.
Specifying the level of involvement is especially useful when more than
one agency is involved as it can prevent the practitioner from working at
cross-purposes to other service providers. Involvement includes the frequency of participation as well as the length of time each participant
spends on each contact or on outside session tasks related to the client's
intervention.

Determining the optimal intervention setting is related to the short- and
long-term effectiveness of the intervention. Accessibility of the setting to
the client is based on geographic proximity, available transportation,
and specific eligibility requirements. These factors should be considered
in formal sites such as agencies, institutions, or other organizations
concerned with human welfare as well as in informal sites. Informal
sites include, for example, the client's home, a fast-food restaurant, a
park bench, and a subway platform. Does the site facilitate implementing the intervention plan and accomplishing objectives? Is the site af-
fordable and accessible to the client? Does it maintain privacy and other
rights while possessing sufficient resources to carry out the intervention? In reality, the best available combination of these factors may still
result in very limited intervention site options. For example, clients
serving prison sentences for sexual abuse of their children are invited to
participate in parenting skills classes in the prison, but may be unable to
practice these skills with their children until months or years later.

Developing practice prescriptions and examining the extent to which they
can be generalized is another way to specify and describe an intervention more completely (Wedenoja, Nurius, & Tripodi, 1988). A practice
prescription is defined as a "statement which instructs practitioners in
what to do, be, think, or say when working with clients or on behalf of
clients" (Wedenoja et al., 1988, p. 429). Practice prescriptions often indicate that the practitioner must think, feel, or act in certain prescribed
ways. For example, when a practitioner develops a group for paroled
sexual offenders, individual contracts must be negotiated with each parolee regarding personal goals. Constructing practice prescriptions is
accomplished by answering the questions Wedenoja and her colleagues
(1988) pose:

1. For what type of client and practice setting is this prescription
   designed? What client characteristics, such as gender, ethnicity,
   previous treatment history, or cognitive abilities, are particularly
   relevant?
2. What intervention or specific interventive technique should the
   social worker implement? Is the intervention sufficiently de-

scribed so that it could be replicated by the same or another worker?

3. What is the rationale for selecting this prescription? What empirical or other evidence is there for using this prescription?
4. With what types of clients, presenting problems, specific treatment objectives, agency settings, and social workers is the prescription known or not known to be effective or appropriate? What modifications might be necessary because of these concerns?
5. How might this be applied in other situations? (adapted from Wedenoja, et al., 1988)

Most practice prescriptions are focused on specific client populations and describe the worker's role and behavior in delivering the intervention in some detail. Prescriptions should be offered under one of two conditions: when there is supporting evidence that justifies the prescription's intervention effectiveness, relevance, and generalizability; or when the prescription is offered as a hypothesis to be tested in the clinical situation. In most of our work with clients, the second situation is the more likely to prevail. This reality increases our need to know how an intervention plan is monitored, and whether it is effective.

IMPLEMENTING RESEARCH-BASED INTERVENTIONS WITH INVOLUNTARY CLIENTS

No matter how hard we attempt to plan for all possible contingencies that might interfere, the best planned intervention can go awry. The reasons for this derailment range from problems in the intervention plan itself or in the environment, to obstacles in the client, practitioner, or the interaction between them. As the practitioner observes the extent to which a chosen intervention plan continues to be applicable, modifications and alterations may be required. In some cases of implementation failure, we may need to select an entirely new intervention. In cases where successful implementation does occur, the extent of progress toward objectives must be assessed and measured as systematically as possible. To assess intervention implementation, we recommend asking the following questions:

1. Is the intervention implemented accurately? Are the procedures implemented consistently across time and, if appropriate, consistently across practitioners?
2. What are the major problems in intervention implementation?

How can these be located, monitored, and corrected when encountered?

3. How is progress toward the intervention objectives assessed?

Accurate Implementation

Accurate implementation refers to the *validity* of intervention implementation: Does the intervention, in reality, exist as planned? In the clinical literature, the terms often used for intervention validity are treatment *integrity* (Sechrest & Redner, 1979) and *fidelity* (Moncher & Prinz, 1991), i.e., faithfulness of the intervention to its original plan. Also a part of accurate implementation, the *reliability* of an intervention depends on the degree to which procedures are consistently implemented from time to time and from practitioner to practitioner. For example, in a parenting skills training program for very young fathers, an intervention procedure used to begin group sessions each week might be verbal reinforcement and support for any time spent as primary caretaker; if the procedure is inconsistently implemented from week to week or across practitioners with two different groups, there is unreliability in the implementation of procedures. The absence of the procedures in one group and their erratic presence in the other indicates that these procedures were not effectively communicated and/or implemented.

Differences, i.e., *variability*, in applying intervention procedures, can impede or prevent the accomplishment of intervention objectives. The terms *treatment drift* (Peterson, Homer, & Wonderlich, 1982) and *treatment shift* (McMahon, 1987) are used to describe this phenomenon; drift is used to describe deviation from an intervention research protocol, while shift is used to describe a practitioner knowingly or unknowingly contributing to variability in clinical practice.

As indicated previously, we recommend that both the intervention procedures and the theoretical approach should be specified. If two practitioners use cognitive-behavioral family therapy to help prevent out-of-home placement of a troubled adolescent, for example, each employs many different types of interventions unless a standard procedure or set of procedures has been clearly identified. As practitioners, we often nod knowingly when we hear a term like *cognitive-behavioral therapy* or *structural family therapy* without truly understanding how the individual components of these intervention approaches are being used with a particular case. This lack of procedural specification has made it very difficult to meaningfully compare intervention implementations across treatment outcome studies. Although this may appear patently obvious, a necessary first step in determining how to reduce variability is recognizing when and how variability occurs.

Identifying Variability in Implementation

Referring to the example of the parenting skills program for young fathers above, one can account for some treatment shift if it can be ascertained that one group leader had not understood that the caretaking reinforcement and support component was to be implemented each week. Further, if upon checking with the second group leader it is found that she had stopped reinforcing and supporting primary caretaking among the young fathers because she did not approve of where they took their infants and small children (video game parlors, streetcorner hangouts, and bodegas known for drug dealing), one might account for even more of the observed variability. This information suggests the occurrence of two types of variability: variability due to unclear communication of procedures and implementation variability.

There are five general sources of implementation variability:

1. lack of knowledge or understanding of the intervention procedures;
2. inaccurate implementation, e.g., wrong context, timing, or affect;
3. interpersonal obstacles that preclude real implementation;
4. nonimplementation; and
5. unreliable client system involvement in intervention.

As noted earlier, a prerequisite for monitoring implementation variability is specification of the essential intervention procedures. Implementation monitoring is systematic observation of the degree to which an intervention is consistently implemented as planned (Blythe & Tripodi, 1989). To begin monitoring, one should specify a simple list of key intervention parameters, such as frequency, time, place of intervention, and procedures. In the above example, the practitioner's verbal reinforcement and positive affective responses to a list of positive fathering activities are intervention procedures. Intended efforts of the practitioner or other interveners and of products that verify the intervention took place may also be monitored. Examples of intended efforts include time in sessions with the client, within-session content, and tasks requiring completion. Figure 3.1 is an example of a mother monitoring her own efforts to initiate nondemand conversations with her 13-year-old daughter. Monitoring must be closely tied to key intervention objectives. In this example, intervention objectives concern improving positive communication with the daughter (defined as nondemand conversations) and improving the mother's feelings about herself as a parent. A more complicated between-session client monitoring form was used with a depressed young woman diagnosed as a borderline personality disorder (see Figure 3.2). In this example, the client monitored her implementa-

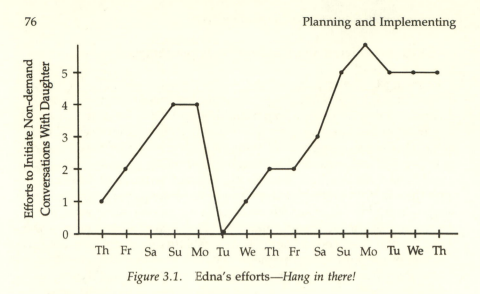

Figure 3.1. Edna's efforts—*Hang in there!*

tion of a range of coping strategies in a variety of self-sabotaging problem states.

Implementation failure occurs when the intervention is not implemented as planned. The initial site of failure may originate within the client system, within the system of interveners (practitioner and others), and/or within the interactions between the worker, the client, and extraneous events. Investigating implementation failure can be carried out systematically by reviewing the five sources of implementation variability listed above. The implementation failure sources are then examined within each potential system site, i.e., client, intervener, or interaction. For example, implementation failure located in the client system often takes the form of a compliance or treatment adherence problem. Compliance issues can range from actual attrition (referred to as absconding or escape in some settings!) to erratic session attendance, inattention to session content, or lack of motivation and willingness to engage in agreed-upon intervention activities. Some sources of these failures include the extent of the client's understanding of the intervention procedures; the correct application of the intervention procedures by the practitioner or client; interpersonal obstacles that impede implementation; and poor responses on the part of other client system members that may prevent the client's full participation.

Implementation failure, once identified, can be corrected by addressing the source of variability within the site. Strategies to correct variability and implementation failure should be implemented as widely as necessary among the involved systems. One primary strategy is to correct knowledge, communication, and informational inaccuracies. Improved specification of intervention procedures may assist with this. It also is important to correct possible inaccuracies due to the client's mis-

	Problem	Dysfunctional Problem Solving		Alternate Problem Solving	
Date	Description of Problem Situation Thoughts or Overt Problems	Desire to Self-Sabotage (1–100) List Sabotage	Behavior— what I did (also amount, duration)	Coping Thoughts	Coping Behavior

Sabotages: Drinking
Suicidal Thoughts
Hoarding Pills
Staying in Bed
Eating Binges
Shoplifting
Overspending
Skipping Appointments

Figure 3.2. Record of attempts to overcome desire to self-sabotage using alternate coping in daily situations.

understanding of the purpose and content of intervention objectives and procedures.

If client nonadherence to intervention procedures prevents accurate implementation, there are six strategies the practitioner can use to increase adherence. These can be used individually or in combination:

1. Make a specific request of the client rather than a vague one in instigating action. For instance, "During the next week you must

call in at least three times to update the program on your job search" is more effective than, "Why don't you check in a few times next week and let us know how your job search is going?"

2. Obtain an overt (either oral or written) commitment from the client to comply with intervention procedures;
3. Train the client to perform the required procedures before expect- ing autonomous performance (teach needed new skills);
4. Positively reinforce completion, and approximate completion of the activity;
5. Ensure that required client intervention activities are manageable, that is, they require the smallest amount of possible discomfort and difficulty;
6. Involve the client in the selection and design of intervention tasks the client will be expected to complete (Levy, 1977).

The practitioner should also assess whether fatigue and boredom are factors preventing accurate implementation. Sometimes an aversive agency setting or a noisy, nonprivate meeting site, the occasions or opportunities for planned between-session tasks, or the simple repeti- tiveness of practicing a new activity again and again can take a toll on the client's (and others) ability to sustain continuous progress. If it is possible to change the source of fatigue and boredom, the practitioner should attempt to do so. In the many cases where it may not be apparent how to change some of these factors, we encourage the practitioner to discuss the sources of fatigue and boredom with the client, perhaps generating other possible change methods, but at least acknowledging the impact these factors have on the client. This reduces the likelihood that the client will feel blamed for the intervention failure.

Increased monitoring of intervention implementation is useful once the likely sources of variability have been identified. This may be con- ducted by the practitioner, the client, or others. In many cases, this can be easily accommodated and built into existing monitoring devices. Monitoring activities can be increased by more frequent monitoring, monitoring in more settings, and/or by monitoring different aspects of the problem.

ASSESSING PROGRESS AND EVALUATING PRACTICE WITH INVOLUNTARY CLIENTS

Determining the extent and nature of client improvement is central to intervention implementation. Client improvement is demonstrated in the variables that make up the intervention objectives. If change is the desired objective, progress is indicated by differences in the intervention objective variables between baseline and intervention phases. If maintenance or prevention is the desired objective, progress is indicated by a lack of change in the intervention objective variables or by a decrease in variables tied to negative risk factors.

Monitoring Progress

Monitoring is done for a purpose. The purpose is to evaluate the extent of progress toward a goal, here measured against the intervention objectives. Monitoring is conducted based on a time frame for expected changes. These changes may be either short- or long-term or both. The practitioner identifies a specific time period in which progress is expected to occur, for example, within six sessions. The variables examined for progress or change can reflect all the different types of data discussed in Chapter 2. The variables measured to evaluate progress in a depression management program might include the biweekly depression symptom level score on the BDI (Beck et al., 1961), a daily log monitoring engagement in positive activities, accomplishment toward goal setting, and a weekly overall self-reported mood level rating. This example illustrates that progress can also be monitored across two or more variables at the same time. Within one intervention plan there may be multiple objectives, e.g., finding a more stable living situation, getting into a vocational training program, and developing an adaptive social support network. Within these multiple objectives, different levels of progress may be considered, such as the length of time necessary for change to occur or the extent of change expected in a particular period of time.

Monitoring improvement should begin as soon as the intervention is implemented by measuring the same variables that were measured during assessment (baseline) as well as other variables that might indicate client progress. The measurement intervals should remain the same or should be similar to what they were during baseline. These intervals should be meaningful in terms of the problem and intervention objectives. For example, adherence to a psychotropic injection medication regimen may only require weekly monitoring, while problems such as crack cocaine use, feelings of complete fury toward a child, and occasions for relapse to unsafe sexual behavior may require monitoring on a daily or even more frequent basis.

Monitoring change during intervention can also serve to bolster client motivation and increase congruence between client and worker. Most clients do not progress through an intervention plan in an even, regular manner. Often there is a point at which the client or practitioner becomes discouraged, impatient with slow progress, or doubtful about the utility of the entire enterprise. To counteract this tendency the practitioner might try these procedures we have found useful:

1. Verbally reiterate the focus and importance of small, manageable objectives by reviewing steps accomplished toward larger goals as indicated in case records.
2. Play audio- or videotapes of earlier sessions that illustrate progress when specific activities or problem manifestations have changed.
3. Review any graphed data, such as the change in frequency or magnitude of a target behavior, with the client.
4. In group interventions, use constructive feedback from other group members to help the individual client realistically appraise progress.

Determining the *significance* of improvement is necessary to decide whether sufficient improvement has occurred. Improvement can be regarded as a reliable change in the measurement of problem variables in the direction of the intervention objectives. This is observed by examining the *clinical significance* of the changes made toward the intervention objectives; and in some cases, this is followed by determining the *statistical significance* of those changes. Clinical significance is discussed in more detail in Chapter 4.

Based on an assessment of progress and accomplishment of intervention objectives, the practitioner has three options concerning intervention implementation: Continue the intervention as it is at present, modify the intervention, or stop implementing the intervention entirely. In cases where sufficient progress is occurring at a reasonable rate, a decision can be made to continue the intervention with no change. In cases where insufficient progress has been made, the practitioner can, upon examination, identify modifications to the intervention that would improve the likelihood of progress. These modifications may include subtracting one or more components, adding components to the current intervention, or changing the way in which the intervention is implemented. Finally, in some cases the intervention should be discontinued. These cases include situations when (1) the problem and intervention objectives have been wholly accomplished, (2) the intervention is identified as unethical or as introducing the client or others to risks that are not likely to be outweighed by benefits, or (3) the intervention is evaluated as unlikely to bring about improvement or may have occasioned deterioration. When faced with this situation, a practitioner has several alternatives, including referral, further assessment, consultation, and the design of a new intervention plan. These may be effectively used alone or in combination.

When the point of expected change occurs, the practitioner can examine the measurements to draw one of four possible inferential conclusions:

1. The intervention objective(s) was attained.
2. Progress was made, but the intervention objective was not completely attained.
3. No progress was made.
4. Deterioration occurred (we're farther away from the objectives than when we began!).

The use of graphs to analyze practice progress can also be extremely instructive. For a graph to be useful in assessing progress, however, it must begin during assessment as it requires multiple observations of the target objectives (dependent variables) both before and during intervention. Progress is evaluated by changes in the level of the dependent variable between assessment and intervention phases. Graphs and other visual indicators of progress can be meaningful to clients when used in session and given to clients to keep and use between sessions. Graphs started during early assessment have an advantage in that they can be used to illustrate progress over larger amounts of time. Other ongoing, visual progress forms include charts, tallies, and various types of report cards.

CONCLUSION

This chapter has addressed the second and third phases of practice: planning and implementation. In work with involuntary clients even the selection of problems is a task laden with coercive potential, and we have attempted to address the importance of client self-determination in problem identification and goal selection to the fullest extent allowable. The available treatment outcome research supports this as critical in producing effective outcomes. Selecting research-based interventions is difficult because the body of applicable and supportive literature remains sparse. This underscores the importance of specific and accurate intervention description. Implementing interventions with involuntary clients depends on accurate implementation, the ability to identify sources of variability within interventions, and the assessment and evaluation of progress toward intervention objectives.

Chapter 4

Termination and Follow-Up

This chapter discusses the final phases of work with voluntary and involuntary clients: termination and follow-up. Definitions of termination and follow-up are offered and conditions under which termination and follow-up occur are discussed. Procedures for maximizing the effectiveness of termination and follow-up are reviewed, and case examples illustrate the application of termination and follow-up procedures.

Termination involves a set of activities aimed at completing work with a client and preparing the client for the next phase of his or her life, hopefully in a less restrictive setting and possibly without any social services intervention. In reality, the work of termination begins at the first session with the client, insofar as the practitioner is always attempting to move an involuntary client toward voluntary client status and/or independence or less reliance on the system. Note that we are referring here to termination that is jointly planned by the worker and the client, as opposed to client dropout or termination precipitated by agency directives or policy.

Termination of social work intervention should not be confused with termination of work on a particular treatment goal. Throughout practice, specific client goals are being completed, and thereby terminated, as specific problems are resolved, gains are made and maintained, or potential difficulties are avoided. When any of these situations occur, work on particular goals should be terminated. Some agency record-keeping systems, however, do not lend themselves to ongoing termination of goals throughout the course of services.

In contrast, termination of work with a client occurs when it is apparent that, upon examining client data and other case information, all necessary goals have been accomplished satisfactorily. Both the worker and the client should agree that work has been completed. For example, a worker has been seeing two lesbian parents, Eve and Linda, who adopted a 6-year-old girl, Kay, 6 months earlier. Eve and Linda were required to receive family treatment when their adoption worker reported them to protective services after seeing a bruise on Kay's upper arm. Both Eve and Linda indicated that they were unsure about how to handle Kay's frequent and violent temper tantrums and her "testing" behaviors. They became frustrated when their usual ways of responding to Kay were not effective and admitted that they both had resorted to hitting her at times. With the concurrence of Eve and Linda, the worker set treatment goals to eliminate their hitting Kay and to reduce their yelling at Kay. As they worked toward these goals, the couple revealed that they also had violent arguments with each other, which sometimes resulted in physical fighting. Although this was not the reason for the original referral, the worker felt it was important to address this issue because of the potential for a family member being injured and the potentially undesirable consequences for Kay. The couple more easily accomplished their treatment goals related to hitting and yelling at Kay, as evidenced by self-report data, practitioner observations of Eve and Linda using their new skills to respond to Kay's tantrums, and corroborating discussions during regular sessions. Accordingly, work on these treatment goals was terminated but work on the goals related to their arguments and fighting took more time to accomplish. Eventually, their self-reported information and practitioner observations confirmed that these goals had also been resolved. At this time, the clients and the practitioner agreed to terminate their work together, and a report was made to the referring protective services unit.

Of course, the ideal situation in which involuntary clients and workers can continue to work together until necessary goals are attained is not always possible. Sometimes, work with an involuntary client must continue *after* goals have been attained, simply because of a mandate from the system. This may be seen in the case of Rick, a client who was released from prison to parole. Within the first four months following his release, Rick had accomplished all of his goals and was employed, was attending AA meetings, and had reestablished connections with his family. Because the order accompanying his release indicated he would be on parole for one year, however, he continued regular meetings and other mandated reporting tasks with his parole officer.

The flip side of this situation can be seen when clients have not completed all of the work on their goals but must terminate because the original mandate for services specifies a termination date that has been reached and cannot be exceeded. Chris became an involuntary client when she was hospitalized due to her overwhelming fears that she was being followed, observed, and harassed by unknown enemies. Chris and her social worker decided to try to reduce these fearful feelings by identifying early warning signs that she was going to experience the feelings and then putting into place a plan for coping with them. Unfortunately, Chris was only eligible to stay in this facility for 28 days, and had to move to a different setting before she and the practitioner had completed their work.

PLANNING TO TERMINATE

If the nature of the mandated service or the intervention model prescribes a particular ending point, the practitioner and the client should discuss this in the first session. Often, clients will be in a state of crisis or perhaps so angry about their involuntary status that the planned termination will have to be discussed again. The point here is that the worker needs to be certain that the client is aware of the likely ending and will not be surprised. In fact, keeping clients aware of termination can actually help to focus their work. When they realize that the end of services is coming within a specified period of time, they are less likely to waste time by such tactics as failing to complete assignments, or not bringing up concerns.

ANALYZING DATA TO DETERMINE IF
GOALS ARE ATTAINED

Decisions to terminate work with a client are based upon information indicating that the client has accomplished his or her goals. The practitioner will have information about the goal attainment in the form of data describing dependent variables. These data can be graphed and analyzed visually and statistically. Visual analysis methods will be discussed here. Quasi-statistical methods of analyzing data related to goal attainment, which are simple to apply and involve only easy calculations, are explained elsewhere (Bloom & Fischer, 1982; Blythe & Tripodi, 1989; Jayaratne, 1978).

Data must first be graphed following the procedures discussed in Chapter 2. The practitioner must determine if the particular goal being considered is related to prevention, maintenance, or change, and what *is the desired direction for the data pattern* in the intervention phase. Prevention goals will call for a stable, relatively flat pattern, indicating absence of the problem. Suppose the goal is to prevent recurrence of verbally abusive behavior. A data pattern similar to that in Figure 4.1 would indicate the prevention goal was being accomplished.

Maintenance goals also should have a stable, relatively flat data pattern with the desired level of the dependent variable being present in the intervention and follow-up phases. Suppose that the goal is for a client to maintain a certain level of social contact with supportive

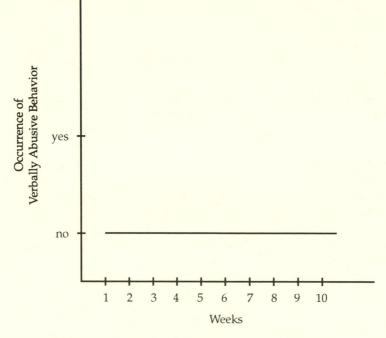

Figure 4.1.   Occurrence of verbally abusive behavior.

friends. A data pattern suggesting that this goal was being maintained in the follow-up period might look like that depicted in Figure 4.2.

Finally, attainment of a change goal would be represented by a shift in the data pattern from a level indicating a problem in the previous phase to a level indicating absence of a problem in the succeeding phase. As an example, a client's urges to use crack may move from a high level to a low level, as shown in Figure 4.3.

Clinical Significance

The above graphs represent data patterns that clearly indicate goal attainment and are less complex than what is typically found in practice. Hence, the practitioner must follow certain guidelines in visually analyzing data patterns. In determining the desired data pattern that would indicate goal attainment, the practitioner also should consider *clinical significance*. Clinical significance is a nonstatistical method that considers whether the intervention has made a difference in the daily functioning of the client (Risley, 1970). It is indicated by an improvement or reduction in the problem state that the practitioner and client regard as mean-

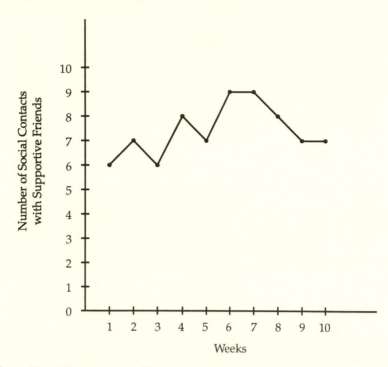

Figure 4.2. Maintenance of level of social contacts with supportive friends.

ingful, given the history, development, and current level of the client's problem. Note that it is possible for change to be statistically significant, but not represent change that is meaningful to the client. Clinical significance is a subjective judgment determined a priori by considering what degree of change or level of the problem would be acceptable for this particular client (Blythe, Tripodi, & Briar, in press). Normative levels of behavior and performance may also be used to assess clinical significance, labeling progress as clinically significant when the client moves from the dysfunctional to the functional range on the variable used to measure the problem (Jacobsen, Follette, & Revenstorf, 1984). For example, among former heroin addicts participating in methadone maintenance treatment programs, abstinence from drugs other than methadone, such as cocaine, is often identified as an important intervention objective, and can be considered within the functional range for this client group.

Clinical significance usually is determined by the practitioner in consultation with the client, but may also involve input from other professionals or significant others. As an example, following participation in an AIDS prevention intervention, a man who had *never* used condoms previously began to use them *all the time* with his casual sex partners

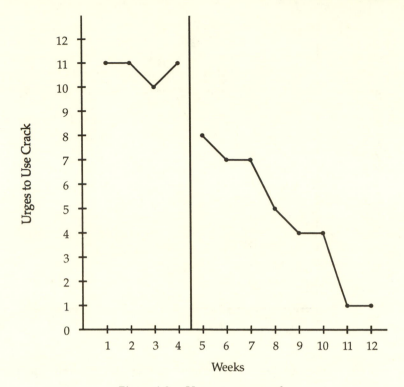

Figure 4.3. Urges to use crack.

although he still did not use them with his primary partner. In the judgment of the intervention staff, the client, and the client's peers, this was a clinically significant outcome. Clinically significant results may also be observed in the form of changeable states or characteristics such as release from or admission to an institution, finding a job or housing, and adoption or divorce.

Assessing clinical significance can be difficult in cases of "mixed" results. Some involuntary clients may go through periods of improvement or relative stabilization, only to experience erratic problem activity that suggests true improvement may not have occurred. The schizophrenic individual who goes through a period of medication adherence and decrease in negative symptoms, and the offender who has maintained work for several months, may both require increased treatment restrictiveness on an episodic basis to manage heightened problem states. Once the practitioner is familiar with the client's pattern of behavior over time, these periods may be anticipated and responses planned in advance. A reasonable intervention goal in such a case often focuses on increasing the length of problem-free or higher-level functioning between episodes.

Examining Trend, Magnitude, and Stability of the Data

The practitioner next examines each phase to determine the *trend*, *magnitude*, and *stability* of the data pattern. Trend refers to the direction in which the data are going. Magnitude refers to the level of the problem, as indicated by the units along the X-axis. Stability refers to the absence of frequent and large changes in the magnitude of the data. Ideally, each phase will have at least 3–5 data points. This number generally is sufficient to provide an indication of the direction in which the data pattern is going and of the level of the problem.

Stability must be examined for data patterns in all phases. Wildly fluctuating data, such as those depicted in Figure 4.4, are difficult to interpret in terms of both magnitude and trend. For involuntary clients, as well as most other clients, however, it is generally not feasible nor ethically sound to withhold treatment or changes in intervention until data patterns become more stable. Fluctuating data should be examined for possible patterns of response, such as increased magnitude indicating problem severity on certain days. Events in the client's life can then be examined in an attempt to detect explanations for the data patterns— explanations that may suggest environmental or other interventions. These events often are called *critical incidents* (Reid & Davis, 1987). Elliot, for example, was an inpatient on a mental health ward. Elliot's social worker noted that he had more paranoid delusions after contact with his girlfriend, regardless of whether the contact was in the form of visits, telephone calls, or letters. The worker used the graph depicted in Figure 4.5 to encourage Elliot to discuss his concerns that his girlfriend might be having him followed because she suspected that he saw other women. This eventually led the worker to involve the girlfriend in some of their sessions.

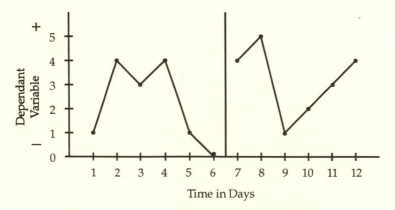

Figure 4.4.   Graph of fluctuating data.

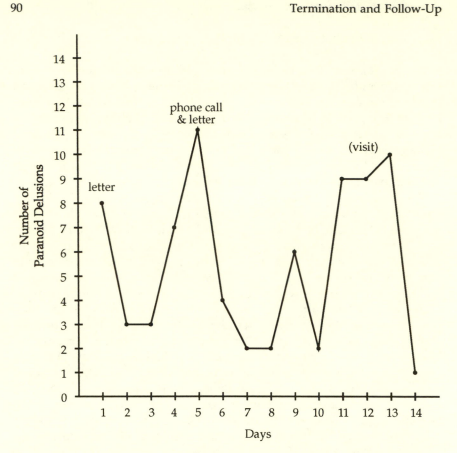

Figure 4.5. Graph of frequency of paranoid delusions and critical incidents.

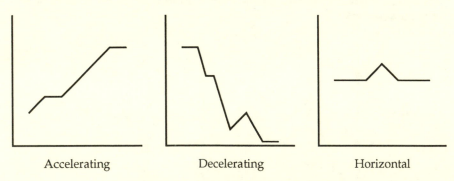

Figure 4.6. Trends in data patterns.

There are three possible *trends* in data patterns: accelerating, decelerating, and horizontal trends. Figure 4.6 depicts each of these trends. Again, the practitioner must refer to the treatment goals to determine what is the desired trend.

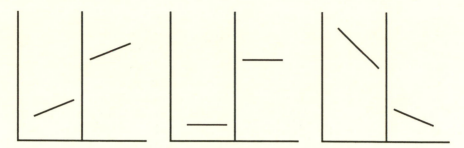

Figure 4.7.   Changes in magnitude.

The goals also dictate whether or not the practice-researcher is looking for a change in magnitude. Prevention and maintenance goals generally involve no change in magnitude while change goals suggest a change in magnitude from baseline to intervention, in the desired direction. Figure 4.7 illustrates some possible changes in magnitude.

Table 4.1 summarizes the steps the practitioner should follow in visually examining graphed data. While they are useful in making treatment decisions, these graphs also can help the client move through the termination process, as is suggested in the following section.

Table 4.1.   Steps in visually analyzing data.

1. Determine the data pattern that would indicate goal attainment.
2. Consider what would constitute a clinically significant data pattern.
3. Assess the stability of the data, and check for possible critical incidents.
4. Examine changes in magnitude and trend in terms of expected data pattern to determine goal attainment. Also consider whether these data patterns constitute clinical significance.

REVIEWING GAINS

Reviewing gains or accomplishments at termination is a critical step in helping clients benefit from their experiences as involuntary clients. To do so, the practitioner should refer to the previously identified treatment goals and the graphs that indicate goal attainment. We believe that graphs should be shared with clients throughout treatment. This review and reinforcement is important in helping the client avoid a return to the problems he or she experienced before entering treatment, albeit involuntarily. Graphs provide a visual representation of the client's accomplishments and, as such, help clients recognize the magnitude of their achievements.

While reviewing these gains, the practitioner also must help clients realize their role in achieving these results. If clients, involuntary or voluntary, have a positive experience (as defined by achieving desired goals) with a social services agency, it is possible that they will attribute this positive experience to the worker or to other collateral services rather than acknowledging their own role in the process. Clients must be helped to take credit for their contribution to their own problem resolution so that they will be more likely to see themselves as able to solve other problems in the future.

Another part of reviewing treatment gains involves going over the strategies the worker and client used to achieve the gains. Particular emphasis should be given to reviewing the problem-solving process and the actual steps taken by the client. At the end of this review, the client should be able to use the problem-solving process and the other skills he or she learned during intervention to deal with future obstacles. We cannot overemphasize the importance of this step. Our work with involuntary clients should have focused on building skills and helping them learn new ways to overcome obstacles. As much as possible, we should be moving them from involuntary to voluntary client status, and/or to less restrictive settings. Therefore, it is critical that at termination we ensure that they not only recognize their role in resolving their problems, but also understand how to replicate these problem-solving actions in the future.

DEVELOPING INFORMAL AND FORMAL SOURCES OF SOCIAL SUPPORT

All too often, individuals in the mental health, child protective, and criminal justice services systems became involuntary clients, in part, because they did not have enough sources of social support. In other instances, these individuals had used up these supports by asking for too much help too many times, or by disappointing these sources of support. Without these supports, they were not able to hold things together and committed actions that brought them into one of these systems as involuntary clients. These actions frequently are methods of coping, albeit not ideal methods, in situations where the individuals see few other options. Hence, an important part of work with involuntary clients is identifying and building, or possibly repairing, informal and formal support networks.

What do we mean by informal and formal social supports? Gottlieb (1981) defines social supports as "verbal and nonverbal information or advice, tangible aid or action that is proffered by social intimates or inferred by their presence and has beneficial emotional or behavioral effects on the recipient" (quoted in Whittaker & Tracy, 1989, p. 29). Formal supports are those offered by organized services and usually, but not always, involving professionals. An outpatient mental health center and a homemaker services program are examples. Informal supports are not housed in any type of organization and tend to involve family, friends, and members of the community. For example, a member of a church might volunteer to be a buddy to a person just released from a correctional facility, or an aunt might make daily phone calls or visits to check in on a person living independently after being discharged from a psychiatric unit. If informal and formal supports are viewed along a continuum in terms of degree of organization and professional involvement, somewhere in the middle are self-help groups such as AA and NA or a group of parents meeting to support each other in their efforts to deal with living conditions in a housing project.

Informal and formal social supports can serve several important functions for these clients both during and after involuntary services are terminated. Frequently, they make it possible for clients to be served in less restrictive settings. Such settings may be more attractive to involuntary clients. Research has documented, for instance, that African-Americans (who are overrepresented among involuntary clients) only seek formal services as a last resort (Sue, McKinney, Allen, & Hall, 1974). After termination of services, informal and formal supports can be invaluable in helping clients maintain treatment gains. And, when services are time-limited or need to end before all goals have been completed, other supports may make it possible for clients to continue to make necessary changes.

Formal and informal social supports may be initiated before the point of termination, or as the time to terminate draws near. In either case, a careful assessment of client needs as well as resources is necessary before a plan for enlisting social supports is developed. In conducting such an assessment, attention should be devoted to the potential sources of support in the client's environment, in addition to the possibilities for developing new supports. A strengths-based assessment is important here (Hill, 1972). Existing or former memberships in organizations, such as service clubs, and churches, are potential sources of support. Old connections that have been damaged or severed should be explored to determine, first, if they are adaptive and have potential to contribute to the client's functioning and, second, if they can be reinstated.

Assessment tools are available that can help both the practitioner and the client identify needs, and potential and actual sources of support. Social network maps specify the level of informal and formal supports available to a client. Another example of such an assessment tool is the ecomap, which illustrates an individual's or a family's relationships with various elements of their social environment (Hartman, 1978). Figure 4.8

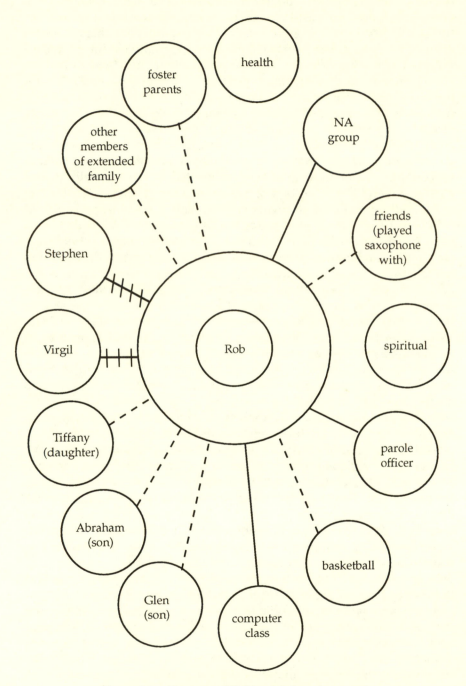

Figure 4.8. Ecomap of Rob's social environment.

shows an ecomap for a young African-American parolee, Rob. Rob has infrequent contact with his three children, each by a different woman. In treatment, efforts will be made to help Rob make some contacts with these children. He has severed all contacts with his family of origin, except for his older brothers, Virgil and Stephen. Although recent interactions with Virgil have been strained, the worker notes a strong connection between the two of them and the possibility for repairing and strengthening this relationship. Virgil has helped Rob on numerous occasions and has a steady job and stable family life. Stephen, on the other hand, is a convicted felon who has a long history of numerous offenses. The practitioner sees no reason for attempting to repair this relationship at this time. Rob lived in several foster homes, but was especially attached to his last set of foster parents. Efforts will be made to locate them and determine if they have an interest in being involved with Rob at this time. Rob also has started attending NA meetings and sees his parole officer each week. Rob used to enjoy jam sessions with some friends in which he played saxophone. The worker will explore his interest in music and the possibility of establishing some connections for him in this area. Rob is developing computer skills at a job training program. He has very little recreational activity, although he used to enjoy basketball—another possible source of support.

Practitioners are urged to be creative in their search for sources of support. All too often, practitioners simply turn to the local resource book published by United Way or some other information and referral organization. While they can uncover some very useful resources, there are limits in the degree to which these publications can be helpful. Sometimes resources in such books are overutilized and consequently have long waiting lists. Or they may have several stipulations regarding service eligibility. Another concern is that such resources continue to cast the client in the role of client, when the client may actually benefit from a more mutual relationship or a resource that does not label him or her as client. If resources are identified in such directories, the client should be involved in this process, as well as in gathering information and evaluating the potential of the resource to meet the need. These are valuable skills for clients to possess after involuntary services have terminated.

At times, it may be necessary to prepare clients to use these informal and formal sources of social support so that they enjoy the maximum potential level of support. Clients must be able to clearly communicate their needs, to accept offers of help, to use communications that promote positive relationships, and to express their appreciation to sources of support (Blythe, 1983). Sometimes the individual most in need of the social support is the least able to access it. Because they may have had unsatisfactory experiences, particularly with formal supports, clients may have difficulty expressing themselves calmly and/or may only be able to respond in negative or hostile terms. Practitioners should assess the client's verbal and nonverbal skills. Ideally, the client would be observed while interacting with a current or potential source of support. Role-play practice with clients can develop and strengthen communication skills. If possible, practitioners may want to accompany clients on initial meetings with supports to coach and encourage them.

Before terminating with an involuntary client, the practitioner should ensure that informal and formal sources of support are in place and functioning, especially if these supports are viewed as important elements in the client's posttreatment success. This is usually possible unless the resource is a formal source of support with a long waiting list. Drug treatment programs, for instance, often cannot meet the demand for services. It is not a good idea to hold open a case when all other work on goals has been completed, if the worker is just waiting for a slot in a program to become available for the client. In such situations, it is preferable to close the case and reopen it briefly when the client reaches the top of the waiting list. In this way, the worker does not build in unnecessary dependence, yet can ensure that the referral is effectively implemented. Also, this procedure gives clients clear signals regarding their client status.

RELAPSE PREVENTION SKILLS

Similar to creating linkages with formal and informal social supports, relapse prevention is an activity that becomes especially relevant at termination, although it may have been a focus of intervention earlier in treatment. In general, the purpose of relapse prevention is to provide clients with skills that help them maintain the gains they experienced in treatment and avoid returning to involuntary client status.

This seems a good point at which to note that we do not think it is reasonable, although it is highly desirable, to expect that none of our clients will ever return to involuntary client status. The fact remains that most of these individuals live in environments marked by poverty, drugs, crime, crowded schools, inadequate housing, and limited employment opportunities—environments that make it extremely difficult to function. While we approach each case as if we expect that this client can and will avoid a return to involuntary client status, we also are not blind to the environmental stressors that they must confront on a daily basis.

Having said this, some variation of relapse prevention work is extremely important with involuntary clients. Relapse prevention is most widely used in substance abuse (Marlatt & Gordon, 1985), but has been extended to other client problems such as depression, chronic pain, sexual deviance, and schizophrenia (Berlin, 1985; Wilson, 1992). One of the most important components of relapse prevention involves identifying the warning signs or cues that the client may be slipping back into the problem area. Depending on the client situation, the problem area will be defined differently. For one client, it might be delusional thinking; for another, extramarital affairs with younger women; and for a third client, suicidal ideation, just to name a few examples. Identifying the cues can be accomplished by reviewing with the client some of the events that occurred before this most recent episode. These include intrapersonal, interpersonal, and environmental events. With the client's knowledge and consent, significant others may be involved in this process, particularly with clients who have difficulty maintaining contact with reality. A simple self-anchored scale or self-report measure could be developed to help the client or significant other estimate the potential for relapse and the severity of the situation. For example, in an effort to avoid a relapse to crack use, Reginald and his worker decided that he should monitor his urges to use crack and desire to return to places or hang out with friends associated with his former use. Sylvia, who experienced severe depression, needed to monitor her use of medication and her moods.

Another important part of relapse prevention involves developing a plan for responding if the client becomes concerned that he or she might relapse. This plan should consist of a simple set of actions that the client can take, if necessary. These actions should be easy to carry out. They should be recorded somewhere that is easily accessible to the client. The practitioner may want to write these as brief steps on the back of his or her business card so that they are easily accessed and may be carried at all times. In no case should the plan require a large expenditure of effort or other resources to put it into effect. And there should be several options in the event that some of the alternatives cannot be used.

Finally, we have to help clients realize that they may experience a slip, but that this slip is not equivalent to a full-blown relapse. Clients need to understand that a slip is not a reason to feel overwhelmed or defeated and is certainly not permission to relapse. Nor should a slip be construed as failure on the part of the client. Tara, for instance, was learning to avoid hitting and yelling at her children as a means to get them to obey her. As termination drew near, her worker talked with Tara about the fact that it was preferable that she not yell at her children. But they also discussed the reality that most parents do yell at their children from time to time. If Tara did so, she should not take this as a signal of failure nor permission to return to her old ways. Rather, it was something that might occur once in a while and, when it did, Tara could refer to her relapse prevention card to identify some ways to handle her feelings before they led her to yell at the children.

CLIENT AND WORKER HESITATION TO TERMINATE

Even when clients have been informed about the pending termination, they may be hesitant to terminate. In these instances, the worker needs to explicitly recognize the client's reluctance. For instance, a worker might say, "I can see that you would prefer to continue working with me." While being clear that the termination must occur, the worker can indicate that he or she would also like to continue (Kadushin, 1983).

Practitioners also may be hesitant to terminate, particularly if they have become attached to a client or client unit. Workers need to be very clear about both program and client goals and their potential implications for deciding when to terminate. Supervision can also be helpful here. If workers are having serious doubts about termination, they need to examine these cognitions to determine what might be behind them. In these cases, it usually will be something more than a simple attachment to a client. Often, workers are concerned that clients will not be able to maintain the gains they have made. (Client hesitation to terminate sometimes comes from similar doubts.) Developing a supportive resource network for the client and identifying relapse prevention plans are two strategies we have just discussed that can help clients continue to manage their lives after services are terminated. If the worker is seriously examining the decision to terminate, he or she should consider whether more work needs to be done in one or more of these areas. Of course, if the mandate for services allows it, the practitioner can extend services. We believe, however, that this extension should be time-limited and should have a definite focus around some limited, yet critical objectives.

Follow-up activities, which will be discussed in the next section, can also help clients and/or workers when they are hesitant to terminate. As will be seen, follow-up can allow for additional checkpoints or can even build in some brief booster sessions.

FOLLOW-UP

Follow-up can serve different, but related, purposes. A primary purpose is to determine if the client is maintaining gains made earlier. Another purpose of follow-up may be to provide booster intervention sessions. Booster sessions are designed to boost skills and new learning back to the level they were at when intervention ended and are particularly useful with interventions that have involved developing new skills. These sessions may have been scheduled in advance, before services were terminated, with the additional goal of providing support and reinforcement for continued maintenance of treatment gains. Booster sessions also may be scheduled in response to indications that clients are having difficulty maintaining their gains. These indications may come from a routine follow-up check, a call from the client or a significant other requesting help, or a report from another professional. In some instances, follow-up is mandated based on the client's involuntary status. Finally, follow-up may be carried out to collect information on the effectiveness of services delivered.

While we recognize that many workers may not have the luxury of making routine, periodic follow-up contacts, we nonetheless urge workers to do as much follow-up as is feasible. If possible, we recommend something like 3-, 6-, and 12-month follow-up contacts. Ideally, at least some, if not all, of these contacts would be in the client's home or current living situation, which will provide a much more complete picture of how clients function in their current environments. Follow-up contacts in the home also may afford opportunities to collect information from other individuals, but this should only be done with the client's knowledge and permission. Office-based follow-up sessions are the next best alternative. The in-person contact can yield considerable information. At a minimum, we suggest that the practitioner attempt to make 1 or 2 telephone contacts (or written contacts, if the client does not possess a telephone) over the course of the first 6 months following termination of services. Follow-up contact is especially important with clients who are at risk of harming themselves or others. In these instances, it seems ethically imperative that the agency provide sufficient time for workers to make follow-up contacts.

The responsibility for follow-up may be less clear when another agency is working with the client. Generally, the practitioner must weigh such things as the degree to which the tie between the client and the new worker is formalized, structured, and/or mandated; the potential for the client to harm someone; and the importance of gathering effectiveness data. For example, a client discharged from a psychiatric facility to community living with an intensive case manager may not have to be followed to ensure that treatment gains are being maintained, because the case manager should be performing this function. The practitioner may be able to simply call the case manager to answer questions about intervention effectiveness. A follow-up contact with the client probably would be redundant. On the other hand, suppose that this same client were discharged to community living and simply referred to a community mental health center for therapy. In this instance, there is

less structure and perhaps some ambiguity about the relationship between the client and the community mental health center. The practitioner may be more likely to follow up directly with the client to get
more reliable information. If there is a concern that the client might
harm someone, then there is even more reason to contact the client
directly. Of course, we realize that the ideal is not always possible in
practice.

Methods of Keeping Contact With Clients

For a range of reasons, from environmental stressors to preferred
life-style, clients who have at one time been involuntary are likely to
move frequently and to not be easily tracked. Therefore, workers should
lay the groundwork for keeping in contact with clients before they actually terminate with them.

Toward the end of service, the practitioner should tell the client that
he or she wishes to stay in touch with the client. It is critical that the
client understand the reasons for the follow-up. Along these lines, clients need to be informed as to who will have access to any information
the worker collects during follow-up contacts.

In discussing follow-up plans, realize that clients may have different
responses. For purposes of discussion, we will present the two ex-
tremes. Some clients, despite a positive relationship with the worker,
will not want to be followed. In fact, they may have been looking forward to getting the system off their backs. As with other such situations,
the practitioner needs to help the client express these feelings and val-
idate them, while remaining clear that follow-up contacts will be attempted to accomplish specific purposes. Other clients may actually
look forward to follow-up, and see it as a means of avoiding termination. Again, the practitioner should assist the client in expressing these
feelings, while stressing the purpose for follow-up. The client needs to
understand the conditions under which he or she can request assistance
in the future (this will vary across social agencies and perhaps across
workers), what type of assistance can be expected, and how to contact
the worker.

Once the purposes of follow-up have been clarified and client responses handled, the practitioner should take steps to facilitate future
follow-up contacts. After checking the agency records to be sure that the
client's current address is correct, the client should be given postcards
with the practitioner's address and postage on them, to be used to
communicate any change of address. The agency record also should be
checked to be sure that addresses and phone numbers of relatives
and/or significant others who may know how to contact the client (of

course, with the permission of the client) are correct. Sometimes, fol-low-up sessions are scheduled in advanced. If so, a written record of these dates should be given to the client. Pocket-sized calendars, dis-tributed at no cost in stationery shops, may be given to clients so that they can record follow-up appointments as well as other dates.

Finally, the agency record should indicate any good leads on where to locate clients if they have difficulty maintaining gains made in treat-ment. In such instances, clients are unlikely to fill out a change-of-address postcard. Knowing that a client tended to frequent certain bars in a specific neighborhood, or cashes a public assistance check at a particular convenience store can be immensely helpful in locating a cli-ent. Unless there are other reasons for not doing so, such information should be recorded in the case record as it will be difficult to recall 3 to 6 months after services have been terminated. These good leads on where to contact clients may also serve as secondary sources of infor-mation, if the client cannot be located.

Approximately 1 to 2 weeks before the scheduled follow-up contact, a reminder of the contact should be sent to the client along with instruc-tions on letting the agency know if the client cannot keep the appoint-ment. To further ensure that the contact will occur, the mailed reminder should be followed by a telephone confirmation or the client should be asked to return a card (enclosed in the mailing from the practitioner) indicating whether he or she will be available for the follow-up session.

Possible Information to Gather in a Follow-Up Session

The content of the follow-up session will vary according to the stated purposes of the session, the setting in which it occurs, any mandates to gather certain information, and the specific needs of the client and the practitioner. Following are some suggested areas that might be ex-plored.

1.   Is the client maintaining the progress made during the interven-tion? If not, what might be contributing to this? If not, is the slippage enough to warrant a booster session(s), a referral to another formal source of support, identifying another informal source of support, or intervention at some other level?

2.   If so, do they need to be addressed? If they need to be addressed, how should this be done: booster session(s), referral, informal supports, or something else?

3.   Are the client's informal and formal supports still effective, or does he or she need to repair them, develop new ones, or take some other action?

4.   Is the client's relapse prevention plan adequate? If not, how does it need to be improved?

5.   Is the client using the skills learned during intervention? If not, does he or she need to do so? Are any adjustments necessary?

6.   Is the general purpose of the referral sufficiently resolved? For example, in a child abuse referral, is the parent still abusing the child? In a corrections case, has the client committed any new offenses?

7.   Is the client involved in adaptive activities that might displace less socially desirable behavior? (Is the client employed, attending AA meetings, attending parent support groups, volunteering in a community service setting, as examples?)

8.   Is there any specific information that the practitioner is mandated to collect?

Gathering the Follow-Up Information

As was true in the earlier phases of service, research-based termination and follow-up rely on empirical data. These data may be qualitative or quantitative. Most likely, the semistructured interview will be the most effective in gathering the necessary information. Such a format typically gathers qualitative information, some of which can be quantified. A semistructured interview has the dual advantage of allowing the client some flexibility to talk about his or her concerns and priorities, but also increases the likelihood that the worker's questions will be addressed during the follow-up contact.

Standardized measures and rating scales also may be used to collect follow-up information. This is especially helpful if such instruments were used during intervention, or developed for use in relapse prevention. When instruments were used during intervention and are repeated at follow-up intervals, it is interesting and helpful to compare the two sets of responses. Again, clients should be helped to understand that some slippage is to be expected and to determine if the current situation is functional or requires some level of intervention.

As we indicated above, the ideal setting for collecting follow-up information is the client's natural environment, but this may not be possible. The worker and client may want to initially take some time for conversation and then signal that it is time to get to work by reminding the client of the purpose for the contact. The practitioner should also review matters like who will have access to the information gathered. As much as possible, the worker should analyze the information the client presents as it is gathered, for clinical decisions, and share this analysis with the client. In this way, they are likely to be able to make any necessary plans or adjustments in a timely fashion, if not during this contact.

In some instances, the practitioner will collect information to complete a mandated report. For example, a probation officer may identify drug use through the report of a urine test. Or, a worker may suspect child neglect during a home visit. As with any mandated reporting, the worker needs to make clear to the client that the behavior in question is being reported, why it is being reported, and what the basis is for the report.

Aggregating Follow-Up Data

If the practitioner collects follow-up information on whether treatment gains have been maintained, these data can be pooled with similar data on other clients to examine the effectiveness of a particular treatment program. This is especially likely if the practitioner has collected information on the attainment of overall program goals as they relate to individual clients. Suppose that the practitioner works in a suicide unit. He or she may collect follow-up information on suicide ideation, gestures, and/or attempts from all clients. These outcome data could be pooled across clients or could be grouped according to variables related to client characteristics or program differences. The results would be of interest to practitioners working with similar populations. In addition, supervisors and administrators might find the information helpful in making programmatic decisions such as those related to staff training, hiring, and allocation of resources.

CONCLUSION

Ideally, termination will be a planned activity with the decision to terminate being based on an analysis of all available case information to determine if goals have been attained. Of course, the ideal is not always possible in the real world. Ironically, people who became clients involuntarily may also be terminated involuntarily. When this occurs, the practitioner can attempt to implement as many of our recommendations as possible. Fortunately, there usually is some advance notice that premature termination will occur, so that the termination can at least be planned.

This chapter has presented methods of visually analyzing graphed data and determining if change is clinically significant to assist in decision-making regarding termination. Activities that are crucial to an effective termination, including reviewing the gains the client has made, ensuring that social supports are available, and helping the client develop relapse prevention skills, were discussed. Follow-up might be carried out for various purposes, which were noted. Strategies for gathering follow-up data, the types of follow-up information to collect, and means of aggregating follow-up data also were presented.

Chapter 5

Research-Based Practice With Clients in the Criminal Justice System

> The mood and temper of the public with regard to the treatment of crime
> and criminals is one of the unfailing tests of the civilization of any country.
> Winston Churchill, 1910.

In this chapter, we examine practice with the most easily recognizable group of mandated clients: those receiving services due to involvement with the criminal justice system. The criminal justice system is difficult to understand, both with respect to practice orientation and the restrictiveness of security and intervention methods. Some of these interventions may take place before an individual is incarcerated. These preincarceration services include services provided in community diversion programs for youth, local probation programs, and residential or daytime alternatives to incarceration programs. Other interventions take place during incarceration, within the confines of facilities such as juvenile or adult detention, jail, or prison. These facilities may be local, state, or federal in jurisdiction. Still other interventions occur after release from incarceration as with parole or other aftercare services for offenders.

Increasing crime rates in the United States continue to draw attention to the problems associated with the process and procedures of the criminal justice system. Reported crime and arrest rates, however, portray only the top strata of a funnel that quickly narrows to include a relatively chosen few. According to the *1991 Sourcebook of Criminal Justice Statistics* (Flanagan & Maguire, 1992), the estimated total number of arrests, or those entering the criminal justice system, was 14,195,000. Approximately 81.6% of those arrests were males. Almost 70% were white, with the remainder being primarily African-American. In the past decade, increasing proportions of women were arrested for criminal offenses of all types, but especially offenses involving drugs. From 1982 to 1991, the number of women arrested for drug offenses, including possession, manufacturing, and sale, increased by 89%, a rate almost twice the increase for males during the same period (Federal Bureau of Investigation, 1992).

Of all those convicted of felonies, 60% are placed on probation while only 40% are sentenced to confinement (Pallone & Hennessy, 1992). From 1980 to 1990 the number of incarcerated females has increased by 130%; the number of males by 81% (Bureau of Justice Statistics, 1989). The total probation services population as of 1990 was 2,521,525. The number of sentenced prisoners in state and federal correctional facilities was 738,894; and daily estimates of local jail and detention facilities include another 405,320 individuals (Flanagan & Maguire, 1992). Clients may enter the criminal justice system once, many times, or may maintain continuous involvement over many years. The path through the criminal justice system begins at commission of a crime and proceeds through reporting, arrest, indictment, plea, trial, outcome, and sentencing. What is less generally known are the many points of exit from the criminal justice system prior to sentencing and prior to incarceration. Figure 5.1 identifies each of these steps and their potential outcomes.

Slightly over 20% of all men and 5% of all women convicted of indictable offenses receive prison sentences; this represents about 4% of all adult offenders. The average sentence length is about 12 months and women are generally given shorter sentences than men (Pallone & Hennessy, 1992). Figure 5.2 depicts the small proportion of those offenders who serve sentences.

WHAT IS TREATMENT WITH CRIMINAL JUSTICE CLIENTS?

The system-prescribed goal of intervention with criminal justice clients is to prevent the recurrence of criminal behavior. From this worldview, the probationer, parolee, and prisoner have offended society by their behavior. If the word treatment is taken as it is usually understood, each of these individuals must undergo a change. The final change target in the field of corrections is the individual's criminal behavior and attitudes. Due to the sheer size of criminal justice and correctional systems across jurisdictions, a limited number of programs are used on a widespread basis as the vehicles or methods of change: diversion, alternatives to incarceration, and custodial care (i.e., incarceration). These programmatic intervention methods include two primary components: (1) variable deprivation of freedom providing for punishment, monitoring, and protection of public safety; (2) variable potential involvement in pro-

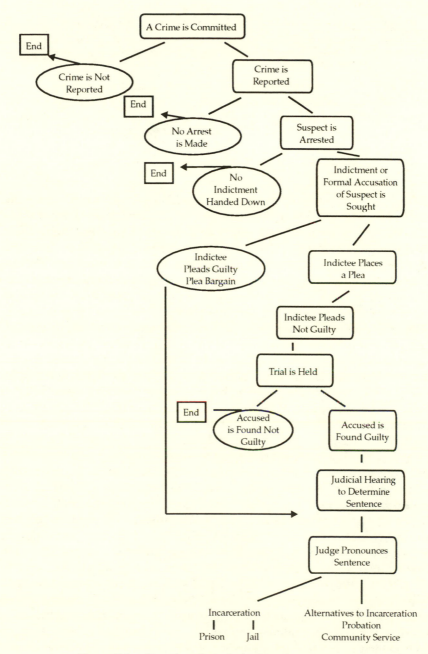

Figure 5.1. Entering the criminal justice system.

≣79% No Arrest
⊞10% Probation
▨6% Convict>Prison
⬚5% Charge Dismissed
▦.4% Tried/Acquitted

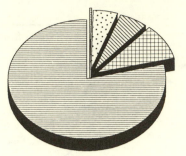

Figure 5.2. Sentenced incarceration as an infrequent consequence of crime.

grams, e.g., educational, vocational, rehabilitative, and supervision, and counseling efforts, that allow matching of client need with service and provide the opportunity to gain skills or resources that help avoid further criminal behavior. The level of involvement possible in programs and counseling is usually determined by available resources, while the level of supervision required is often set by legislative mandate or policy.

Examining the criminal justice system along a continuum of least to most restrictive, one can see that the number of options decrease markedly as restrictiveness increases. Alternatives to incarceration, probation, and parole involve some monitoring of behavior and often involve variable levels of residential placement. In work release programs, for example, inmates who have relatives to live with are moved to less restrictive status sooner than those who have no relatives with whom they can reside. An assumption is made that individuals in these least restrictive programs maintain many of their freedoms and rights. Among moderately restricted programs, more freedoms are withdrawn; and generally more monitoring devices are required. These programs are most often, but not exclusively, residential in nature. Once incarcerated, restrictiveness can vary depending on the size, density, and security level associated with a correctional facility. The highest degree of restrictiveness is found in punitive segregation units inside prisons where offenders live in relative isolation and are allowed very limited access to recreation or interaction with others. Individuals are usually sent to these units following infractions committed once inside prison or jail.

Including those listed in Table 5.1, a wide variety of programs have been used in the United States and other countries as alternatives to incarceration (ATI). Fines and other forms of restitution are the most frequently used alternatives. Probation, instead of sentencing, and parole, which is granted after serving a portion of a given sentence, are also widely used. ATI programs, whether residential or day reporting, and partial confinement programs, such as work release and educational release, often involve additional specialized treatment for alcoholics,

Table 5.1. Restrictiveness of the Criminal Justice System

Person is found guilty of a crime and is sentenced to the following:

Low degree of restriction
  Fine or other restitution
  Probation
  Parole
  Alternatives to incarceration
    1. Electronic Monitoring devices
    2. Restitution and fines
    3. Work furlough
    4. Work release programs
    5. Halfway house
Moderate degree of restriction
  Detention facilities
  Group homes
  Alternative incarceration
High degree of restriction
  Jail
  Prison
Highest degree of restriction
  Punitive segregation in prison

other drug abusers, or sex offenders (Koehler & Lindner, 1992). Community service programs may use work release inmates to staff work projects for nonprofit or government agencies. Some community corrections programs offer innovative alternatives to incarceration by shifting offender services from the state to the local community, often providing residential care and vocational training in addition to more traditional correctional counseling. As part of some ATI programs involving house arrest or curfews, individuals wear electronic bracelets that transmit information identifying their proximity to a monitoring device to central monitoring sites. If an offender exceeds the acceptable distance from the device during the hours of confinement, the information alerts an alarm. Of course, programs using such technology are only as good as their capacity and ability to promptly respond when information is received. While ATI programs are more humane and appealing to many than incarceration, research on their effectiveness is mixed; strong conclusions cannot be drawn at this time. Several reviews and summations of available research find ATI programs no more or less effective than incarceration at reducing recidivism (Netherland, 1987; Smith & Berlin, 1988).

Probation, a division of the field of correctional care, is a legal, social, and personal service operating within the framework of a judicial setting. Probation consists of investigation and supervision for the purpose of protecting society, preventing delinquency and crime, and rehabilitating the offender. Evolved from practices in English common law, probation was originally intended to mitigate the severities of the penal code. Determination of appropriateness for probation is usually made on the basis of a *presentence report*. Probation tasks include investigation (assessment or, as it used to be called, a "social study"), recommendations to the judge, surveillance, friendly admonition, and environmental manipulation, including resource brokerage and advocacy (Netherland, 1987). While these practices have not changed since the early part of this century, today's probation officer has behavioral and social science research to draw on, making probation practice amenable to research-based practice.

Parole, originally an outgrowth of British attempts to dispose of convicted felons in the colonies, is the conditional release, most often granted by a board of parole, of a convicted offender from a penal or reformative institution, usually after serving a portion of the given sentence in confinement (Cromwell, Killinger, Kerper, & Walker, 1985, p. 390). The offender released to parole typically is required to fulfill certain conditions, including regular meetings with a parole officer. Failure to meet these conditions results in a return to confinement to serve the balance of the sentence and may involve an additional sentence for the violation of parole. Many of the numerous problems attributed to the parole system involve the large discretionary power of parole boards. During the 1980s, however, sweeping changes in sentencing were made that have limited some of this discretionary power.

Martinson and Wilks (1977) compared inmates released under parole supervision and those released at the end of their sentences without supervision. Research demonstrated that the parolees recidivated less than the nonsupervised offenders. In general, other research has also found that probation and parole are as effective as incarceration (Lindquist, Smusz, & Doerner, 1985). Pallone and Hennessy (1992) also note that statistical evidence suggests that those sentenced to probation are less likely to recidivate than those sentenced to prison.

Innovative prison programs include treatment units such as drug therapeutic communities. "Stay'n Out" (Wexler, Falkin, & Lipton, 1990) and SHOCK incarceration programs, which provide shorter sentences for nonviolent offenders, are examples. SHOCK programs are paramilitary in nature, with a strong emphasis on discipline, physical activity, and adaptive structure. At less cost to the community and less time away from the community for the offender, SHOCK programs also demonstrate recidivism rates at the same or lower levels as traditional incarceration (State of New York, Department of Correctional Services, Division of Parole, 1993). The effectiveness of in-prison therapeutic communities and other forms of substance abuse treatment also has recently been examined. While results across populations are mixed (Leukefeld & Tims, 1992; Rachin, Inciardi, & Martin, 1993), their conclusions cannot be dismissed as "nothing works." More realistically, the questions raised by these findings suggest refined work to answer, What *specifically* works for whom, and under what circumstances?

Conventional wisdom dictates that offenders commit more serious criminal offenses as time goes on. The high rates of recidivism generally support this. However, Pallone and Hennessy (1992) summarized the research on crime trajectory and concluded the evidence shows a pattern of retrogression rather than progression. Trends descriptive of antisocial behavior among delinquent preadolescents and adolescents are altered significantly during development with fewer preadolescents engaging in overt antisocial acts and more adolescents engaging in covert antisocial acts over time. Among adult male offenders, specialization in nonviolent offenses was found in the U.S. and international samples, with little tendency toward consistently violent behavior. Furthermore, progression from nonviolent to violent offenses is infrequent, while significant retrogression from violent to nonviolent offenses occurs.

The effectiveness of sentencing as an intervention has been reviewed and summarized by Eysenck and Gudjonsson (1989). It is generally acknowledged that there is wide sentencing disparity on the basis of offender age and sex. Studies of various ATI programs in Great Britain have not found strong indications that these have reduced recidivism. Longer custodial sentences do deter certain types of crimes, such as murder, rape, assault, burglary, and robbery. Examining sentence length often poses methodological problems, as sentence length bears little correlation to the sentence length actually served. It is not possible to compare the effects of different sentences as offenders are not randomly assigned to sentence. Based on interaction effects reported in the literature, certain offenders may gain most from certain types of sentences. Eysenck and Gudjonsson (1989) also notes that growing information about how to identify hard-core or career criminals could be used to select those given sentences.

Mental Disorder Among Criminal Justice System Clients

There is little doubt, to even the most casual observer, that jails and prisons contain many individuals who require significant mental health care. The increasing numbers of homeless, sheltered homeless, and incarcerated individuals have all been proportionately attributed to reinstitutionalization of the mentally disordered population (Eysenck & Gudjonsson, 1989; Johnson, 1990; Teplin, 1992). Available research does not allow attributions of causation between mental disorder and criminal behavior, nor between incarceration and mental disorder, although there is evidence that vulnerable individuals may be worsened as a result of the prison environment and engage in self-destructive behavior as a consequence (Toch, 1992; Toch, Adams, & Grant, 1989). All authors above agree that the current resources allotted are inadequate to provide the legally mandated care for the large numbers of mentally disordered individuals in jails and prison. Better screening procedures, to identify disordered individuals, and the development of specific methods to treat incarcerated offenders are strongly urged.

Pallone (1991) summarizes the available epidemiologic information into four points:

1. While the incidence of clinical mental disorder, according to NIMH data, for the general population is about 19%, among offender populations it more nearly approximates 74%; that is, it is four times greater among imprisoned offenders than in the general population.
2. The incidence of mental retardation among incarcerated offenders appears to exceed that in the general population by 50%.
3. Alcohol and other drug abuse problems are estimated at 7% in the general population, while among incarcerated offenders, the incidence of alcohol abuse is about 19%, other drug abuse about 17%, and concomitant problems about 54%; that is, alcohol, other drug, and combined drug/alcohol problems are between 5 and 8 times more prevalent among incarcerated offenders than in the general population.
4. When compared to public psychiatric inpatients, incarcerated offenders have 3 times the prevalence of affective disorders, 4 times the rate of drug problems, 4.5 times the rate of organic mental disorders, and 11 times the prevalence of personality disorders. Schizophrenia is over 50% higher among the psychiatric inpatients and there are no significant differences in alcohol problems or anxiety disorders (Pallone, 1991, p. 147–8).

While Pallone (1991) suggests the higher prevalence of mental disorder among incarcerated offenders reflects the prevalence of mental disorder among the same demographic group in the general population, Teplin (1991, 1992) consistently finds a significantly disproportionate mental disorder among individuals in the criminal justice system, even after controlling for demographic differences between offenders and nonoffenders.

ENGAGEMENT WITH CRIMINAL JUSTICE SYSTEM CLIENTS

Social work practice in criminal justice settings has roots dating back to the 1890s. Coercive casework has been described as the use of re-

straining and constraining legal authority in the process of helping offenders function in their social environments without resorting to illegal
or antisocial behavior (Mangrum, 1976). Mangrum believes that the basic ideas that traditionally constitute casework are necessary for effective
practice, including the belief that motivation to improve or solve problems must come from within the client. Further, effective casework must
be desired and voluntarily requested by the client. As we have discussed
in earlier chapters of this book, we do not think it is reasonable to expect
mandated clients to willingly enter into, engage in, or initially respond
to contact with a practitioner. Casework, as traditionally defined, may
not be a reasonable service to provide if it demands voluntary participation on the part of mandated prisoners. There is no research demon-
strating more or less effective means of engaging criminal justice system
clients. While this is not surprising, the reasons for this are illustrative of
philosophical differences that exist in most literature on treating criminal
offenders. In general:

1. Engagement is not defined as necessary to accomplish goals.
    Terms such as cooperation and compliance are more frequently
    used to describe work with criminal justice clients.
2. Engagement is not separated from other treatment components.
3. Related to the above two reasons, engagement may be regarded
    as necessary by some authors, but is never regarded as sufficient,
    i.e., the active ingredient of intervention that facilitates accom-
    plishing outcome goals, in any criminal justice treatment pro-
    gram.
4. Effective engagement with criminal justice clients involves a facil-
    itative worldview or perspective on the part of the practitioner. If
    the practitioner is worried about deception and malingering, de-
    termined that the client not successfully manipulate or get over,
    or overly concerned that the client like or enjoy the contact, en-
    gagement is naturally impeded. Other practitioners want very
    much for their clients to succeed and may feel angry or blaming
    when the client does not follow suggestions or comply with man-
    dated requirements. Understanding client malingering, discussed
    in Chapter 2, is particularly important for criminal justice practi-
    tioners. Related to this is the importance of maintaining honesty
    and straightforwardness on the part of the practitioner. Any ev-
    idence of dishonesty or manipulation by the practitioner can be
    viewed by the client as justification for rejecting the entire change
    process (Bush, 1991).
5. Clients mandated by the criminal justice system often feel
    strongly that the practitioner does not have the right to know all
    the personal details of their lives. This is particularly true if the

client only views the worker's role as one of monitoring such things as criminal behavior, drug use, and job search. We have observed that this often significantly affects the practitioner's ability to engage and develop trust.

The following situation is an example of how a practitioner (*P*) offers to assist in areas the parolee-client (*C*) felt were unrelated to his avoiding crime and other proscribed activities:

P: How are things going this week?

C: Fine, no problems.

P: How are things at home?

C: Ah—well, my woman's nagging me about not having a job yet, but everything's okay.

P: Your wife called and said she went to the emergency room the other night with a black eye.

C: That lyin' bitch! I didn't give her no black eye!

P: What happened the other night?

C: Listen, she didn't call the police or nothin—I'm not in trouble and nothin happened! What business is it of yours if I keep looking for work and don't do no drugs? She got outta line and I hit her. I've never done it before, but she just kept on me.

P: What else can you tell me about the situation?

C: What the hell you want from me? This isn't your business! Why are you messin with my private life?

P: *You're* my business. I want to make sure you don't get so pressured that you go off and get sent back up. I want to know what's going on with you so I can help.

C: Shit—it's bad enough I have to give you my pee in a bottle, now you want me to tell you my business. I don't tell no one my personal business, especially not no parole counselor!

P: I know it's not a good time. I really don't want to see you go back up though, so anything that is bothering you enough that you would hit someone, bothers me. What if you hit someone who *did* call the police? What if your wife calls the police the next time? This job search has been going on for a while and everyone you know asks you how it's going. That would get to me too.

C: You know, I just get so fed up with people turning me down—I hate getting up in the morning sometimes.

P: Hitting your wife is not so good though—what do you think?

C: I felt bad after it happened. She called her sister. She wouldn't let me go to the hospital with her or nothin. I went out and stayed out all night.

P: What was that like?

C: It was fine. (*Long pause and sigh.*) Shit, I wanted to get high. Shit, if I'd seen anyone to score from, I probably woulda—I was so pissed at her—and at myself for hitting her.

P: This sounds connected to things that are important to you staying out of prison—feeling that close to using . . . feeling so angry at yourself you don't care.

C: Yeah, but I don't know what to do and I don't want no trouble . . .

P: We're both agreed that you don't want any trouble. But you don't sound like you have much hope of anything changing. What if we put our heads together and see if together we can come up with a way to try to deal with this?

C: I dunno, I'm not sure . . .

The reluctant parolee above and certainly most criminal justice clients are reasonably concerned about disclosing information that may get them in trouble with their counselors and even potentially returned to prison. This is a very real worry. If the goal is to build a relationship containing some degree of trust, the practitioner should be clear and specific about the limits and boundaries of confidentiality. This may mean carefully spelling out the details on more than one occasion. As in the example above, clarifying the link between other problems and possible criminal behavior or other violations can be helpful with individuals who may have a tendency to compartmentalize their problems, not seeing the relationship between domestic or interpersonal issues and stress and anxiety, having feelings related to a need to escape or inability to cope, and possibly displaying behaviors that may ensue from these feelings such as violence, drug use, or decreased compliance with monitoring requirements.

What works or what is helpful when, despite clarity, honesty, and effort on the practitioner's part, the client still rejects assistance? The practitioner fulfills the legal mandate to monitor compliance to criminal justice system rules and offers assistance mobilizing other environmental resources and obtaining concrete services. Once practitioners have demonstrated their utility, commitment, and effectiveness in helping solve concrete problems of the offender and family members, the reluctance to engage often gradually fades. Practitioners are viewed first as brokers, and then as enablers and facilitators. We realize that practitioners with caseloads of over 100 offenders, all struggling with community reentry, do not have unlimited time to spend on individuals; however asking a client during each session (regardless of other content), What is one thing I can help you with today? is one way clients can come to view the practitioner as a practical helper. Within the session, the practitioner may provide a referral, make a phone call, or go so far as to call and make an appointment to arrange a collateral contact for the client.

Case Example

Carlos Vasquez is a 24-year-old married Latino man, who was born in Puerto Rico, but moved to the states with his parents when he was 3 years old. He is currently facing release from custody in the state correctional system after serving 3 years of a 5–8 year sentence for armed robbery and burglary.

Background

Mr. Vasquez's father reportedly left the family to return to Puerto Rico within two years after arriving in the states and he has few memories of living with his father and mother. From an early age, he observed his mother injecting drugs, which he assumes were heroin and cocaine,. He reports a brother, 6 years younger, was born "sick" and placed in foster care immediately after birth. At this time Carlos was told his mother was getting sicker and could no longer care for him. He went to live with a paternal aunt. He remembers feeling he was bad during this time and couldn't do anything right, but says he now knows "they just didn't give me no love there." Contact with his mother was sporadic, usually not more than once a month and sometimes not for as long as a year. On several occasions, his mother would tell him that she had gotten straight and would be coming to take him to live with her. However, within a few weeks it would be clear that his mother was using drugs again and shortly thereafter her visits would cease.

He reports not enjoying or doing well at school, feeling stupid, and spending time trying to fool teachers or stealing things such as office supplies, books, and cafeteria food from the school. He got in trouble frequently at school, for which his aunt beat him. She told Carlos he was "no good, just like your father."

Mr. Vasquez's first contact with the criminal justice system was when he was 14 years old and in the eighth grade. He was arrested with four others for stealing expensive hubcaps and other parts from parked cars and adjudicated to a youth diversion program. At age 17 he was convicted of stealing several cars and sentenced to 18 months in the youthful offenders' facility in the local prison where he completed his G.E.D. and indicated a strong interest in learning electronics maintenance, pursuing an honors vocational training program. Following release, Mr. Vasquez was placed in an apprentice position in a large electronics servicing center, but lost this job less than 6 months later. The employers' records indicate this was due to drug use on the job, but Mr. Vasquez indicated that they just "pushed too hard and wanted too much" from him.

At age 19, Carlos was arrested for possession of cocaine and suspected of involvement in small operation dealing. He served 90 days of a 9-month sentence and was released to enroll in an outpatient substance abuse treatment program. He attended the program for about 3 months, returned to living with his aunt, and returned to the same network of street friends, several of whom he had known since early childhood. He was arrested twice during this time, and served one sentence of 3 months in the county jail. When asked about his drug use, he admitted he has used "almost everything you can do." During the past 2 years this has included marijuana, methamphetamine, cocaine, and crack. Shortly after he was released following his last incarceration, Carlos became involved in an organization that stole expensive cars with electronically controlled accessories and dismantled them to sell for parts.

Carlos's support system outside the prison involves his wife of 5 years, Maria, with whom he lives while on furlough, a girlfriend of 3 years who came to visit him when he was in prison and whom he sees about twice a week, and the aunt who now lives four blocks away from his wife's apartment. He sees his aunt approximately once a week. A child, by his wife, was killed almost 3 years ago at age 3 in a neighborhood drive-by shooting. Carlos also mentioned a counselor from the school at the local jail who maintained correspondence with him while he was in the state prison. He reports no close male friends, and no desire to resume contact with previous street (criminal) associates, but has hopes of locating his brother.

Mr. Vasquez feels he has lost a valuable period of his life by spending time in prison. When questioned, he expresses some remorse about the suffering his crimes inflicted on others, but generally regrets "being in the wrong place at the wrong time." He had a difficult period of adjustment to prison, particularly around the time of his child's death. He states he saw a counselor in mental health 3 or 4 times during that period. He reported that shortly after this he was able to obtain a job as a baker in the prison food service, which helped keep him busy. He also enrolled in a drug abuse treatment program.

Initial Contact and Engagement

Mr. Vasquez appeared pleasant, cooperative, and earnest to the practitioner. He explained that he didn't want to do more time in prison and was serious about making things right this time. He was an attractive, carefully groomed man who looked slightly younger than his age. He excitedly spoke of his hope of getting a real job that involved skilled training. Although he had been on job search only a week, he had found a job picking up and delivering pets for a grooming service. He acknowledged the job was boring.

The practitioner was able to listen a great deal during this first session as Carlos clearly had many things he wanted the practitioner to know, but kept returning to his strong motivation to succeed. Rapidly, he pressed the practitioner to tell him if she would help him, "Do you think you can do anything for me?" When the practitioner did not answer immediately, he spoke teasingly and with a smile on his face, "Or are you just one of those paper pushers who really doesn't give a shit about us 'hardened' criminals?"

The practitioner smiled back, but didn't answer Carlos. She began by acknowledging that this period of community return is a very difficult, confusing time for most people. She stated that she would be honest and straight with Carlos, and by being this way would try to reduce some of the confusion and different messages he would receive from others in the system, friends on the street, and people at home. The practitioner indicated that before the end of today's session, she wanted to make sure that Carlos was totally clear about his reporting and other monitoring requirements.

ASSESSMENT WITH CRIMINAL JUSTICE SYSTEM CLIENTS

The purposes of assessment with criminal justice system clients are varied and may include at one time or another, all the purposes cited in Chapter 2: to provide information for other staff, to provide the basis for work between the individual client and practitioner, to determine suitability for programs or placements, and to prescribe the intensity or length of treatment options.

Some of the problems related to general assessment with criminal justice system clients concern the lack of reliable normative information about individuals who engage in criminal behavior. To understand this, it is necessary to briefly withdraw from the individual client as focus and identify some of the broader methodological problems in studying crime and delinquency that affect individual assessment.

First, as noted throughout this chapter, the number of individuals who become part of the criminal justice system is very small compared to the number of individuals who commit crimes. This involves who is arrested, who is charged following arrest, who is taken to court, and who is convicted. All available normative assessment information on individuals who engage in criminal behavior is necessarily gathered on this small, unrepresentative group of *caught* criminals.

Second, the use of differential methods of research has often hampered our efforts to understand individuals who are involved with the criminal justice system. These methods search for differences between normal and deviant individuals, attempting to identify traitlike characteristics that separate criminals from others. Except in cases of certain crimes such as homicide and rape, there is little evidence that these differentiations can be reliably made.

Third, the focus in correctional settings is on managing many individuals. This has led to the development of profiles of behavior that, while statistically accurate and helpful in planning large programs or service needs, frequently do not reflect the best fit categorization for an individual offender. Practitioners should be cautious in using such information in assessing individuals.

Two examples serve to illustrate how objective case information may not provide useful practice information. One common interpretation problem concerns the *offense of record*, which designates the leading offense under which a convicted offender has been sentenced most recently. Offenders are classified according to the offense of record rather than the offense as committed or the offense for which they were arrested. The results of plea bargaining, common in a high proportion of cases, yield rather misleading conclusions. The eventual offense of record may bear little resemblance to the individual's behavior or to the charge originally filed.

Our second example occurs when a history of prior incarceration is confused with actual criminal behavior history or with the likelihood of future criminal behavior. Incarcerated felons have a high rate of recidivism, which appears to be a function of the individual's prior record. In many cases, judicial sentencing discretion dictates that an individual's prior record determines the level of system assignment or sentence. First-time offenders are more likely sentenced to probation than are those with a prior record, who are more likely sentenced to incarceration. It is probable that felons who are *convicted but not incarcerated* do not recidivate, while those felons who are *incarcerated* have a higher rate of recidivism (Pallone & Hennessy, 1992). Taken together with the information presented earlier in this chapter, practitioners must be particularly careful not to assume more lengthy or severe patterns of criminal behavior among those incarcerated as opposed to those on probation or routed to other ATI programs.

Finally, many practitioners find themselves involved in preparing information to support or refute competency to stand trial. Competency is a legal, not a clinical concept, indicative of whether a defendant in a criminal proceeding understands the nature of the charges, and the consequences that may result from conviction as well as whether the defendant is able to participate with an attorney in the preparation of a defense. Insanity, mental retardation, and/or memory deficits typically are cited to support a claim of incompetence to stand trial. An important distinction practitioners should understand is that competency applies to the defendant's state of mind *at the time of the trial*, not the state of mind at the time of the criminally alleged behavior (Stone, 1988, p. 196).

Improving Assessment Data

Some of the strategies for improving the reliability and validity of assessment data with criminal justice clients are the same as those useful with all involuntary clients. There are, however, other strategies and information specific to criminal justice issues that require specific information and relative sophistication on the part of the practitioner.

The first of these strategies concerns diagnosis and the use of the terms *antisocial, sociopathic,* and *psychopathic* to describe either the personality (traits) or the behavior (state) of the offender. While antisocial behavior refers to normatively deviant behavior or nonconformity, antisocial personality disorder, as reflected by the DSM refers to a stable pattern of underlying construction that results in this behavior. In some settings, including forensics, law enforcement, and community mental health, there is a tendency to label as antisocial all those who have served sentences (the longer the more likely) or who have engaged in blatant incidents of antisocial behavior.

Rampant confusion is found in the research and clinical literature on this subject resulting from the use of various labels describing the same behavior, arguments centered on the unique meaning and significance of these definitions, and a lack of clarity in the definition of terms.

Models of sociopathy based on behavioral deficits and excesses identify deficits in interpersonal warmth, empathic capacity, learning, impulse control, fear arousal, and autonomic conditioning, with excesses in seeking aggressive, sexual, and other sensation-arousing experiences. Significantly, there is no current unitary conceptualization of this phenomenon defined by pervasive personal deficits that guides either research or clinical practice (Sutker, Bugg, & West, 1993).

Given this confusion and tendency to overlabel, we recommend careful specificity when using these terms, operationalizing the definition in use, and, where possible, using behavior and symptom checklists specifically designed to assess psychopathy and antisocial personality. These checklists can focus the practitioner on problem areas salient for work with individual clients and do not necessarily rely on overall scores or norms for clinical utility. For use with delinquents, the Behavior Problem Checklist and the Checklist for the Analysis of Life History Data (Quay & Parsons, 1970; Lee & Prentice, 1988) are helpful in distinguishing among delinquent groups, particularly to identify psychopathic behavior patterns. Hare (1991) developed the Psychopathy Checklist-Revised (PCL-R) to assess psychopathy in adult male offenders. The PCL-R consists of 20-items rated on a 3-point scale from both interview and case record information, including items that assess such traits as lack of remorse, guilt, and empathy as well as overt behaviors such as pathological lying, juvenile delinquency, and irresponsible parenting. The PCL-R is widely used in the criminal justice system because of its ability to make reasonably reliable predictions of recidivism, parole violation, violence, and treatment outcome.

The second strategy involves assessing the presence of mental disorder among individuals involved in the criminal justice system. As discussed earlier, the extreme circumstances of incarceration can readily precipitate mental distress and symptoms of disorder in vulnerable individuals (Toch, 1992). Regardless of the severity of the manifestation of the mental disorder, the assessment issue becomes one of identifying the contributions of individual and environmental factors. In reviewing the clinical literature on mental distress and disorder in prisons, there is no doubt that such factors as prior mental illness, the threat posed to outside social support by incarceration, noise, overcrowding, intimidation and assault, and previous coping or other experiences in the prison environment all figure prominently in how an individual will respond (Cox, Paulus, & McCain, 1984; Toch, 1992).

Most suicides occur during the first 72 hours of incarceration. Jail and detention facilities, therefore, have particularly high incidences. While full mental health assessment is rarely feasible during this period, it is important to screen for and assess factors related to suicidal behavior and severe mental distress. In response to the problem of suicide in jail and

Form 330 ADM(CC) (3-86)

State of New York
Commission of Correction
Office of Mental Health

SUICIDE PREVENTION SCREENING GUIDELINES

DETAINEE'S NAME	SEX	DATE OF BIRTH	MOST SERIOUS CHARGE(S)		DATE	TIME
NAME OF FACILITY		NAME OF SCREENING OFFICER		Detainee showed serious psychiatric problems during prior incarceration. Yes _____ No _____		

Check appropriate column for each question.

	Column A YES	Column B NO	General Comments/Observations
OBSERVATIONS OF TRANSPORTING OFFICER			
1. Arresting or transporting officer believes that detainee may be a suicide risk. *If YES, notify Shift Commander.*			
PERSONAL DATA	No Family/ Friends		
2. Detainee lacks close family or friends in the community.			
3. Detainee has experienced a significant loss within the last six months (e.g., loss of job, loss of relationship, death of close family member).			
4. Detainee is very worried about major problems other than legal situation (e.g., serious financial or family problems, a medical condition or fear of losing job).			
5. Detainee's family or significant other (spouse, parent, close friend, lover) has attempted or committed suicide.			
6. Detainee has psychiatric history. *(Note current psychotropic medications and name of most recent treatment agency.)*			
7. Detainee has history of drug or alcohol abuse.			
8. Detainee holds position of respect in community (e.g., professional, public official) and/or alleged crime is shocking in nature. *If YES, notify Shift Commander.*			
9. Detainee is thinking about killing himself. *If YES, notify Shift Commander.*			
10. Detainee has previous suicide attempt. *(Check wrists and note method.)*			
11. Detainee feels that there is nothing to look forward to in the future. (expresses feelings of helplessness or hopelessness). *If YES, to 10 and 11, notify Shift Commander.*	Nothing to Look Forward to		
BEHAVIOR/APPEARANCE			
12. Detainee shows signs of depression (e.g., crying, emotional flatness).			
13. Detainee appears overly anxious, afraid or angry.			
14. Detainee appears to feel unusually embarrassed or ashamed.			
15. Detainee is acting and/or talking in a strange manner (e.g., cannot focus attention, hearing or seeing things which are not there).			
16. A. Detainee is apparently under the influence of alcohol or drugs.			
B. If YES, is detainee incoherent, or showing signs of withdrawal or mental illness? *If YES to both A & B, notify Shift Commander.*			
CRIMINAL HISTORY	None		
17. No prior arrests.			

TOTAL Column A _____

ACTIONS
If total checks in Column A are 8 or more, notify Shift Commander.

Shift Commander notified: Yes _____   No _____

Supervision Instituted: Routine _____   Active _____   Constant _____

Detainee Referred to Medical/Mental Health: If Yes:

	EMERGENCY	NON-EMERGENCY
Yes _____ No _____	medical _____	medical _____
	mental health _____	mental health _____

Medical/Mental Health Personnel Actions: (To be completed by Medical/MH staff)

Figure 5.3.

INSTRUCTIONS FOR COMPLETING
SUICIDE PREVENTION SCREENING GUIDELINES — FORM 330 ADM

GENERAL INFORMATION

This form is to be completed in triplicate for all detainees prior to cell assignment.

Insert top copy in detainee's file. If detainee is referred, give second copy to medical or mental health personnel. The third copy is available for use according to our facility's procedures.

Comment Column:	Use to note:
	1. information about the detainee that officer feels is relevant and important
	2. information requested in questions 6 and 10, and
	3. information regarding detainee's refusal or inability to answer questions (See Below - General Instructions)
Detainees's Name:	Enter detainee's first and last name and middle initial.
Sex:	Enter male (m) or female (f).
Date of Birth:	Enter day, month and year.
Most Serious Charge(s):	Enter the most serious charge or charges (no more than two (2)) from this arrest.
Date:	Enter day, month and year that form was completed.
Time:	Enter the time of day the form was completed.
Name of Facility:	Enter name of jail or lock-up.
Name of Screening Officer:	Enter name of officer completing form.
Psychiatric Problems During Prior Incarceration:	Check YES if facility files show that during prior detention detainee attempted suicide and/or was referred for mental health services. If "unknown", write unknown across space.

INSTRUCTIONS FOR ITEMS 1-17

General Instructions

Check the appropriate YES or NO box for items 1 - 17.

If information required to complete these questions is unknown to screening officer, such information should be obtained by asking detainee to answer questions. However, detainee has a right to refuse to answer.

If detainee refuses to answer questions 2-11, enter RTA (refused to answer) in the Comment Column next to each question. In addition complete the YES or NO boxes only if information is known to you.

If during an otherwise cooperative interview, detainee refuses to answer one or two questions: Check YES in the box(es) next to the unanswered question(s) and enter RTA in the comment box next to each unanswered question.

If detainee is unable to answer all question 2-11, enter UTA (unable to answer) in the Comment Column next to each question. Also enter reason (e.g., intoxicated, not English speaking) for not answering these question in the Comment Column next to question 2. In addition complete the YES or NO boxes only if information is known to you.

Observation of Transporting Officer

ITEM (1) Suicide risk: Check YES or NO box based upon the verbal report of the arresting/transporting officer or upon the screening form completed by the police agency. If YES, notify shift commander.

Personal Data Questions

ITEM (2) Family/friends: Check YES box if someone other than a lawyer or bondsman would (1) be willing to post detainee's bail, (2) visit detainee while he/she is incarcerated, or (3) accept a collect call from detainee.

ITEM (3) Significant loss: Ask all three components to this question—loss of job, loss of relationship and death of close friend or family member.

ITEM (4) Worried about problems: Ask about such problems as financial, medical condition or fear of losing job. Check YES if detainee answers YES to any of these.

ITEM (5) Family/significant other attempted suicide: Significant other is defined as someone who has an important emotional relationship with the detainee.

ITEM (6) Psychiatric History: Check YES box if detainee (1) has ever had psychiatric hospitalization, (2) is currently on psychotropic medication, or (3) has been an outpatient psychotherapy during the past six months. Note current psychotropic medication and name of the most recent treatment agency in the Comment Column.

ITEM (7) Drug or Alcohol History: Check YES box if detainee has had prior treatment for alcohol/drug abuse or if prior arrests were alcohol/drug related.

ITEM (8) Respect and shocking crime: Check YES if detainee is very respected for work, community activities, etc. and/or the crime is shocking in nature, e.g. child molestation.

ITEM (9) Suicidal: Check YES if detainee makes a suicidal statement or if he responds YES to direct question, "Are you thinking about killing yourself?" If YES, notify shift commander.

ITEM (10) Previous attempt: Check YES box if detainee states he has attempted suicide. If YES, note the method used in the Comment Column. If either YES or NO, check detainee's wrists and note any scars in Comment Column.

ITEM (11) Hopeless: Check YES box if detainee states feeling hopeless, that he has given up, that he feels helpless to make his life better.
If YES to **both** items 10 and 11, notify shift commander.

Behavior Appearance Observations

YES or NO must always be checked for each of these items. They are observations made by the screening officer. They **are not** questions.

ITEM (12) Depression includes behavior such as: crying, emotional flatness, apathy, lethargy, extreme sadness, unusually slow reactions.

ITEM (13) Overly anxious, afraid or angry includes such behaviors as: handwringing, pacing, excessive fidgeting, profuse sweating, cursing, physical violence, threatening, etc.

ITEM (14) Unusually embarrassed or ashamed: Check YES box if detainee makes non-elicited statements indicating worry about how family/friends/community will respond to his detention.

ITEM (15) Acting in strange manner: Check YES box if you observe any unusual behavior or speech, such as hallucinations, severe mood swings, disorientation, withdrawal, etc.

ITEM (16A) Detainee under the influence: Check YES if someone is apparently intoxicated on drugs or alcohol.

ITEM (16B) Incoherence, withdrawal, or mental illness: Withdrawal means physical withdrawal from substance.
If YES to **both** A & B, notify shift commander.

Criminal History

ITEM (17) No prior arrests: Check YES box if this is detainee's first arrest.

SCORING

Be sure to count all checks in column A and enter total in the space provided. Notify shift commander 1) total is 8 or more, or 2) any shaded boxes are checked, or 3) if you feel notification is appropriate.

DISPOSITION

Officer Actions

Shift commander notified: Check YES or NO. Shift Commander should be notified about detainee prior to cell assignment.

Supervision instituted: Check appropriate supervision disposition. This section is to be completed by shift commander. For definition of active, constant and routine see N.Y.S. Commission of Correction Minimum Standards for Local Correctional Facilities.

Detainee referred to medical and mental health personnel: Check YES or NO. If YES, check emergency/nonemergency, medical/mental health. This section is to be completed by shift commander.

Medical/Mental Health Actions

This section should be completed by medical/mental health staff and should include recommendations and/or actions taken.

Figure 5.3. Continued.

detention facilities, a screening form was developed for law enforcement officials to assess immediate risk (Cox, McCarty, Landsberg, & Paravati, 1987). The form is a simple, 17-item checklist, derived from clinical as well as research sources, and requires about 10 minutes to administer (see Figure 5.3). These suicide prevention screening guidelines clearly net information about other areas of distress as well, resulting in a high number of "false positives" for suicide being referred for further screening. In a clinical screening program such as this, however, the sensitivity of this measure is of less concern than is its ability to include any and all individuals who might be at risk. In the 6 years this instrument has been in use, the rate of suicide in local jails and detention facilities in New York has significantly decreased (Cox & Morchauser, 1993).

Improving Reliability and Validity

The methods used to gather assessment information in the criminal justice system include multiple reporting instruments, tests, and measuring devices, as well as traditional narratives and clinical reports. The high numbers of people in the criminal justice system coupled with high accountability demands from the public and policymakers have produced a wide array of instruments available for use at different points in time (preassessment, assessment, monitoring compliance, and outcome), in different settings (preadjudication, presentence, pretreatment, during treatment, and posttreatment), and at different levels of the criminal justice system (prearraignment, pretrial, probation, ATI, corrections, and parole). Although many of these measures appear to be standardized in format and administration, this is often not the case. One example of this is the presentence report (PSR), a usual part of a criminal justice system client's record. PSRs, in narrative format, contain information about the crime, the offender, and circumstances that may be relevant to sentencing or other disposition. Although certain information is required for the courts, many PSRs contain additional potentially useful information gathered much less systematically, often from unspecified sources.

Information contained in large system databases, whether state, local, or federal, also relies on secondary information obtained from other records. Often entered into these systems at different points in time by many different individuals, this information should be verified against archival paper records and the client, as well as against other sources of direct information. Criminal history, descriptions of family members, and information about known enemies in the system (used when assigning offenders to specific correctional facilities) may be in error, with potentially serious consequences. Both the mother who travels 10 hours by bus to see her son, but is mistakenly placed on the "no visit" list, and the inmate nearing a parole hearing who has successfully completed several training and treatment programs that are erroneously listed under another person's name, suffer considerable distress over the implications of these multiple record-keeping systems.

Our recommendation is to gather, examine, and compare all information at one point in time. Ask the client first to clarify any discrepancies in other records or in self-reported information. Information may have changed and simply needs to be updated or it may have been initially recorded in error. Changing criminal justice records is often not an easy task and may involve obtaining formal corroborative information, delaying the change. For this reason, we suggest that the practitioner review this information with the client as soon as possible. While necessary to manage the high numbers of individuals, practitioners should remain aware of the limitations of large record-keeping systems and carefully check their reliability.

In Chapter 2 we suggested four ways the practitioner can work to minimize assessment bias occurring as a result of agency context that are particularly relevant here. Working with criminal justice clients, several agencies may be involved in providing information, including those concerned with presentence hearings, diversion or ATI programs, and victim's assistance. Information obtained about the offender's behavior and impact on the victim is obviously quite different than that used to argue against incarceration. Nowhere more than in correctional settings must a practitioner take care to evaluate information carefully and consider the environmental factors that may have biased assessment.

Case Example

Assessment and Contracting

The practitioner's assessment of Carlos was guided by the format and forms of the state department of corrections and parole administering the program. According to departmental regulations, by the end of the first meeting with the client, the assessment and initial treatment plans must be completed and filed within 24 hours. The assessment and plan may be altered with justification, as necessary, but must be filed before intervention can legally begin. Intervention is programmatically defined as entry to training, vocational, or treatment programming requiring formal referral. Showing Carlos the form, the practitioner began asking case history questions, keeping in mind the information she read in his records just prior to their appointment. Asking Carlos the questions on the form (Type II information), she turned to other information in his file to confirm information (Type IV information), and asked clarifying questions as needed. This form is replicated in Figure 5.4.

As the form was completed, Carlos again indicated that he wanted to

Figure 5.4. Assessment form for initial treatment.

Case Number: _____

Participant Name: _____

Arrest Data

Agency Name: _____
Offense (Primary): _____
Offense Code: _____
Arrest Date: _____

Sentence Data:

Date: County: Court: Defendant's Explanation of Crime:

                                         _____

Start Date: End Date:
Sentence Length:_____   Co-Defendants:
                                           1. _____
                                           2. _____
Financial Obligations:
Total Amounts:
Fines
Costs
Restitution

Referral Data: Duration Period: check all needed at case
                                       closure:

Psychological/Psychiatric Counseling
Medical Treatment
Psychological/Medical Evaluation Only
Drug Treatment/Counseling
Alcohol Treatment/Counseling
Employment Counseling
Credit/Financial Counseling
Financial Aid
Marital/Family Counseling
Education Training/Vocational Rehabilitation

Family Data
Name: Relation: Age: Criminal History   Phone/Address
1. _____
2. _____
3. _____

Employment Data:
Current Employer: Address: Phone:
Type of Work: Weekly Wage: Date Began/Left: Reason:
Previous Employer: Address: Phone:
Type of Work: Weekly Wage: Date Began/Left: Reason:
Special occupation skills: Change of employer:

get into skilled job training or work in a job setting that would train him. The practitioner let Carlos know that she heard his motivation and impatience, particularly his feeling he had lost so much time, and that they would begin work toward his goal as soon as possible. She then explained that, unfortunately, in order to participate, the state required the forms be completed. They went over the assessment form she had just completed: Carlos disagreed with both the reason his previous employment was terminated ("He didn't have no proof I was using!") and with the practitioner's indication that Carlos needed financial counseling. Looking through past records the practitioner found information (Type IV) that supported both her entries. Carlos was wrong in both cases based on the substantive documentation, and he acquiesced when she showed him the earlier entries.

Handing Carlos a copy of the case analysis form, she explained that this form might be of use to the two of them in planning their work. She prefaced discussing the categories listed on the form by saying that these were the areas many people had difficulty with when they returned to the community. She invited his participation by asking, "What would you like to start talking about; things that are going well? Or things that you think need some work?" Carlos shrugged, so the practitioner suggested they start with the job that Carlos had mentioned as most important to him right now. The practitioner inquired about the conditions, pay, stability, and future in Carlos's present job. Initially he was upset, insisting that it was a "nowhere job for anyone with a brain," and demanding that they not waste time talking about it. What became clear, however, was that Carlos's employer was a tough, but apparently fair individual who had made his expectations very clear. The hourly wage was reasonable, and the employer allowed Carlos time off during the middle of the day for required appointments (as long as time was made up at the end of the day). The employer also promised a raise after 6 months, and offered to teach Carlos some aspects of the grooming business. Although the practitioner pointed out these advantages to Carlos, he remained taciturn and restated his intentions not to stay in the job.

They briefly discussed each of the areas on the case analysis profile, identifying first his strengths. These included:

1. Carlos's G.E.D. and college credits earned in prison,
2. his good physical health,
3. evidence of good emotional coping skills, e.g., seeking out counseling in prison when his son died, understanding the role of work in helping him cope with difficult life events,
4. the fact that Carlos's wife, by allowing him to live with her, provides the opportunity for his early release.

They then moved to discussing issues that might interfere with Carlos

Employment	Vocational Training	Academic Training	Physical Health	Mental Health	Legal	Substance Abuse	Housing
Without work. No prospects.	No marketable skills.	Functional illiterate.	Incapacitated. Needs medical services.	Unstable. Lashes out or retreats into self.	Habitual civil & criminal problems.	Needs detoxification & treatment.	Constant transient.
Work unstable. Casual labor.	Laborer— minimal skills.	Backward but able to function at basic level.	Chronically ill. Needs medical care.	Confused, anxious and/or self-deprecating.		Extensive substance abuse.	Moves often.
Work part-time. Little promise for future.			Occasional incapcitation.	Rational but occasional confusion.	*History of repeated problems.*	*No evidence of use; no treatment.*	
full-time; not at potential.		G.E.D. and functions well.					*Moved back in with wife.*
Working near potential.	Achieved full potential for work.		In sound health. Seldom ill.	*No evidence of any SX.*			

First Iteration ⟶ X   Second Iteration ----- O

Figure 5.5.   Case analysis profile, month 1 and month 3.

successfully accomplishing his own goals and participating in the program. These included:

1. a fairly negative attitude about his current job,
2. a 10-year history of involvement with the criminal justice system,
3. a significant history of substance abuse and (now) return to the environment where it took place,
4. with the exceptions of his wife and aunt, a lack of any identifiable social support that would encourage adaptive functioning and progress.

With few exceptions, all of the people Carlos knew in his neighborhood were involved in dealing or using drugs, and usually both. Based on discussion of these issues, the practitioner registered current levels on the form, indicating Carlos's beginning profile (see Figure 5.5).

The practitioner was concerned about maintaining the strengths noted above, as well as addressing the problems. At the top of this list was Carlos's ability to maintain himself in his current living situation. Realizing she was treading on intrusive ground, she explained she was concerned about the stability of his living situation, particularly in view of his relationship with his girlfriend. Carlos immediately became agitated and said,

> She told me you would try to get me to stop seeing her! She was right! I can't believe it! I come in here telling you how I'm working, how I want a better job, how motivated I am to do right this time, and all you want to talk about is my private life. This is about my family and I protect my people.

The practitioner nodded, saying that she understood Carlos's desire to protect his family and keep his life private. Making eye contact she said,

> I am only concerned with this because you must have a stable living situation to participate in the program. I do not know if your wife knows about your girlfriend—or how she feels—and you're right, that's really *not* my business. But if she kicks you out, both you and I have a problem. Does that make sense?

Carlos said he knew he had to live with a family member. Based on the angry expression on his face, the practitioner turned to another topic.

Due to Carlos's past history of drug use, a mandated part of his early release was involvement in drug treatment. Carlos had agreed to this prior to entering the early release program, so raising the issue was not new information, but a reminder of priorities. AA/NA, group treatment, and day treatment programs were all acceptable forms of involvement. Attendance would be verified by a form completed by treatment staff or by the meeting convener. Carlos admitted he had not attended any form of drug treatment since his full release 2 weeks ago. This concerned the practitioner, not because she suspected Carlos was using, but because of Carlos's expressed frustration and impatience with his current job situation. She was worried that this might lead to eventual relapse. She asked Carlos what types of drug treatment he thought were best for him, given the mandate. Carlos's work schedule precluded involvement before 8 P.M., so they examined the practitioner's resource file for evening groups. After discussing two evening group programs located in another part of town and an intensive weekend program, Carlos suggested that NA would probably be best for him, expressing concern that a more rigid, less structured program might not work. The practitioner was impressed with Carlos's insight and desire not to set himself up for failure, and told him so. She raised the issue of risk situations, asking Carlos when, where, and who made him feel like using. He insisted there was nothing that could make him feel like using right now. In exploring past episodes of drug use, Carlos was unspecific, saying that he used because he wanted to "celebrate or have a good time."

The practitioner inquired about Carlos's mental health status, asking him what thoughts he was having about his son, and his own future since he had been home. She asked if he had any trouble sleeping or was having any disturbing kinds of thinking, and whether he had ever thought about hurting himself. Carlos grimaced at the first question, stating that his wife still had pictures of the baby around the apartment and that pained him. He reported looking forward to his future, "Now that I have one." Other than nervousness about wanting to "get going" and "make it right this time," Carlos reported no upsetting thinking. He said that the only time he had ever had thoughts about checking out were when he was in prison and heard about his son's death.

Based on this discussion, the practitioner suggested and Carlos agreed to the following initial goals/priorities for their work together:

1. Getting into approved drug treatment (already out of compliance)—will attend NA 3 times weekly, gets sponsor within 3 weeks.
2. Maintaining current job/employment (despite attitude)—no negative consequences, e.g., reprimands, cut-back hours.
3. Maintaining other required compliance activities (see contract below).
4. Pursuing training, education toward skilled employment.

Before the first session was over, they reviewed the parameters and consequences of Carlos's mandated monitoring. While these represent the most structured portion of Carlos's intervention program, they also provided the context in which other goals were pursued. The practitioner needed to assess Carlos's understanding of the mandates and consequences and to contract with him to uphold his responsibilities. The monitoring requirements and their consequences are given below:

Monitoring

1. Weekly meeting with program counselor (practitioner).
2. Random urine testing 2–3 times weekly.
3. Verified attendance in acceptable drug treatment program.

Consequences

1. If misses weekly meeting with no contact, within 24 hours is reported absent without leave. After 3 days this status changes to absconder and, if found, individual is returned to custody to serve remainder of sentence + one year.

2. If + urine screen, may be immediately sent back to prison to complete remainder of sentence.
3. If not involved in drug treatment on agreed-upon basis, may be limited from involvement in other programs or training and may be returned to custody.
4. If not involved in drug treatment and has + positive urine screen, must be returned to custody.

Carlos had signed a legal contract with the state prior to his release outlining the requirements of his early release, and the practitioner went over this contract with him. The state contract required that before state-funded vocational rehabilitation or job training could take place, Carlos had to first demonstrate 3 months of adaptive community living. When the practitioner pointed this out to Carlos, he was dismayed and quickly became agitated. She explained that the reason for this regulation was to make sure that people in training were already well settled into meeting other program requirements so they were not taking on everything new at once. Carlos countered with his opinion that the rule was to drive people crazy so they went back to drugs and just back on the street, saving the state money. The practitioner noted that there were many necessary steps to complete before beginning training and that Carlos could begin work on these immediately. The formal state contract, signed almost 2 months earlier and long before this first appointment with the practitioner, did not specify two important components: the positive consequences (besides continued freedom) of meeting the requirements and the practitioner's agreed-upon activities. In addition to outlining the above mandated components of the contract, the practitioner's contract also spelled out several other conditions, including specified amounts of involvement necessary.

After Carlos left her office, the practitioner briefly outlined what she viewed as Carlos's strengths and weaknesses to alert her of areas to informally monitor during the coming months. Her notes were as follows:

?expressed desire to succeed—anxiety?
+ job
+ living with wife
− not currently in any drug treatment (although knew he needed to be)
− overly confident he will not relapse/be successful
− no evidence of problem-solving skills to avoid drug use
?little insight into situations that may occasion drug use
?instability caused by relationships with wife and GF? Could wind up without place to live?

Choosing Change Targets and Setting Goals

In many ways, targets of change are already set for the mandated offender entering treatment. Social mandates for offenders returning to the community consist of several goals: firm insistence on controlling impulses and obeying rules of parole, i.e., steady work, no deleterious habits, no involvement with undesirable associates, regular reporting, and general cooperation and participation in treatment plans deemed helpful. Goals for clients in institutions, whether criminal or psychiatric, involve adjusting to and complying with inside regulations that may have little to do with health or changing criminal behavior. Some of these rules exist solely to ease administrative burdens.

For community-based criminal justice system clients, the goals are often very similar. The most common include finding housing, drug treatment, a job or vocational training, avoiding criminal, i.e., legal system involvement, and maintaining adaptive social relationships. The categories of need used in Dell'Apa, Adams, Jorgenson, & Sigardson's (1976) case profile remain relevant in practice today. Broadening this perspective only slightly however, one sees that other targets are extremely important in providing the foundations of these major life domains. These other targets include such areas as family relationships (partner, children, extended family), informal support systems (friends, work partners, church or recreation groups), and even contacts with other formal support systems (agencies, school). During periods of life transition, the players in these categories may be shifting; there may be a strong need to address and work on problem-solving some of these subgoals or instrumental goals *in service* of the larger category goals. For example, a 16-year-old delinquent may need to work on completing her G.E.D., but she also may need to worry about child care, housing, and her 10-year-old brother who she is concerned is going "bad." Identifying goals in smaller units that the client can identify with this week, such as "Let's find you a place to live" or "Let's work on finding someone who can take care of your baby" are more real than "Let's get you employed!"

Although this is generally true of involuntary clients, the repeated experience of failure (and being so labeled by family members and the criminal justice system) can have a depressing effect on motivation and behavior. Clients may believe that it is almost better, and certainly *feel* that way inside, not to try at all rather than to try again and fail. In addition to mandated goals, broken down into manageable, real units for the client, other goals the client identifies should also be incorporated into treatment planning. Many practitioners also develop individual goals that they wish to address. In the case of Carlos Vasquez, for example, the practitioner is concerned about the potential volatility of

Carlos's living situation, but Carlos clearly does not wish to admit to or tackle this problem. The practitioner, however, will continue her surveillance of this issue as long as she believes it can harm Carlos's future in the program. Although it is not identified as a separate item on Carlos's list of goals (subsumed under "other requirements of program participation"), Carlos is aware that the practitioner is concerned about this and that his program participation depends on maintaining an approved address.

SELECTING RESEARCH-BASED INTERVENTIONS FOR CRIMINAL JUSTICE SYSTEM CLIENTS

Almost twenty years ago Handler (1975) pointed out the value of certain unique social work skills in work with criminal justice populations. Chief among these is the importance of viewing clients as part of a total social system that contributes to both the problem and the solution. Emphasizing contacts with employers, teachers, family members, and significant others to identify problems and seek solutions, social workers also stress the importance of case coordination. In criminal justice system work this is critical, as multiple disciplines meet and multiproblem clients require a multiplicity of carefully orchestrated services. Skills in information and referral, steering, accessing community resources, and advocacy are critical in working with this population. In addition, more basic microcounseling skills such as giving feedback, clarifying, summarizing, confronting, appropriate questioning, interpretation, goal setting, and limit setting are used in work with correctional clients. Conflict resolution and crisis intervention on intrapersonal, interpersonal, and systemic levels also are common tasks. There are three major prevention and control intervention points in criminal justice practice as identified by Lundman (1984): predelinquent, preadjudication, and postajudication. While the goals of these three intervention points are different, the methods to achieve them often are the same.

There have been numerous reviews of intervention programs designed to reduce criminal behavior in both juvenile and adult populations. The earliest of these reviews, similar to those in general social work practice, concluded that nothing works (Martinson, 1974; Lipton, Martinson, & Wilks, 1975; Martinson & Wilks, 1977). A panel convened to review these findings (Sechrest, White, & Brown, 1979) concluded that due to both implementation and evaluation difficulties, the studies were so inadequate that few warranted unequivocal interpretation. Among the few successful studies, results suggested some treatments might prove effective with certain subgroups of offenders. These studies return us to the question, What interventions work best, with whom, and under what circumstances?

Using stricter methodological inclusion criteria for later reviews, results improved somewhat. Among 170 studies with juveniles, Romig (1978) found that more successful interventions included teaching behavioral and communication skills, with or without other family members involved. Examining 40 studies from 1973 to 1978, Blackburn (1980) found that treatment studies often targeted convenience behavior, i.e., management for facilities, rather than behavior directly related to crime. Of the 40 studies, 70% involved behavioral intervention methods and 28% found less recidivism among experimental group members than control group members. Upon reflection, these minimal reductions in recidivism may be the results of basing models of intervention on wrong psychological theories of crime and change, and/or focus on opportune, but inappropriate targets. Comparing institutional, open residential, and community settings, there is no evidence that intervention programs are more or less successful in one setting than in another (Martin, Sechrest, & Redner, 1981). Program failures in all settings are generally attributed to treatment staff: (1) lack of control over administrative resources, (2) sabotage or poor motivation, and (3) failure to gain control over other sources of influence (Blackburn, 1980; Martin, Sechrest, & Redner, 1981).

Meta-analyses of intervention outcomes were conducted by Garrett (1984, 1985) for adult offenders, Gottschalk, Davidson, Gensheimer, and Mayer (1987) for delinquents, and Andrews et al. (1990) for both. Among the adult studies, more noticeable improvements were found in psychological variables and adjustments to institution and community than in recidivism. Across all studies, of all the treatments studied, cognitive-behavioral and contingency management programs were the most effective. Gottschalk et al., (1987) found that community-based interventions had small effects on outcome. They drew conclusions suggesting that accurate implementation, along with sufficient duration and intensity of treatment, would improve effectiveness.

Gendreau and Andrews (1990), Eysenck and Gudjonnson (1989), and Izzo and Ross (1990) qualitatively reviewed the treatment outcome literature, concluding that cognitive-behavioral methods hold most promise for work with adult and juvenile offender populations. They also cited Nietzel (1979), who, based on a review of social-learning-based programs targeting criminal behavior among adults examined across institutions, nonresidential, and community-based programs, found that social-learning approaches were effective with many types of criminal behavior and superior to the alternative interventions (Eysenck & Gudjonsson, 1989).

Manual-driven treatment protocols for work with juvenile and adult offenders based on social-learning principles are available. These contain varying amounts of accompanying information about their demonstrated effectiveness and their applications. For work with adults, McGuire and Priestly (1985) and with adolescents Stumphauzer's *Helping Delinquents Change* (1986) are two well-known manuals for instituting behavior change. In different ways, both emphasize the importance of considering the complex and varied effects of punishment on behavior (Bandura, 1986), including its differential effects on individuals (Eysenck & Gudjonsson, 1989), and strongly encourage the use of positive reinforcement wherever possible. *Time to Think: A Cognitive Model of Delinquency Prevention and Offender Rehabilitation* by Ross and Fabiano (1985) identifies sets of cognitive variables likely impaired or delayed in offenders. These include the cognitive content and process (what and how offenders think), their worldviews, reasoning, values, understanding of others, and coping skills. The model emphasizes individual assessment and treatment planning, arguing that cognitive deficiencies may exist in one or more areas and that intervention must be tailored to address specific deficiencies.

According to Ross and Fabiano, successful cognitive-behavioral programs frequently place strong emphasis on one or more of the following four components: (1) self-control (thinking before acting), (2) critical, i.e., rational, logical, objective, thinking, (3) rational self-analysis (teaching people to critically assess their thinking), and (4) means-ends reasoning (part of general problem-solving skill).

Practitioners assist offenders with behavioral changes, particularly the immediate problem-solving necessary to cope with the constraints of system involvement. This may mean coping with the daily living problems in prison such as boredom, fear of assault, physical and psychological victimization, noise, depression, anxiety, and worries about significant others outside. There is little outcome data on the effectiveness of such interventions from an individual or psychological perspective, although the jail suicide screening program described earlier is an example.

Practitioners also help confined and community-based offenders develop problem-solving skills that can be transferred to other areas of life. Problem-solving skills are arguably the most adaptive life skills lacking in substance abusers and therefore provide an important intervention target in work with correctional populations (Husband & Platt, 1993). Identifying problems accurately, generating options, choosing the best alternative, and implementing it are all components of problem-solving skill the worker can teach the offender to practice and improve. Offenders are colloquially thought to have less problem-solving ability than other individuals, despite mixed research evidence on this topic. While some studies have found no differences between offenders and nonoffenders on problem-solving tests (Grier, 1988; Ingram, Dixon, & Glover, 1983), at least one study reports very low means-ends problem-solving scores among male inmates (Ivanoff, Smyth, Grochowski, Jang, & Klein, 1992), and several others among substance abusers (Platt, Scura, & Hannon, 1973; Intagliata, 1978). Sharing the perspective of Ross and Fabiano (1985), we believe that careful individual assessment and targeting of intervention, even within problem-solving, is important.

Practitioners may also play a key role in working with the family, helping family members deal with the psychosocial and economic impacts an incarceration has on those remaining in the community. During the critical periods of early incarceration or community return, practitioners may assist both the offender and family members in dealing with the adjustment. When offenders first become part of the system, the family may be overwhelmed with the legal and financial burdens thrust upon them, while simultaneously coping with conflicting feelings toward the offender. During community return, the family is again placed in a difficult position and their response is often mixed, caught between wanting to help and not wanting to do anything that might increase monitoring or sanction against the family member. Family members, as well as those involved directly in the criminal justice system, have learned to mistrust those in official positions. Although it is generally accepted that family involvement is better than no family involvement in delinquent, preadjudication, and alternatives programs, once sentenced to confinement, some male offenders prefer to limit contact with family members outside. This can also make community return and family reentry more difficult.

In work with criminal justice system clients, it is important to attain a realistic perspective about what can and cannot be done. Since little has been little done with individual offenders or groups of offenders that affects crime or offers real protection to the community, we believe that interventions should be tailored to address individual needs.

IMPLEMENTING AND MONITORING INTERVENTIONS

As we stated in Chapter 3, for an intervention to occur, the practitioner must be aware that an intervention is being performed. It also is a good idea that the client understand as much as possible about the intervention. This is relatively easy with concrete intervention components such as urine testing for drug use, but less clear when the practitioner identifies major problem-solving and values deficits. First, however, the practitioner must clearly specify the intervention activities and list their critical components. These need to be explained to the client so that it is clear how the intervention connects to a particular problem. For example, in teaching problem-solving skills to offenders, a practitioner can begin by explaining the concept of problem orientation: "How do you know when you have a problem?" Another strategy is to begin immediately by generating many problem-solving options or brainstorming to engage clients in actually learning a problem-solving step. Examples of this include setting a scene from which the client needs to escape: "You're at a friend's house and these people know you're clean, but about 9 o'clock someone brings out a pipe. What are all the different things you could do in this situation to avoid using?" This is then followed by evaluating the options and choosing the best option.

An advantage to mandated monitoring is that it often includes monitoring of easily verifiable intervention implementation. This provides a ready source of feedback for client and practitioner and provides a check on the accuracy of implementation. Even with simple implementations however, validity problems can still occur. For instance, a client might get an intervention program attendance chit verified at the beginning of a meeting and then leave rather than attend. Or, the client might miss a urine screen, ostensibly due to illness, when the screen would, in fact, test positive for drug use.

A more difficult issue in work with criminal justice clients is determining outcome. In addition to (although some might argue, instead of) the stated goal of preventing recidivism, which is extremely difficult, many practitioners focus on related life changes. These demand skilled individual assessment, goal setting, and monitoring, particularly if these outcome goals are linked to legal mandate and the degree of restrictiveness judged necessary. Because these intervention procedures often involve new learning in several domains of the client's life, there is a higher likelihood that something unplanned will occur, whether in implementation, in monitoring, or in assessing the outcome of a client's progress.

Assessing outcome in criminal justice is often done on a programmatic rather than individual basis. On an individual level, common successful outcomes include completing mandated reporting without reincarceration or other criminal activity and achieving intermediate success points on other life goals such as employment/education/training, stable living situation, and participating in other adaptive activities (e.g., drug treatment, community organizations). Because the nature of practice with criminal justice clients usually involves more monitoring than most practice, evaluation of progress toward individual goals occurs less often than that of overall mandated goals. Experienced practitioners have learned the value of spending the little extra time it takes to evaluate progress toward goals that the client may view as more salient to maintaining life without crime.

In substance abuse treatment, a time-worn analogy of planting seeds is used to philosophically explain the pattern of repeatedly reintroducing and retraining clients over and over again in the concepts and procedures of behavior change: practitioners hope that a seed will germinate and take hold, but understand that given external exigencies, certainly not all will take root and bear fruit. For most, if not all, clients in this system, the end of intervention is the end of the mandated reporting period. This period is not based on the length of time the client needs to successfully prepare for life in the community. Unfortunately, treatment often ends abruptly when the client begins using drugs or engaging in criminal behavior and absconds, afraid of return to custody, or at the time when the practitioner is forced to make the decision to return the client to custody. In short, many of these termination points are artificial from an intervention standpoint.

Case Example

Implementation, Monitoring, and Outcome

The next month (and 6 sessions) proceeded as per contract with no crises or major upheavals. Carlos complied with almost all requirements of the mandate and understood that in terms of his goal (job training) these next 2 months were a waiting/testing period. He began to use the sessions with the practitioner appropriately as a place to vent his frustration about his life, lost time, being stupid, and how awful some of the customers of the grooming parlor were. The practitioner began each session by collecting the needed verifications for monitoring and with an open-ended, "So how are things going?" Based on her concern about Carlos's ability to problem-solve around drug risk situations, she introduced *protection training*, drawing analogies between identifying cues to problems, and problem-solving steps as protection against drug use. Carlos, who had been an HIV peer educator in prison, enjoyed the analogy and used it frequently. One lunchtime he came in announcing, "Hey, I got to use my protection last night!" and proceeded to relay an incident where he successfully avoided using drugs by problem-solving his way out of the incident. He was particularly pleased with how early in the situation he had recognized he was in a risky setting.

During this first month, there was much discussion about daily life (What do you do? Where do you go? etc.) so that the practitioner was able to frame problem-solving in real-life events. Anticipated social events over a weekend were discussed and planned for during an end-of-week appointment. Each week, the practitioner would also ask, "And how is your family?" The first 3 weeks, she received only brief responses in return. The fourth week, Carlos's aunt was sick and he explained how he had asked for an hour off and the use of the grooming service van to drive her to the doctor. He did not seem surprised that the owner loaned it to him, nor that his wife had spent a portion of each day making special foods for his aunt to eat and taking them to her. At the end of the first month, the practitioner redid the case profile with Carlos, noting that there had been no involvement with legal systems and, while he was still in situations where people were using drugs, that he was attending NA 3 times weekly. He did not, however, have a sponsor by this time, and the practitioner was somewhat concerned that Carlos still lacked this social support. He explained that he often attended three different meetings in one week and had not yet found a home meeting. The second iteration is represented (along with the first) in Figure 5.6.

Over the next 3 months, a series of events occurred: Carlos was precipitously fired from his job one week and rehired the next (no explanation was forthcoming from the employer and Carlos said it was "all a mistake"); Carlos found and passed entrance examinations for an electronics technical training school; Carlos missed an appointment with the practitioner and a scheduled urine screen; Carlos was kicked out of his wife's home when she was confronted with evidence of his ongoing relationship with his girlfriend; and Carlos could provide no evidence of participation in NA or other approved drug treatment program. Carlos also announced that his girlfriend was pregnant.

The practitioner responded to each of these from inside the problem-solving framework she and Carlos had been practicing. Legally, Carlos could have been returned to custody for one or more of these infractions; however, the practitioner's judgment was that Carlos appropriately problem-solved the situations once faced with them. Carlos arranged to stay with his aunt while he attempted to reconcile with his wife. He had resolved whatever issue existed with his employer independent of the practitioner. Carlos admitted to the practitioner that he did not like NA. He expressed concern about slipping back and admitted he had used drugs once or twice in the past month. The prospect of entering school sometime within the foreseeable future excited him and he did not want to lose the opportunity. Working together, the practitioner and Carlos were able to locate another, more desirable drug program in his neighborhood that Carlos could attend 4 evenings a week for relapse prevention and skills-building interventions.

Carlos's involvement in the program continued for the next year. During that time, he successfully participated in the drug treatment program for 6 months, entered electronics training school and was reunited with his wife, who was also now pregnant. He attended meetings with the practitioner on a regular basis and felt she was openly

Employment	Vocational Training	Academic Training	Physical Health	Mental Health	Legal	Substance Abuse	Housing
Without work. No prospects.	No marketable skills.	Functional illiterate.	Incapacitated. Needs medical services.	Unstable. Lashes out or retreats into self.	Habitual civil & criminal problems.	Needs detoxification & treatment.	Constant transient.
Work unstable. Casual labor.	Laborer— minimal skills.	Backward but able to function at basic level.	Chronically ill. Needs medical care.	Confused, anxious and/or self-depre- cating.		Extensive substance abuse.	Moves often. *Out of wife's home—Aunt*
Work part- time. Little promise for future.			Occasional incapcita- tion.	Rational but occa- sional confusion.		*Some use; no evidence of tx participation*	
problem at job? solved success- fully	*passed exam for training*	G.E.D. and functions well.	*Somatic complaints*				
Working near potential.	Achieved full poten- tial for work.		In sound health. Seldom ill.	*Stress*	*No arrest or evidence of crime*		

Figure 5.6.   Case analysis profile, month 5.

helpful and supportive, although he realized that she didn't "like the way I run my personal business." Urine screens for drugs were returned positive 4 times during the year, but at each point Carlos and the prac- titioner were able to plan forward to avoid the next slip. The practitioner did not believe Carlos was using drugs on a regular basis, or engaging in criminal behavior. The progress Carlos made during this period is represented in Figures 5.6, 5.7, and 5.8.

About 9 months after he began the program, Carlos indicated that his wife would like to meet the practitioner. The practitioner was delighted and used the opportunity to prepare for the meeting as a way to begin termination and follow-up planning. Carlos initially stated that his wife wanted to meet the worker because she was extremely worried he would fall back once he stopped the program and regular sessions. Reluctantly, Carlos admitted that he was feeling differently than Maria, but a little concerned about this too, expressing worry that the better things became in general (he spoke of the training program, his wife's child on the way), the more anxious he became in situations that might occasion drug use. The practitioner assured Carlos these were quite normal reactions and noted they could work on identifying what Carlos needed to prepare him for the future.

Employment	Vocational Training	Academic Training	Physical Health	Mental Health	Legal	Substance Abuse	Housing
Without work. No prospects.	No marketable skills.	Functional illiterate.	Incapacitated. Needs medical services.	Unstable. Lashes out or retreats into self.	Habitual civil & criminal problems.	Needs detoxification & treatment.	Constant transient.
Work unstable. Casual labor.	Laborer—minimal skills.	Backward but able to function at basic level.	Chronically ill. Needs medical care.	Confused, anxious and/or self-deprecating.		Extensive substance abuse.	Moves often.
Work part-time. Little promise for future.			Occasional incapcitation.	Rational but occasional confusion.			*Living with Aunt* X
no problems working full time X	*in school part-time*	G.E.D. and functions well.				*Some use; Attending to regularly* X	
Working near potential.	Achieved full potential for work. X	*in school* X	In sound health. Seldom ill. X	*No sx or reported complaints* X	*No evidence of criminal activity* X		

Figure 5.7. Case analysis profile, month 7.

Carlos continued with great difficulty, but managed to communicate that his wife had recently begun to indicate she might be feeling somewhat threatened by the relationship between himself and the worker. Carlos quickly dismissed this as related to her pregnancy and feeling unattractive, but the worker said this too was quite reasonable after such a period of time and suggested that it was important that Maria know and feel that the worker was supportive of Carlos's entire good life: his training program, his recovery, *and* his family. The practitioner and Carlos agreed to (1) outline a plan for termination and follow-up contacts that would assuage concerns of all involved; (2) involve Maria, to the extent possible, in identifying resources and needs important to maintaining the progress Carlos has already made; and (3) access these other resources and implement adjunctive services so that these supports would be in place by termination.

The plan the practitioner and Carlos developed began by specifying some parameters. The practitioner was not able to continue seeing Carlos on a regular basis once his official program involvement ended at the end of the designated 16-month period. They initially identified several programs that might help Carlos address his current and projected needs, including two that focused specifically on the needs of ex-offend-

Employment	Vocational Training	Academic Training	Physical Health	Mental Health	Legal	Substance Abuse	Housing
Without work. No prospects.	No marketable skills.	Functional illiterate.	Incapacitated. Needs medical services.	Unstable. Lashes out or retreats into self.	Habitual civil & criminal problems.	Needs detoxification & treatment.	Constant transient.
Work unstable. Casual labor.	Laborer—minimal skills.	Backward but able to function at basic level.	Chronically ill. Needs medical care.	Confused, anxious and/or self-deprecating.		Extensive substance abuse.	Moves often.
Work part-time. Little promise for future.			Occasional incapcitation.	Rational but occasional confusion.			
		G.E.D. and functions well.				*Some use; regular tx involvement* X	
Working near potential. *school and job* X	Achieved full potential for work. X	*Good progress in school* X	In sound health. Seldom ill. X	*No complaints or observable sx* X	*No arrests or evidence of crime* X		*Living at home with wife; reconciled* X

Figure 5.8. Case analysis profile, month 9.

ers. The practitioner offered to obtain more information about each of these and Carlos asked,

> Do you think they have groups of guys who talk about how hard it is to do this? I mean, shit, I know most of those guys out there ain't no good and are just waitin until the next time they can score, but do you think there might be a couple of guys there who are straight?

The worker, impressed by Carlos's direct request for social support, offered to find out what she could. A plan for follow-up included monthly contact for the first 3 months, then moving to quarterly contact for remainder of the year.

Within the next month, the meeting with Maria, Carlos, and the worker took place. Maria was very shy and deferent to the practitioner at first, but quickly became engaged in planning for Carlos's termination and follow-up. Maria noted that the counselor Carlos had known for many years was now working at one of the two community agencies for ex-offenders, mentioned Carlos's need for dental work, and expressed a desire to be more actively involved in Carlos's future progress, asking if there were programs for wives "like me—with good men who sometimes make mistakes."

Upon review of progress and gains still to be achieved, Carlos and the practitioner arranged a network of supportive services to help maintain progress toward his goals. Continued substance abuse/relapse prevention work (with supplemental individual contact at that agency), involvement in the ex-offenders community support program (with his former counselor, an administrator in the program), and referral to a vocational placement agency specializing in work with skilled ex-offenders to begin following completion of the electronics training program. Carlos and the worker both felt the relationship had been productive, although not without tension and conflict. Carlos stated he felt "okay about leaving" because he had plans to come back (follow-up) and because he knew many other men he did time with who really needed the program. A week after termination he called the worker to ask if she could take a referral, Stephen, who was a brother of a new *compadre* he met at the community program—and to say he was doing well. Follow-up contacts at months 1 and 2 indicated all was going well. At month 3, there was evidence Carlos had been using drugs again, although the frequency was unclear. He described it as related to his impending job search, the difficulty of school, and concern about Maria and the baby in her final months of pregnancy.

The practitioner expressed her concern and together she and Carlos problem-solved the best ways to handle these heightened issues. The plan designed in their meeting included (1) temporarily increased involvement in the drug program; (2) visiting the physician with Maria to ask questions; and (3) immediate contact and assurance (breaking down the steps into manageable units) from the vocational placement agency about the job search process.

CONCLUSIONS

At present, the criminal justice system in the United States is difficult to understand, inefficient, ineffective, and mazelike administratively. Programs are fragmented, activities are duplicated, and resources are often wasted. Many prison environments are violent, boring, depressing, regimented, and overcrowded. Most prisons are located away from population centers, making links between prison and community impossible. The alternatives appear more humane: alternatives to incarceration in less restrictive settings including community and home, and better proximity of institutions to the populations (and their families) they serve. The evidence suggests many such programs are no less effective than more restrictive settings at preventing recidivism.

Individual interventions with those involved in the criminal justice system demonstrate mixed effectiveness, but rather than drawing a "nothing works" conclusion, leading treatment specialists cite the heterogeneity of the population, limited controls used in designing and testing interventions, and the lack of control treatment staff have over criminal justice environments. Assessment, treatment planning, and intervention in many criminal justice systems are often more concerned with public safety and issues of managing large numbers of offenders than with creating the conditions for individual change. Nowhere is the demand for effective, cost-efficient intervention higher.

Chapter 6

Research-Based Practice with Child Protective Services

Child protective services are child welfare services, typically delivered under the auspices of state governments to children and families. The two general goals of child protective services are to protect children from abuse and/or neglect and to strengthen families so that abuse and/or neglect does not occur or recur (Pecora, Whittaker, & Maluccio, 1992). To accomplish these goals, children and families are given preventive or protective services, under the authority of child protective services. Preventive services are aimed at keeping children and families together, while reducing the risk that the children will be harmed. Protective services involve some degree of removal of the children from the family unit to protect them from experiencing further abuse or neglect.

Another conceptualization, and a more traditional one, that has been used to classify services to children and families offered under the auspices of child protective services is supportive, supplementary, and substitute forms of care (Magazino, 1983). Supportive services are less intensive services that strengthen, bolster, or otherwise support the family so that children can remain at home. Examples are parent training, advocacy, and counseling. Supportive services might be delivered by the public child welfare worker or through a private agency. Supplemental services are a sort of adjunct to the family and take over some limited degree of family responsibilities. Again, the goal is to keep the family intact. Day-care services and homemaker services are examples. For the most part, although not exclusively, these are purchased by the public agency and offered under private agency auspices. Substitute services are those services that take over the role of the family. Foster care is the chief example of this, and it can be offered through the public or the private sectors, although more often it occurs in the private sector. Supportive forms of care are preventive in nature while supplemental services usually are preventive. Substitute forms of care are protective in nature.

The identity of the client changes somewhat depending on the type of services being delivered. In preventive services, the client is usually identified as the family unit, although the parents or caretakers may be the primary focus of interventive activities. In protective services, however, the children are more likely to be identified as the client, although the parents or caretakers will also be considered clients to the extent that the services work with them to prepare them for the children's return home.

Children and families who come into contact with child protective services may be offered or mandated any of an array of services, which can be arranged along a continuum of restrictiveness. Parent education, advocacy, and referral lie at the least restrictive end of the continuum, respite care and intensive family preservation services are somewhere around the middle of the continuum, and foster care is one of the services at the more restrictive end. These are just a few examples of the possible services to be offered or mandated.

To understand how children and families become involuntary clients in this system, we must consider another aspect of child protective services—intake, investigation, and case decision-making. Since the mid-1960s, most states have had laws requiring that suspected child abuse or neglect be reported to the appropriate state agency or the police (Sussman & Cohen, 1975). Reports or referrals usually are handled by an intake unit of the local child protective services agency, which determines if an investigation is necessary. If an investigation is called for, the referral will be investigated by protective services agency staff, but police may be involved when the reported abuse is quite severe. In most states, this investigation involves an assessment of risk of harm to children, often using a structured tool or format for doing so (see, for example, Holder & Corey, 1986; Magura & Moses, 1986; Martinez, 1989; Miller, Williams, English, & Olmstead, 1987).

At the conclusion of the investigation, the child protective services worker must decide if the referral is substantiated or unsubstantiated. If it is found to be unsubstantiated, the referral is denied and the case is closed. If substantiated, the child protective services worker decides whether to provide services or refer the family for services (Stein, 1981). Pecora and his colleagues (1992) identify several factors that influence this decision: protective services agency policies, statutory limitations, local standards of service delivery, availability of services, and the family's willingness or ability to benefit from services. Depending on these factors and the severity of the findings concerning the abuse or neglect, the child protective services worker may ask the court to mandate services. Mandated services tend to be more restrictive and clearly place families in the category of involuntary client. If the risk to the children is less, protective services may simply offer services to the family. Even if services are not mandated by the court, most families feel some degree of pressure to accept services, under the possible threat that their children will be removed. Clearly, they are more appropriately categorized as involuntary, not voluntary, clients.

Who are the clients who come to the attention of the child protective services system? Not surprisingly, poor and minority children are over-represented in the foster care population. For instance, in 1986 the proportion of minority children in foster care was nearly twice the proportion of minority children in the general population (Tartara, 1990). Generally speaking, the number of children and families who come into contact with child protective services is growing rapidly. Between 1976 and 1989, reports of child abuse and neglect increased by 259% (National Commission on Child Welfare and Family Preservation, 1991). If these reports are substantiated, many of these children will end up in foster care. Although there were decreases in the number of children in foster care during the late 1970s and early 1980s, that trend has been reversed. From a low of approximately 175,000 in 1983, the number of foster care placements had grown to an estimated 340,000 by 1989 (National Commission on Child Welfare and Family Preservation, 1991).

In this chapter, we use two examples of services to involuntary clients, one court mandated and the other not court mandated. In the first instance, therapeutic foster care (sometimes called treatment foster care) is offered to an adolescent mother and her baby. These services are court mandated, and provided by a social worker in a private agency that supervises therapeutic foster care. In the second case, intensive family preservation services are offered to a mother and father and their four children in an effort to avoid placement and keep the family together safely. Services are not court mandated, but the parents knew that their children would likely be removed to foster care if they did not participate in this program. Again, services were provided by a social worker in a private agency. In both case examples, the practitioners are providing services and are not involved in investigation.

CASE EXAMPLE WITH THERAPEUTIC FOSTER CARE

Tamika, age 15, and her 18-month-old daughter, Jasmine, were placed in foster care when Tamika's mother locked them out of her home. where they had been residing. Tamika's mother, Alice, said that Tamika had to learn to be responsible for Jasmine, and that the only way to accomplish this was to force her to do so. The mother claimed that Tamika left Jasmine with her for days at a time while she went off with her friends. The young mother and her daughter had to be placed in separate foster homes as there were no homes for teenage mothers and young children available at the time. Tamika only attended school sporadically. She said she had no interest in school and that they didn't teach anything there. She often got in fights at school, leading to her expulsion. These fights were fairly serious and Tamika had begun to carry a knife, a gift from her older boyfriend, for her protection. During her first 5 months in foster care, Tamika frequently got into fights and stole things, leading to her placement in 4 different homes. The fourth placement was in a therapeutic foster care home, which has specially trained foster parents who take more challenging cases. The foster parents, Harvey and Joyce, worked closely with the therapeutic foster care worker, who made weekly visits to their home. The worker, the foster parents, and Tamika developed a treatment plan.

The worker also engaged Alice in treatment. Alice had two sons living at home, both in their early 20s. The younger son had two children who occasionally lived there, too. Alice had a full-time evening job cleaning offices and another part-time job cleaning homes during the daytime. Alice, who weighed about 215 pounds, had "heart problems," which led her to experience shortness of breath. Alice did all the cooking and cleaning in her own home, although her sons were unemployed. She had little time or energy for leisure activities, but attended church every Sunday. Alice had two other daughters, ages 17 and 19. They both had children of their own and were living with boyfriends. As a teenager, Alice had to move out on her own when she became pregnant. She left high school and got a job to support herself and her baby. She believed that her daughters should be able to do the same.

Her two sons were using crack and selling to support their habits. They often brought "shady" people into her home, according to Alice, but she said she had been unable to control her boys since they were young. Alice said she prayed every day that her sons would be "saved from their lives of sin" but that so far the good Lord had not seen fit to answer her prayers. Meanwhile, she took care of them.

CASE EXAMPLE WITH INTENSIVE FAMILY PRESERVATION SERVICES

Gloria was the 28-year old mother of four children ranging in age from 3 to 14 years of age. She lived in a crack house and prostituted to support her drug use. Gloria's 14-year-old daughter provided most of the child care as Gloria usually was too strung out to do so. The children were not attending school and had little food in the home. They had not received routine medical care in over a year, and the 6-year-old boy suffered from asthma. The house was without any furniture and had only a few toys.

There were, however, several guns of different sizes including some large rifles, a supply of drugs, and other drug-related paraphernalia throughout the house.

Gloria had a mother and two sisters living in the same city but they had discontinued contact with her since she moved into the crack house. Her mother wanted to take the children to live with her, but she was afraid to go to the crack house to get them. Gloria's husband, who was the father of the two middle children, had disappeared from her life and his whereabouts were unknown.

At one time, Gloria had held a steady job as an administrative assistant. She and her husband owned a small home in a working-class neighborhood. When their alcohol use turned to heroin and cocaine, their lives began to unravel. Eventually, they lost their jobs and had to sell their possessions to support their habits. They could not keep up with the mortgage payments and lost their home, too. Over time, they drifted apart. Gloria lived with a pimp, the father of her youngest child, for about 6 months, until he was killed in a fight with another pimp. She moved her family into the crack house, which was run by the cousin of her former paramour.

A neighbor, very disturbed by the presence of the inhabitants of the crack house in her neighborhood, called in the referral to child protective services. A protective services worker investigated the case and referred the family to intensive family preservation services. Gloria said she didn't think anybody could help her anymore, but she agreed to one visit with the worker. Interestingly, Gloria's children had not come to the attention of the protective services system until this time.

ENGAGEMENT WITH CHILD PROTECTIVE SERVICES CLIENTS

Even if this is their first contact with child protective services, parents often have some knowledge of the system. Perhaps their own parents or other relatives had children removed by protective services. Or, they may have had neighbors or friends who have been investigated by the public agency. In any case, clients who have been offered or mandated services by child protective services tend to have preconceived notions of what is entailed.

A common response is to think of the protective services worker as being too nosy or of the services as not being sensitive to their social, cultural, and economic realities. Topeka, an African-American adolescent mother, for example, complained that she failed a parent training class because she did not want to make her 2-year-old son into a sissy by rubbing his back at nap time, which the trainer required them to do. In her family, boys were taught from an early age that they had to be tough and self-sufficient to survive in their environment. Giving massages to help a toddler fall asleep might lead him to be soft, in Topeka's opinion.

In other cases, clients may have heard stories or experienced how disorganized and chaotic child protective services can be at times. If so, clients might believe that if they can just keep them out of their business or give them the right answers, the social workers will leave them alone or even forget about them. Sharon, a mother of 6 children, suspected that her oldest son, age 19, was involved in a child prostitution ring organized by her own father. And she feared that her youngest children, ages 5 and 7, were being recruited for or possibly even involved in the business. Her father had sexually molested her as a teenager, but when she told a minister and the child welfare agency became involved, Sharon was removed from the home and placed in foster care. She felt punished, not helped, by the system. Now her 7-year-old son was "daydreaming" and wetting his pants in school and a protective services worker wanted her to accompany him to family counseling. Sharon privately acknowledged her own suspicions but was convinced that confiding in a family counselor would not be helpful.

Another common response of clients is to be angry because child protective services has repeatedly threatened to remove their children, actually taken away their children, or perhaps removed the children and made it difficult for the parents to maintain any contact with them. Odalys had used crack during her pregnancy, which was detected when her first baby was born. He was taken away from her and placed in a foster home at birth. Odalys was so depressed and ashamed about these events that it was not easy for her to arrange for visits or to feel comfortable with the infant under the seemingly judgmental eyes of the foster parents and worker. They seemed to take her hesitation as indifference toward the child. Odalys attended parent education classes (although her child was not at home with her and she could not really try out the parenting techniques being taught in the class), completed a drug treatment program, had random urine tests over the 10 months following the birth of her son, and moved into housing that was acceptable to the foster care worker. When the baby was finally reunited with Odalys, she was very upset and angry to learn that protective services still wanted her to attend parent support group meetings.

Parents' responses are likely to differ, depending on whether or not their children are removed. Diorio (1992) conducted interviews with 13 parents whose children were in the temporary custody of the local protective services authority and were in foster care or an institutional placement. These parents felt that the actions of the protective services worker were unjust and that their own rights were violated or ignored.

Consequently, these parents were fearful that any action they might take could be held against them, almost at the whim of the protective services worker.

These are the responses of the parents. Unfortunately, we sometimes forget that children also are involuntary clients in child protective services, regardless of whether the services are protective or preventive in nature. Depending on their age, children tend to respond with bewilderment because they do not understand what is happening, or with fear and anxiety because they may be separated from the familiar, even if it is not an ideal situation at home. Older children, with some experience with the system, may be more likely to feel anger as well, and perhaps wonder if they can manipulate the system to their advantage.

As can be seen from the above examples, involuntary clients in child protective services, both mandated and nonmandated, are likely to react to social work intervention provided via protective services with such feelings as anger, frustration, confusion, suspicion, and hostility, to name just a few. At the same time, practitioners must acknowledge their own feelings about the families with whom they are working. While each practitioner will have a different problem orientation and worldview, it is possible to make some generalizations. For many of us, children seem more vulnerable than adults. Setting aside those instances in which children clearly should not and cannot live with their families because the situation is so terrible, sometimes the conditions practitioners see or are told about in the homes make it difficult for them to like the parents. Yet, in order to give children every possible chance to grow up with their families of origin (if they can safely do so), practitioners must be able to establish a good working relationship with the parents or caretakers based on mutual respect and trust. And to do so, they must be able to see the strengths and resources that the family possesses. To develop a working relationship with these families, practitioners must realize that parents are doing the best job that they can, given the stressors, barriers, obstacles, and challenges facing them.

So, clients may come into the encounter with the practitioner full of negative feelings and expectations, and practitioners may come in with some negative reactions and concerns. What can be done to facilitate the development of a good working relationship?

First, practitioners must give families the opportunity to demonstrate their strengths and positive attributes. Kinney et al., (1991) identify some beliefs that they think practitioners must have to establish a good working relationship with these families. In a sense, these beliefs help to counteract some of the negative or problem-oriented responses we have to clients and/or their environments, and allow us to identify some of their strengths. These beliefs are:

1. Even though the clients' environments and lives may look different from ours, there are more similarities than differences between us. For instance, we experience the same emotions. Sometimes, we (both clients and professionals) are careless and hurt people we love. From time to time our lives get chaotic and disorganized.
2. These clients, like other people, are doing the best they can do to cope with the situations confronting them. Usually, they must deal with multiple obstacles and stressors, which would be challenging, if not extremely difficult, for anyone to face.
3. People do not intend to harm one another by their words or actions. We sometimes lack skills and choose ways to try to resolve problems that end up hurting family members and others we care about.
4. Most family members really do care about each other. That caring may be hidden under layers of painful experiences, and they themselves may not realize it is there anymore. Yet, we can still find instances of acts of caring and of wanting to belong to the family. (Adapted from Kinney et al., 1991, pp. 59–60.)

If we can keep these beliefs uppermost in our minds and reflect them in our verbal and nonverbal actions, clients will realize that we are treating them differently than past human service professionals may have treated them, they will realize that we respect them. And, they will appreciate that we are helping them to see some of the good things about themselves and their families.

Operating from these beliefs seems to have benefits for assessment, too. Berlin and Marsh (1993) note that assessments can be limited by what theoretical frameworks practitioners subscribe to and by what practitioners know how to treat. We would add to this that assessments can be limited by what we allow ourselves to focus on. A practitioner can choose to focus solely on the problems or can also focus on some of the positive attributes, the strengths, and the resources. If they focus solely on the problems, practitioners are at risk of feeling just as overwhelmed and frustrated and hopeless as their clients. Moreover, they will not be aware of some of the resources and strengths that the families possess that can help them deal with some of their difficulties. We are not suggesting that practitioners overlook or deny the severe problems that must be addressed. Rather, we are arguing that if practitioners solely focus on these, it will be difficult to engage their clients, and to get a complete assessment of the families.

In addition to these beliefs, which are important in influencing practitioners' verbal and nonverbal behaviors during contacts with families, there are some concrete things that practitioners can do or say to facilitate engagement. As noted in Chapter 2, in order to prepare clients to assume their role as client, they need to understand what is expected of them and how they will interact with the practitioner. Practitioners can begin by being very clear about their own relationship to the child protective services agency that provoked this contact between the practitioner and the family. At this time, the practitioner should explain that he or she is a mandated reporter (i.e., is required to report any suspected child abuse or neglect). The practitioner also should indicate what other kinds of information may need to be reported to protective services, the courts, or some other entity. The practitioner should describe how he or she typically works, how often and where sessions will be held, and who will be involved (Wasik, Bryant, & Lyons, 1990). In therapeutic foster care, for instance, there is much more work with the family of origin than is typical in regular foster care, so all parties need to be aware of this. Family preservation practitioners may need to inform families that there will be frequent sessions, lasting more than the traditional 50 minutes, and that these sessions will be in their homes or communities. Another type of information practitioners may want to communicate is what kinds and levels of activity will be expected of family members. Generally, there is likely to be more emphasis placed on family members actively carrying out tasks, completing assignments, making changes in their lives, and the like, all geared toward making it possible for children to return to or be maintained safely at home. At the same time, practitioners will be available to help them carry out these activities. Again, this may be dramatically different from the family's previous experiences with social services.

Regardless of the conditions under which services are mandated or offered, clients must be made to feel that they have as many choices and as much control as possible. In fact, it is the practitioner's job to enable these clients to resume control over their lives. There are several ways in which this sense of choice and control can be communicated. In some forms of intensive family preservation services, clients are told that they can fire their worker at any time. Simply asking clients what they feel needs to be changed, and then listening to what they say and using it to plan services sends a clear message that they are making choices. Giving clients permission to cancel a prespecified number of sessions, by following certain procedures and redeeming cancellation coupons, is another way to give the clients some control (Hodges & Blythe, 1992). To the extent that it is developmentally appropriate, children and adolescents also should be made to feel this way. Helping parents listen to their children's concerns, just as the practitioner has listened to their concerns, not only engages the children in treatment but helps the family begin to work together as a unit again.

In contrast to work with clients in mental health or criminal justice, many of the contacts with protective services clients will occur in their own homes. An important way to communicate respect and to facilitate relationship development is to act as guests when in their homes. The practitioner should allow clients to take the lead in inviting him or her into a particular room, to sit, and the like. On the first visit, it is very appropriate for the practitioner to make small talk about everyday events or things of interest, perhaps about the family's pet bird or something in the neighborhood, always with a goal of putting the client at ease (Wasik et al., 1990). Sometimes the home will be chaotic, unsanitary, or even practically empty of furnishings. The practitioner needs to realize that the family is accustomed to child protective service workers coming into their home to conduct evaluations that often are perceived as criticism. Thus, it is imperative that the practitioner not communicate judgments. At the same time, truly unbearable conditions cannot be glossed over. For example, if a mother apologizes because there is no furniture to sit on throughout the house and no food in the kitchen, the practitioner might say, "That is something you and I can work on."

If the family referred to the practitioner is in a state of crisis, engagement may actually be much easier. Crisis theory suggests that, because their typical coping responses have not been effective, individuals in crisis are more open to trying new methods of coping (Dixon, 1987). If the practitioner is able to offer some concrete ways of dealing with the crisis in a manner that is acceptable to the family, engagement as well as initial problem resolution will be enhanced.

Practitioners may also have to engage collateral contacts or significant others with the family. Because families interact with so many different systems, collateral contacts are especially significant in their lives. School personnel, physicians, foster parents, neighbors, employers, convenience store owners, extended family, day care and Head Start providers, and landlords are just a few examples of collaterals who may be important to the family and could be a source either of stress or of assistance. All too often, family members have exhausted or even agitated these systems. And, family members may have developed habitual ways of interacting with them. Francesca, for example, was frustrated and angry because her son's teacher, Ms. Allan, had only critical things to say about him and because she repeatedly told him that he did not belong in her classroom. Not surprisingly, Francesca had several angry interactions with Ms. Allan and had called her various names. Ms. Allan was equally angry and seemed to be doing everything possible to remove Francesca's son from her classroom. The practitioner had to engage Ms. Allan so that she could begin to improve the school situation for Francesca's son.

Case Example

By the time Tamika arrived at her fourth foster home, she was even angrier than usual. She felt jerked around by the system. She said that the fights had not been her fault in the previous placements, but that people just thought of her as bad. She was especially angry that she had been unable to see her daughter. She did not like her present school. She said she was the only African-American kid there, which was close to the truth, and that the other students made fun of her name, her hair, and her clothing. She said it was only a matter of time before she "put them in their places."

The practitioner and the foster parents explained to Tamika that this foster home was different than the others in which she had been living. They explained the rules of the household, which included chores for Tamika. They described how they would have frequent meetings, one to two times per week, with the foster parents, the practitioner, and Tamika. While acknowledging that this was a tough school for Tamika, they made it clear that she would be expected to attend and to avoid getting into fights. The foster parents indicated that they would help Tamika get current with her schoolwork and would meet with her teachers to solicit their cooperation. Tamika was pleasantly surprised by their willingness to help, but skeptical that things would really change. The practitioner emphasized that the overriding goal was to return Tamika and her daughter to Alice's home, if possible, or to get them into a stable living situation. The worker noted that she could tell how much Tamika cared for Jasmine by the way she talked about her and the many photos of Jasmine that she carried with her. Tamika became somewhat less angry over the course of this visit, but said she didn't expect things to be any better.

The first thing the practitioner did during the initial week of services was to arrange for Jasmine to move into Harvey and Joyce's foster home with Tamika. Although Harvey and Joyce were licensed to care for young children, they had never had any in their home. They did not have necessary supplies or appropriate toys for a toddler. The practitioner told Tamika she would give her a certain amount of money to purchase things for Jasmine and that, with the foster mother, she could plan how to spend the money. Tamika was pleased to be given this responsibility and said that it made her feel like a real mother. The practitioner also had to engage Alice in treatment. Alice said that she was just glad to have Tamika out of her house, although she said that living in a foster home was not exactly her idea of taking care of oneself. She said she had no time to see a social worker and that Tamika was not coming back to live with her under any circumstances. The practitioner used active listening to indicate that she realized that Alice was extremely frustrated and angry. She praised her for being able to raise her children independently, and said she could tell that Alice wanted Tamika to be a good mother to Jasmine. At the same time, the practitioner explained that the state still viewed Alice as responsible for Jasmine, but that the practitioner would help them figure out the best living arrangements.

The practitioner explained how services would proceed, in a conversation similar to the one she had with Tamika. The practitioner indicated that she would like to arrange some visits between Alice and Tamika and Jasmine. Alice agreed to these visits as long as they were not in her home. The practitioner let Alice set this condition, giving her some control in the situation. This seemed to help Alice relax a bit. The practitioner did not push the idea that she hoped Tamika and Jasmine could return to Alice's household, but simply said that they would be exploring all options with the goal of finding a stable home for them. In response to questions from Alice, the practitioner explained that the current foster home could only be used as a temporary placement. By the end of the meeting, Alice was still indicating that Tamika and Jasmine could not return home, but said that she was looking forward to seeing her granddaughter.

Following is an excerpt from this meeting. The practitioner (P) had just explained to Alice (A) about the foster home where Tamika and Jasmine were living.

A: I'm glad that you found someplace safe for Tamika and that baby of hers to live. Although I do hope those people don't do everything for her.

P: I am working with the foster parents to help them encourage Tamika to take as much responsibility for the baby as she can. Maybe when you get to know them and see Tamika and Jasmine together you can make some suggestions, too.

A: Well, I didn't baby my other two girls and I'm not about to start with Tamika. Besides she is no good. She runs with the wrong crowd. She's got to learn the hard way like I did. It wasn't easy for me to take care of a baby and work and live alone, but I did it.

P: It must have been a real struggle for you to manage all of that alone. It's difficult—

A: (interrupting the practitioner) Yes, it was a struggle, but I didn't get beat up and cheated on by older men and I didn't get messed up with drugs and I didn't carry a knife. Half the time, I don't think Tamika knows what she is getting into.

P: I can tell that you want your daughter and granddaughter to have the best lives that they can have. It's hard to know how to help our children sometimes, isn't it? Especially when the world is so different today.

A: That's for sure. We had booze and cigarettes, and some neighborhoods were no good. But it wasn't like this. I just wish my kids would start going to church. The people at church are good people.

P: I do want to help Tamika find some groups, maybe in church or maybe elsewhere, that she can get involved in, if she is interested. Sometimes, if teenagers have too much free time, they are more likely to get into trouble.

A: I tried to get her involved in the church choir, but she wouldn't have anything to do with it. And I told her to go to the programs at the Y. They have lots of things for kids. But, would she go? No, she just wanted to go out with that old man of hers. And who does she decide is her best girlfriend? Suzette, the neighborhood slut! If there is trouble to find, that Tamika will find it.

P: I can see that you are pretty frustrated from trying to help Tamika in so many different ways.

A: Yes! And that is why I just have to wash my hands of the whole matter. My doctor says I can't take too much stress.

P: I'm sure it is stressful at times to be Tamika's parent. However, I have to be sure that you understand that the State of Florida still views you as responsible for Tamika because she is under 18. That doesn't mean she necessarily has to live with you, but that you and I will work together with Tamika, just like we have started to do, to figure out what is the best living arrangement for Tamika and Jasmine.

A: Well, I guess I can talk to you some, but it's like I said—Tamika needs to learn to take care of herself.

ASSESSMENT WITH CHILD PROTECTIVE SERVICES CLIENTS

With an involuntary client in child protective services, assessment may involve collecting specific information required by the nature of the referral from protective services as well as collecting the necessary information to develop treatment goals and plan interventions. In addition, regardless of what the referral might indicate, the practitioner should always assess the safety of the children. Unfortunately, this is true if children are in foster care or in the homes of their parents or other kin (Kadushin & Martin, 1988). In some situations where the children are at home or elsewhere, but considered to be at risk, the practitioner may need to assess the safety of the children immediately, at the same time as the family is being engaged. If the referral does not indicate that the child is at risk, the practitioner only needs to perform a routine assessment for safety.

Several publications describe available measures that potentially are appropriate for child protective services clients. For the most part, these measures would facilitate assessment aimed at developing treatment goals and planning interventions. Magura and Moses (1986) have a comprehensive review of available paper-and-pencil instruments that will aid the worker in assessing children and families. Grotevant and Carlson (1989) present summaries of numerous types of measures, including self-report measures, observational measures, coding schemes for assessing interactions, rating scales, and questionnaires. Although they provide less details about specific instruments, Weiss and Jacobs (1988) identify a wide range of measurement possibilities for children and families and make some recommendations for assessments in specific areas. And Corcoran and Fischer (1987) provide reviews and copies of measures for children, as well as families. Their book is especially helpful because of their focus on practice applications of measurement.

Perhaps the most widely used measure for children is the Child Behavior Checklist developed by Achenbach (Achenbach & Edelbrock, 1983). The Child Behavior Checklist describes behavioral problems and competencies of children aged 4 to 16, and can be completed by parents or others who know the child well, such as foster parents. A teacher's form also is available. Normative data are published for boys and girls of various age groups, but similar data for children of various ethnic groups is difficult to obtain.

If the objective is to assess functioning of the children within the family, perhaps the measure most widely used is the Child Well-Being Scales (Magura & Moses, 1986). These scales assess the degree to which the children's physical, psychological, and/or social needs are being met. Each of the scales has several levels with clear, behaviorally specific anchors. The Child Well-Being Scales can be used as a whole package, or relevant scales can be selected and used.

There are no widely agreed-upon and used measures of parenting and family functioning. Perhaps the most accessible and appropriate measures for child protective services families would be the Hudson's Index of Family Relations, Index of Parental Attitudes, Child's Attitude Toward Mother, and Child's Attitude Toward Father scales (Hudson, 1982). These are brief, 25-item paper-and-pencil measures that can be administered during the assessment phase of treatment and then repeatedly during intervention to monitor client progress. The items on the scales are written in simple, straightforward language that can easily be understood by individuals with limited reading skill.

Often, more direct measures such as observations or self-reports of specific behaviors or cognitions are more appropriate. A daily count of the number of arguments, the number of times a parent had an urge to strike his or her child, or the length of time children played quietly and cooperatively can provide information about the level of the problem. These measures, collected repeatedly, can be used to assess the extent to which change, maintenance, or prevention goals are attained.

Looking beyond the immediate family, the ecomap is a diagnostic tool that can help both the practitioner and family members better understand the family's sources of stress and support by showing the relationships between the family and other social systems in the environment (Hartman, 1979). Figure 6.1 depicts an ecomap of Gloria's family at the outset of intervention. When Gloria and her children completed the ecomap with the worker, they all realized how many of their social supports had been disrupted. Moreover, some of their relationships with social systems were quite stressful.

Reliability of Assessment Information

As in mental health and criminal justice services, the reliability of the assessment information collected from families in child protective services is a concern. Interestingly, the reliability of the information available in the case file, if the family has had previous contact with child protective services, also is a concern. In fact, case record information is likely to be incorrect or even contradictory. It is not unusual for case records to be missing significant pieces of information such as the names, ages, and relationships of all members of the household including other children. Of course, there is considerable variability and some child protective services agencies have extremely good files. In our experience, however, child protective services case information, both in computerized information systems and hard copy files, is more likely than not to have questionable reliability. One can only speculate about the reasons for this: Large caseloads, high staff turnover, child welfare workers lacking training in social work are a few that immediately come to mind.

For this reason and because it can be a powerful tool in engaging the client and in collecting more reliable information from the family, we

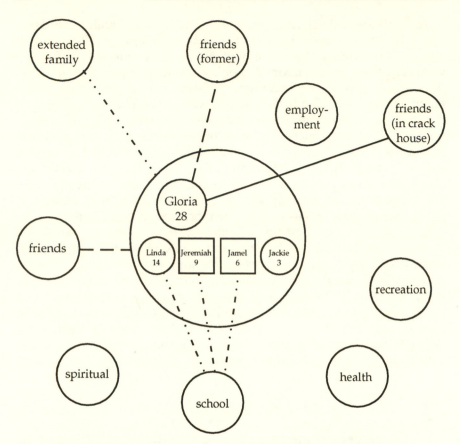

Figure 6.1. Ecomap of Gloria's family at the onset of intervention.

suggest that practitioners have only minimal information when they meet the family for the first time. It is helpful to know the reason for the referral, which children are at risk, the nature of the alleged maltreatment, and who is in the household before the first session. In this way, practitioners can honestly say that they were only told these certain things by the referral source and that they are interested in hearing the family's story. Practitioners should communicate to their clients that they believe the clients are the experts on their own lives and that the practitioner is very dependent on them to help them identify what needs to be done so that the family can be together. They also can tell practitioners what kinds of strategies the family has used in the past to try to resolve problems, what the outcomes have been, and what the family thinks might work now. Kinney et al., (1991) consider this to be an aspect of treating the clients as our colleagues.

Practitioners should not expect clients to tell all of their story or to be

100% truthful at the first session. It is simply a good, adaptive response to hold back some information until they trust the practitioner. Practitioners need to balance what they need to know to ensure safety of family members against what they can allow the family members to tell at their own pace.

Because there are several family members and sometimes collaterals involved, the practitioner may get some conflicting stories or some vague information. In the areas where the conflict or ambiguous comments are related to some important facts that the practitioner thinks need to be addressed, it often is helpful to use interview techniques aimed at further specifying what the family members are saying (Kinney et al., 1991). The practitioner can summarize what has been said, making the contradictions apparent, express puzzlement about the contradictions, and ask family members' help to resolve the confusion. In another approach, the practitioner might ask the clients to help in breaking down the story into specific facts, such as a sequence of events. Or it can be productive to ask the family members to give some specific examples of behavior when they are making generalizations about someone or using labels. Note that the same techniques can be used with collaterals.

If a practitioner has concerns about potential problem areas, but is not sure if or how they exist, it can be helpful to set assessment or tracking goals. For instance, a practitioner might set a goal to "Assess for possibility that Leticia is prostituting." Then, the practitioner will be reminded to search for information, by questions and observations, in each session until this issue is resolved. Information can be stored away and evaluated periodically by the practitioner. This also helps practitioners avoid interrogations, which generally are not helpful in getting clients to reliably report sensitive material. On the other hand, it can be helpful to ask family members some very specific, pointed questions or to point out contradictions. Here, timing is essential.

We also find that asking several family members, or all if that is appropriate, the same questions eventually moves the assessment process toward collecting more reliable information. Depending on the nature of the issue to be clarified, the practitioner may decide to do this collectively or individually. Particularly with adolescents, it seems to be helpful to take them out of the home or to have a private session to discuss sensitive material. Often they respond much better if they are seated in a car, facing forward and not having to make intense eye contact, when going over issues that are difficult for them to discuss.

Families in child protective services tend to live in chaotic environments with multiple stressors or potential stressors, and often are in crisis when the practitioner first meets them. Sometimes, the crisis is the fact that their children have been removed from the home, or may be removed. Sometimes, it is another issue. In any event, practitioners working with involuntary clients from child protective services may find that they need to do a brief assessment, focused on a particular issue or set of issues, and develop and implement an intervention plan to resolve that crisis.

Case Example

The worker's immediate concern for Gloria and her children was that the house in which they resided was not a safe environment. He also was concerned that the children were not attending school and had not received medical attention. Early on the second day of services, the worker arrived with some clothing for the children (they did not have appropriate clothes for winter). He took Gloria and her children out to find an apartment that Gloria could afford on her public assistance. The worker involved the entire family in evaluating the two apartments they found, but indicated that the final decision should be Gloria's. Gloria was unused to taking responsibility for such matters, having delegated much of this to her oldest daughter. Flexible funds, available at the worker's agency for such emergencies, were used to pay the first month's rent, and to purchase some mattresses at a Salvation Army store. He also gave Gloria a sum of money for food and took the family to the grocery store. As much as possible, he let Gloria make the choices, only making suggestions when necessary.

On the third day of services, the worker took Gloria and the children to school, and enrolled the three older children. Again, he let Gloria take the lead in dealing with the school officials, having discussed the kind of questions they were likely to ask in the car on the way over to the school. He then took them to a neighborhood health clinic for school examinations and to have the 6-year-old boy's asthma condition assessed.

Having taken care of some basic needs, the worker could now return to the task of assessment. While working with the family on their immediate needs, he had been collecting some assessment information, but he needed to assess some areas, such as Gloria's drug use, in greater detail. Engagement also had occurred while he was dealing with these immediate needs, but he now had to devote some extra time to engaging the oldest daughter, who was quite angry that she had to assume the role of mother while her own mother was using drugs.

SELECTING INTERVENTIONS FOR CHILD PROTECTIVE SERVICES CLIENTS

Essentially, work with child protective services clients that is focused on maintaining children in the home or returning them home involves dealing with some very practical, everyday issues. Much of the intervention activity is aimed at resolving some concrete resource needs that the families have, teaching family members new skills for successfully dealing with the challenges in their lives, and/or helping families improve or develop their social networks. In many ways, the intervention activities per se are similar to things that all families do from time to time. In the case of child protective services clients, they do not necessarily choose to be involved in these activities and they have some assistance, from the practitioner and others, in accomplishing their goals.

Concrete resource needs of clients can cover any of a number of things. They might need a new place to live, furniture, medical attention, clothing, repairs to their current home or apartment, food, utilities to be functioning, or even a new septic tank. Unfortunately, very little empirical work that examines the effectiveness of interventions to meet the concrete resource needs of clients is available. Essentially, the practitioner must fall back on principles of good social work intervention. The practitioner acts as a broker of services and resources and/or an advocate on behalf of the family (Whittaker & Tracy, 1989).

With regard to teaching new skills, considerable information about the effectiveness of various intervention strategies is available (Gambrill, 1977). Skills that families will find helpful cover a broad range of topics. Parenting, stress management, communication, anger control, problem-solving, budgeting, job seeking, assertiveness, and interpersonal skills are only a few examples of skills that may be helpful to family members. Several treatment protocols have been written to further specify skills training interventions (Fleischman, Horne, & Arthur, 1983; Forehand & McMahon, 1981; Goldstein, Keller, & Erné, 1985; Henggeler, 1991; Patterson, 1977; Wolfe, Kaufman, Aragona, & Sandler, 1981). Rather than following prepackaged skills training modules, however, practitioners should tailor skills training interventions so that they meet the particular needs of the clients. Especially if time is of the essence, it is important to conduct focused skills training.

Much empirical literature documents the importance of having adequate social supports. Unfortunately, less research has been carried out to evaluate the most effective methods of helping clients develop, improve, or maintain their supportive networks. Whittaker and Tracy (1989) discuss skills and tasks necessary for implementing social support interventions and Whittaker and Garbarino (1983) outline social support strategies for dealing with a range of difficulties. Because there is less empirical support to guide practitioners, it is especially important that they monitor goal attainment for goals involving social support interventions.

Case Example

The worker selected numerous interventions to stabilize Gloria and her family in their new home. The list of concrete resources was long and included housing, medical care, clothing, furniture, and food. He also helped the family paint the children's bedrooms and repair the toilet. He did these activities with the family, rather than for the family. He gave Gloria information to enroll her youngest child in Head Start and to get her two middle children in after-school activities. He referred the oldest daughter to counseling so that she could deal with some of her feelings around having been the family caretaker for a period of time. He helped Gloria set in motion efforts to locate her husband to see if he could pay child support, and he helped her apply for social security death benefits for the youngest child. When services were being terminated, 4 weeks later, he gave Gloria some additional referral information that she might find helpful in the future, such as information about a job training program.

Skills training also was an important part of his work with the family. He taught Gloria some basic household and child management techniques such as using a chore chart and a schedule to organize her day and household activities. He also taught her how to budget her limited public assistance check and food stamps. Because she was not accustomed to so much responsibility, Gloria easily became overwhelmed. To help her deal with this, the practitioner taught her stress management techniques. He involved the oldest daughter in this activity as a way of bringing them together, because she too became anxious about things such as her school performance.

In the area of social supports, the practitioner helped Gloria reach out to her mother and two sisters and attempt to repair those relationships. He helped Gloria and her children find a church that suited them, and this became an important source of support for them. Gloria joined the choir, and three of the children joined youth groups. The practitioner also talked to Gloria about the importance of avoiding her friends who were using drugs, so that she would not be tempted to slip back into those patterns. Eventually, Gloria also attended NA meetings.

Finally, the worker used some other interventions that do not exactly fit into one of the above categories. With regard to Gloria's substance abuse, the worker helped her move toward a decision to enter treatment. As they worked on the above issues, the worker always pointed out the consequences of her drug use for her children and herself (Blythe et al., 1991). He stressed that if Gloria did use while he was working with the family, she would have to make sure that her children were being supervised by a responsible adult and that she should leave the home to do so. At his urging, Gloria attended a Saturday morning meeting for people who are thinking about entering substance abuse treatment. Seeing that there were other people like her at this meeting who were struggling with the same issues seemed to help Gloria make the decision to enter treatment.

DEVELOPING GOALS

Goals are particularly important in work with child protective services clients because they provide a structure that helps practitioners think in clear, specific ways about their families. Goals also help the families to focus their efforts and to be clear about expectations. Just as families are seen as the experts on their own situations, they are full participants in the process of identifying and specifying goals.

In essence, good goals are clear, specific, and realistic. Furthermore, good goals describe changes that must be made, in the judgment of the practitioner and family members, to ensure that the children can safely live in the family home. Before reviewing some guidelines for developing good goals, we want to note that this discussion may make goal setting seem simple. In fact, we believe that goal writing is extremely difficult. It is relatively easy to think about a family in general, vague, or obscure terms, but relatively difficult to think about a family in specific terms, and even more difficult to make hard decisions about the major issues that the practitioner is going to try to address in the family. Taking this a step further, it is even more challenging to further distinguish between goals (or outcomes) and interventions (or treatment techniques), and then identify which interventions with family members are aimed at achieving which goals. We believe that forcing oneself to specify things at this level leads to more effective practice and helps practitioners more quickly realize if they are getting off track in their work with clients.

To begin, goals should be identified as soon as possible, but it should be understood that not all goals can be or need to be identified in the first sessions or weeks of service. Some important goals will be identified over time, as the family is ready to acknowledge the need to do so or to divulge necessary information so that work on a goal can proceed. Such goals can be added as the family is ready to do so. Obviously, goals related to issues that impact on the safety of family members cannot be postponed. Once identified, goals can be listed on a goal sheet, which is stored in a prominent or easily located place in the case record. Figure 6.2 is an example of what a goal sheet might look like.

All work with families that is significant should be written as a goal statement. Significant work can be defined as work that must be done in

FAMILY NAME: _____

Goal #	Goal	Date Started	Date Accomplished	Date Discontinued	RATING										
					Date	Date	Date	Date	Date	Date	Date	Date	Date	Date	Date

Goal sheet.

order to accomplish the general objectives of service. For example, in family preservation, the general goal is to maintain children safely in the home. If a mother has some unresolved grief regarding the death of her own father, but dealing with this grief does not seem necessary to maintain the children in the home, then it should not be a goal. The family preservation practitioner may want to refer the mother to a counseling agency at some point where she could deal with this issue. Particularly due to the involuntary nature of services, it is important that we are clear about what needs to be addressed in service, and what does not need to be addressed.

Significant work could be further defined as work that occupies an agenda item for a large amount of one or more sessions. If this is the case, then the issue being addressed should be developed as a goal. If goals are to actually be useful in helping the practitioner and family maintain a focus on the critical issues to be addressed, then these need to be identified as goals. Again, because these families often have so many needs, practitioners may find themselves addressing multiple concerns.

Obviously, some work is significant simply because it is aimed at addressing issues that are mandated by the referring worker from child protective services or by the court. As an example, a referral may stipulate that the family needs to have a functioning telephone so that the mother can call for assistance if the man who molested her daughter should return. The phone may have been turned off simply because the mother was unable to pay the phone bill. If the agency has access to money such as flexible funds, this may only be a matter of paying the bill and counseling the mother to monitor long-distance telephone usage. Although this requires little time or effort, it should be defined as a goal if for no other reason than to ensure documentation that a goal was attained.

Most goals will refer to actual changes to be made by family members, often changes in behavior, or to prevention or maintenance efforts. Some goals may focus on other types of outcomes, such as obtaining specific, concrete services for the family. In addition, some goals can relate only to the practitioners' tasks. The example of assessment or tracking goals was noted earlier. Relationship goals are another example of this type of goal. A relationship goal might be to target specific activities with a family member who is more difficult to engage in treatment. Again, writing this as a goal reminds the practitioner to plan specific activities or simply make comments aimed at developing this relationship, and to do this each time a contact is made with the family member. Moreover, the relationship goal will remind the practitioner to assess the quality of the relationship at each contact. All goals, except for assessment goals, should be rated on a regular basis, probably weekly,

Figure 6.3.   Extent to which client demonstrates desired behaviors.

1	2	3	4	5	6	7	8	9
Demonstrates none of the behaviors		demonstrates some of the goal behaviors		demonstrates half the goal behaviors		demonstrates most goal behaviors		demonstrates all goal behaviors

in terms of goal attainment. Figure 6.3 presents a sample rating sheet, using a 9-point scale. These ratings can be recorded on the goal sheet, although sometimes it is more helpful to graph the ratings.

Goals should focus on outcomes, not interventions. Practitioners often fall into the trap of writing a goal such as "Mother will learn to give specific reprimands, in a firm tone of voice, with nonverbal expressions of disapproval." Even if this goal further specifies what constitutes an effective reprimand, it does not specify the outcomes the practitioner hopes to bring about by teaching the mother to make effective reprimands. Suppose that the real problem is that the 9-year-old son is fighting with his siblings. Thus, the goal should be something like "Son will decrease fighting with siblings." The problem with writing the goal in the first manner is that the mother may learn to make effective reprimands, but the reprimands may not be sufficient to change the son's behavior. The worker could rate the goal as attained, based on the fact that the mother can make effective reprimands, but the son may still be fighting with his siblings and the necessary behavior change was not accomplished. Sometimes it is more comfortable for practitioners to write a goal around teaching a skill or delivering an intervention because we are fairly confident that we can handle this. In the above example, teaching the mother to make firm reprimands was an intervention, perhaps not the only necessary intervention, to help her reduce her son's fighting.

Goals can be closed out because they are accomplished or can be discontinued because the worker and/or the family decide that a goal is not appropriate. The latter category, discontinuing goals, is intended to encourage workers to write goals for all their efforts, but not to be concerned if they make an error in identifying a particular goal. Sometimes, a practitioner and the family identify a certain goal based on the available information, and this goal may seem necessary to help maintain the children in the home or return them home. There are also cases in which instrumental goals, described in Chapter 3, are useful in identifying the most proximal goals or goals necessarily accomplished before moving to others. As the family reveals more assessment information over time, however, it may become clear that the previously specified goal is not critical and that another area must be addressed. The point here is just that we want to encourage practitioners to write goals and not to worry about erroneously identifying certain goals.

To further benefit from the potential of well-specified and well-thought-out goals, we suggest that staffing of cases and supervision also should focus on goals, once the initial assessment is completed. Again, this increases the likelihood that workers will not lose their focus with a family, and will not do a significant amount of work for families in areas that are unrelated to significant family problems. Similarly, we suggest that ongoing recording also be focused around goals, unless it is general assessment information.

While it may seem that undue attention has been placed on goals, we believe that good goals are critical to work with child protective services families. As we mentioned previously, this is partly due to the fact that their lives often are so complex and chaotic. Moreover, if we really are going to work as efficiently and effectively as possible to ensure that children have every chance of living with a family, whether it be their family of origin or a new family, we need to develop and maintain a focused intervention plan.

CONTRACTS

Contracting is an effective tool for helping families move toward goal attainment. We prefer written contracts that specify goals to be addressed and who will be involved in addressing the goals. Like goals, contracts can be revised as new information is uncovered or conditions change. All family members who can understand the contract at some level should be asked to sign the contract. Contracts should also specify practitioner involvement, and therefore should be signed by the practitioner. Collaterals may also be involved in signing contracts if their involvement will be significant. Contracts also provide another opportunity for the practitioner to spell out the terms under which services are delivered—issues such as confidentiality and mandatory reporting can again be explained in a written contract.

We are not in favor of contracts that specify activities or interventions to be carried out to facilitate goal attainment. This requires either a crystal ball that will allow the practitioner to know in advance which interventions will work, or considerable reworking of the contract to update it as interventions are revised or discarded.

Case Example

In the therapeutic foster care case, a contract was developed with the foster parents, Harvey and Joyce, Tamika, her mother, Alice, and the

Figure 6.4.   Contract.

Date: _____

   Tamika Johnston, Alice Johnston, Harvey and Joyce Benson, and Don Slade
agree to work together toward finding a stable, long-term home placement for
Tamika and her daughter, Jasmine. Mr. Slade will meet with Tamika and the
Bensons at least two times per week and with Alice Johnston at least one time
per week. If there are any problems between meetings, they will call Mr. Slade's
beeper at 624-6262. Both Tamika and Alice Johston understand that any suspected child abuse or neglect will have to be reported to child protective services
by Harvey and Joyce Benson and by Don Slade.

Signed by:

_____   _____
Tamika Johnston   Alice Johnston

_____   _____
Joyce Benson   Harvey Benson

_____
Don Slade

practitioner (see Figure 6.4). Jasmine was not included as she was too
young to understand the contract, let alone sign her name. The contract
only stated in general terms what was expected of each participant. It
also reminded all participants that the Bensons and the practitioner were
required to report any suspected child abuse or neglect.

IMPLEMENTING INTERVENTIONS WITH CHILD
PROTECTIVE SERVICES CLIENTS

   Particularly with child protective services clients, it is critical that they
understand the rationale for the specific interventions being implemented, to increase the likelihood that they will be implemented cor-
rectly and with as much client participation as is possible. Even though
they have participated fully in identifying and selecting the problems to
be addressed and in specifying treatment goals, they still need to understand the reasoning behind the selection of certain interventions over
others. Recall that child protective service clients may already have been
required to participate in some interventive efforts that *seemed* irrelevant
to their daily concerns, if not disadvantageous. Even if these interven-

tions were relevant, they probably were communicated as requirements, with little or no attention being devoted to explaining how the family might benefit in a specific way and why this approach was selected over others. Therefore, practitioners should take more time than they might usually devote to helping clients understand why particular interventions are being implemented.

During the implementation of interventions, two tasks are important: (1) analyzing client data to see if goals are being met; and (2) determining that interventions are being implemented as planned and in the most effective and efficient manner. The first task involves the same general activities for all types of involuntary clients. The second task has some special implications for child protective services clients. Because we are concerned about developing permanent plans for children and minimizing their drift in care outside a permanent family unit, we want to avoid unnecessary delays in the intervention phase of work with protective services clients.

Monitoring the implementation of concrete services is relatively straightforward. Generally, interventions related to concrete services involve a set of tasks that must be accomplished. Some involve a very small number of tasks. Josephine, for example, was receiving threatening phone calls from her former partner and his new lover and she was worried about her own safety as well as the safety of her children. Rather than continue to be victimized by this situation, all Josephine had to do was change her telephone number to one that was unlisted. This involved only two steps—acknowledging that these persons were unstable and presented a threat, and making a simple phone call to the telephone company to change the telephone number. On the other hand, some concrete services are very involved. Getting the heat turned on by a slum landlord may involve numerous actions, ideally carried out by the appropriate family members with the support of the practitioner.

Monitoring the implementation of skills-training interventions is fairly straightforward because these are structured interventions. Like interventions related to concrete resources, it is relatively easy to identify the necessary activities to be implemented and to simply document if they have been carried out. In brief, skills-training involves identifying the components of skills that must be taught, teaching these skills through a combination of modeling, role playing, and feedback, and building in generalization of newly acquired skills to other situations (see, for example, Cartledge & Milburn, 1986). Practitioners can use this same format for implementing particular skills training interventions, regardless of the skills being taught, and for monitoring their implementation.

The implementation of social support interventions is more difficult because the interventions tend to be less well specified and because they involve multiple individuals. Yet, because they are so complex, both intervention implementation and monitoring will be enhanced by breaking down the interventions into procedural steps and then determining if these steps have been carried out as intended.

Implementing interventions with child protective service clients can be especially challenging because multiple actors, including collaterals, may be involved. And these actors may have experienced some extremely negative interactions at one time, resulting in some predisposed negative feelings toward the other members of the network. With interventions involving multiple actors, the worker must carefully specify tasks and activities for several different individuals and must closely monitor whether the tasks are being completed and whether the desired goals are being accomplished. In addition to these concerns, the practitioner should be aware that collaterals and family members may have experienced prior interpersonal difficulties that impair their ability to implement interventions. If process measures indicate that interventions are not being implemented as intended, the practitioner will need to assess the reasons for this, paying close attention to the role of all individuals responsible for implementing the intervention.

Case Example

Joyce and Harvey Benson, as therapeutic foster parents, had to develop and implement a number of interventions with Tamika and her daughter. The practitioner worked with them to develop these interventions and problem-solved if any difficulties were encountered. Figure 6.5 is a copy of a form that Joyce and Harvey had to complete in order to document that they were implementing the planned interventions. (Pressley Ridge Schools, 1993)

TERMINATION

As in other forms of involuntary treatment, termination in child protective services is more likely to be dictated by outside influences than by treatment decision-making and case planning. Sometimes, because the child welfare system tends to move slowly and not be overly concerned about the cost of various forms of care, even mandated termination involves considerable notice, which ultimately allows for advance planning.

As outlined in Chapter 4, an important segment of termination activities is reviewing and reinforcing the gains the family has made and their own participation in these gains. In child protective services, the expectation at termination is that children will experience a long-term, permanent relationship with their family of origin or with some other family. If intervention has truly focused on bringing about the necessary

Figure 6.5. PRYDE log of daily events (LODE)

Person completing LODE: _____
Youth: _____
Day of week and date: _____

1. Finish your LODE as close to the end of the day as possible.
2. Report treatment activities of PTP and STP as completely as possible.
3. Fill in all blanks and report who used each skill (Sections A & B).
4. Highlight treatment issues.
5. **REMEMBER: Your LODE is PRYDE's official record of youth treatment.**

A. PARENTING SKILLS

PTP STP   1. I used a social reward in the following instance. Youth behavior I rewarded:
_____
What I did and/or said: _____

PTP STP   2. I told another person about an achievement or positive accomplishment by the youth. Whom I told: _____
What I told about: _____ Told it in front of the youth? Yes No

PTP STP   3. I used an idea or suggestion made by my PRYDE child. _____

PTP STP   4. I used active listening when the youth displayed or expressed the following emotion or feeling: _____
Situation which caused the feeling: _____

PTP STP   5. I used an I message in the following situation: _____
What I said: _____

PTP STP 6a. I used the following skill-teaching components to teach the youth the following behavior: _____
   ___ Previously taught skill   ___ New skill
   ___ affectionate opening statement   ___ verbal description of skill
   ___ social reward or I-message   ___ demonstration of skill
   ___ youth practice of skill   ___ explain short & long-term consequences of behavior
   ___ why youth behavior was inappropriate (replacement beh.)

    6b. I helped generalization by teaching the above behavior in a new setting or with new people. New people (circle): PTP STP PSCL my own child teacher teacher neighbor Other ___ New setting: _____

PTP STP   7. I reached a cooperative decision or re-   ___ positive start
solved a conflict by using these negoti-   ___ generate solutions
ation components on the following is-   ___ decide best solution
sue.   ___ define problem
Issue: _____   ___ evaluate alternatives
(If you used more than 4 components,   ___ plan implementation
attach a description which includes the   ___ Follow-up
decision.)   Who Suggested the chosen solution? _____

B. DISCIPLINE: In addition to points or in a situation where points didn't apply, I used:
PTP STP Positive procedure: reinforced a positive opposite behavior, contracting, other: _____
Youth Behavior: _____
Worthiness of behavior:
awesome   awfully good   appropriate
PTP STP Negative procedure: extinction, time out, response cost, restitution, other:
_____
Youth behavior: _____
Severity of youth behavior: serious medium mild

C. RATING OF THE DAY: Rate your feelings or attitude toward the youth for this day only. Then indicate in your narrative what events influenced your rating.
ecstatic satisfied disappointed no interaction
PTP   6   5   4   3   2   1   NI
STP   6   5   4   3   2   1   NI
       pleased   so-so   disgusted
Circle one: A. Consistent day: rating fits for most the day
B. Inconsistent day: rating reflects overall attitude toward youth at day's end, though day has been variable

Figure 6.5. PRYDE log of daily events (LODE) *(continued).*

D. NATURAL FAMILIES:
Check if your youth had the following today: ___ Home Visit ___ Phone Call
___ Other (what?)
What member of natural family? _____ Conduct was ___ positive
___ negative. Comment in "observations" If negative.

E. ACTIVITIES
For each period of the day record the youth's activities. Be brief and specific. For each activity record the amount of time and the people involved, as well as whether or not you consider the influence of others involved to be prosocial. Finally, circle one of the "Class of Behavior" codes for each behavior (key to codes follows).

OP—Out of home, Parent organized and run.   OC—Out of home, Community involvement: YMCA, school activities, team sports, church activities, etc.

OU—Out of home, Unorganized: visiting, hanging out, movies (no parent), playing with friends, etc.

IA—In home Active: phone talk, chores, games, reading, etc.   IP—In home Passive: TV, radio, napping, etc.

Activity	Amount Time	With Whom?	Pro-Social?	Class of Behavior

MORNING
1. ___ ___ ___ Y N   OP OC OU IA IP
2. ___ ___ ___ Y N   OP OC OU IA IP
3. ___ ___ ___ Y N   OP OC OU IA IP

AFTERNOON
1. ___ ___ ___ Y N   OP OC OU IA IP
2. ___ ___ ___ Y N   OP OC OU IA IP
3. ___ ___ ___ Y N   OP OC OU IA IP

EVENING
1. ___ ___ ___ Y N   OP OC OU IA IP
2. ___ ___ ___ Y N   OP OC OU IA IP
3. ___ ___ ___ Y N   OP OC OU IA IP

F. YOUR OBSERVATIONS   Author's Initials: _____

1.) Describe important events as specifically as possible. 2.) Focus on treatment behaviors and possible new ones. 3.) Include positive as well as negative youth behaviors. 4.) When describing a youth behavior include events preceding the behavior and the reactions or consequences the behavior produced. 5.) Describe the topics of any significant conversations. Note who initiated the conversation and its approximate length.

changes so that children can remain with their families, then termination activities should make every effort to help families maintain their gains so that they do not have to experience another disruption or even the events leading up to a potential disruption.

For child protective services clients, an important facet of termination is being clear about the conditions under which termination of services is occurring and the nature of the future relationship, mandated or otherwise, between the family and the child protective services agency. If families are clear about the conditions under which they exited from involuntary status in child protective services, this information will help them to realize what they must do or avoid doing, in order to stay outside the child protective services system.

Some programs for children and families often make provisions for families to call them if they experience difficulties in the future, after termination. Family preservation services often have such an arrangement whereby families can get some additional assistance in the form of booster sessions. If this is the case, the practitioner will want to make clear to all family members the conditions under which they would be welcome to call for some assistance and how they can best make contact with the practitioner.

FOLLOW-UP

Recall that follow-up has the joint purposes of serving both agency and client needs. At this time, if follow-up occurs in routine practice for child protective services clients, it tends to be directed more toward monitoring families to determine that children are safe, than toward addressing treatment outcomes or even client satisfaction. Follow-up activities should consider the extent to which overall program goals are accomplished, in our opinion: Are children in permanent homes? Are children and other family members safe? Are the basic needs of the family being met? Families First, the family preservation program in the state of Michigan, requires that practitioners routinely visit or call families at 3, 6, and 12 months following termination of services. The practitioners always ask if the children are still in the home and, if not, where they are residing. They also ask if the family has been experiencing any difficulty. This generates some basic information about the effectiveness of Families First in achieving the overall program goal of maintaining children in their home and affords the family an opportunity to request some additional assistance, if needed. The form completed by the Families First worker is depicted in Figure 6.6.

We believe that simple, direct measures of program effectiveness are the best alternatives. They are easy to administer, take very little time, and directly relate to program goals. The Pressley Ridge PRYDE program, a therapeutic foster care program, follows up its clients 1 year after services are terminated. Program staff make a telephone call to determine where the child or young person is living. These living arrangements are rated on a Restrictiveness of Living Scale (Hawkins et al., 1992). They also ask some fairly straightforward questions about whether the youth is employed, has been in trouble with the police or incarcerated, and the like.

Figure 6.6. Families first follow-up evaluation.

MONTH: Three   Six   Twelve   (Circle One)

County: _____   Agency: _____

Name of Family: _____

DSS Case Number: _____

Date Service Completed: _____

FAMILIES FIRST Worker: _____

Worker Completing Follow-up Form: Date Form Completed:
_____

Name of person providing information about the family:
_____

Relationship to family:
_____

Name of child at risk: _____

    Child's placement: _____ (enter code from list below)

Name of child at risk: _____

    Child's placement: _____ (enter code from list below)

Name of child at risk: _____

    Child's placement: _____ (enter code from list below)

Other information: _____
_____
_____

☐ Check this box to indicate that back of sheet was used to list additional children or record additional information.

30	at home	35	jail
31	foster care	36	camp
32	relative placement	37	detention
33	court ordered paid placement	38	training school
34	mental health	39	unknown

Locating former child protective services clients can be challenging, because they often have to make frequent changes of residence. Private agency staff generally do not have access to public agency records, which may include current addresses for former clients if they are receiving some type of assistance from the government. Assuming that the practitioner has followed the advice on maintaining contact with protective services clients, as outlined in Chapter 4, yet the family has been lost, the best method of locating the family is to ask other people in the family's life. For the practitioner, it may be easiest to make some phone calls to other professionals who he or she believes are working with the family. After that, family members and friends, or neighbors, are possibilities. Unless their telephone numbers are in the file, however, this may involve in-person contact, which becomes more costly.

Another possibility, if the family cannot be located, is to gather the information from others in their network. In conducting the follow-up described above, Pressley Ridge interviewers ask their follow-up questions of collaterals or significant others if they are unable to make contact with the family.

CONCLUSION

The range of treatment options and interventive programs for child protective services clients is broad. Because it was not possible to discuss all of them in detail, we focused our case examples on two types of interventions: one in which the children have been removed from the home and one in which the children are at imminent risk of being removed from the home. In discussing various issues, we were aware of the tension between typical practice and ideal practice. We chose to focus on the latter, although we acknowledge that it is not always possible to follow the prescriptions of ideal practice.

This chapter began with a discussion of various ways of categorizing child protective services. The typical manner in which families enter child protective services was reviewed, along with their typical responses to becoming involuntary clients. Methods of engaging both families and collaterals were presented. Assessment methods and tools were discussed, and ways of increasing the reliability of data were indicated. Selecting and implementing interventions with child protective services was reviewed. Finally, termination and follow-up activities with families were presented.

Chapter 7

Research-Based Practice with Involuntary
Mental Health Clients

In this chapter, we illustrate the phases of research-based practice with involuntary mental health clients using case material and examples that address the many decision points and intermediate objectives present in work with this population. We begin by defining the parameters of involuntary mental health treatment: the settings, services, and recipients. Following this we examine common issues related to involuntary treatment in each phase of practice. Several actual client examples are presented to illustrate components of research-based practice. Finally, a case example with a 42-year-old African-American woman suffering from bipolar disorder is discussed to demonstrate all phases of research-based practice with involuntary mental health clients. In this chapter, the terms *client* and *patient* are used interchangeably.

Practitioners who provide mental health services often work with both voluntary and involuntary clients, unlike correctional and child protective settings, where the majority of clients do not request or willfully seek service. Clients who initially request mental health treatment may later be treated under involuntary status if others judge that more restrictive treatment settings are necessary. Mental health services for involuntary clients are provided in both outpatient and inpatient settings.

Acute mental health services are provided for urgent problems and include short-term treatments offered in both inpatient and outpatient settings. The function of acute care is restorative; clients are expected to return to their level of preacute episode functioning, whether normal or otherwise. Typical acute services include emergency room mental health services and emergent care walk-in clinics. Many outpatient clinics and casework agencies actually provide acute mental health services as clients are most likely to use these services when they are in crisis. Suicidal intent, loss of contact with reality involving dangerous behavior, severe anxiety, and desperation about life problems commonly cause individuals and families to seek acute mental health services.

Services for chronic mental illness, now called *severe and persistent mental disorder*, focus on managing an ongoing mental disorder. Based on the particular disorder, service providers and others may hold lower expectations for return to predisorder state, or may expect further deterioration and no recovery. Clients may enter the system as acute and become chronic after one or more acute episodes. Often acute episodes recur at predictable and unpredictable times for many years. Schizophrenia (and other disorders involving loss of contact with reality), manic-depressive illness, and major depression are three disorders that often follow such a pattern. Services for severe and persistent mental disorder are provided both in outpatient and inpatient settings.

Outpatient settings are nonresidential and represent the least restrictive service mode. They may provide both acute, emergency, and long-term or chronic care. Typical involuntary mental health services provided on an outpatient basis include assessments or evaluations for mental disorder, programs for sex offenders and physical abusers, and same-day treatment programs for severely and persistently disordered clients.

Located between inpatient and outpatient settings on the restrictiveness continuum are halfway houses and group homes. Individuals who live in these facilities have been evaluated as needing some supervision in living arrangements and are often suffering from severe and persistent mental disorder. Houseparents or counselors usually also reside in the homes and provide immediate intervention for problems in living, although clients generally receive ongoing mental health care and other services from outside affiliated agencies and practitioners. Sometimes these residential arrangements are transitional (i.e., halfway) houses and serve to prepare clients for return to unsupervised community living, while group homes may provide permanent housing for severe and persistently mentally ill individuals.

Inpatient mental health settings represent the most restrictive type of mental health care. These include residential care facilities such as psychiatric hospitals and psychiatric units in general hospitals, and prisons or other institutions whose primary mission is not psychiatric care. Involuntary patients in these facilities are generally housed on locked units and are prevented from leaving if necessary. Physical restrictions and seclusion rooms may be used if patients become violent toward others, although psychotropic medications have reduced much of the need for physical methods of control. Both acute and persistently (or chronic) mentally disordered individuals may become involuntary clients. A significant proportion, 29%, of psychiatric hospitalizations are involuntary; of these, 3% are criminal and involuntary and 26% are noncriminal and involuntary (Snowden & Cheung, 1990). Publicly financed psychiatric inpatient admissions are more likely involuntary than are privately paid admissions. Ethnic minorities and males are overrepresented among involuntary mental health clients; these clients are most publicly visible in urban communities where homelessness is a frequent concomitant of severe mental disorder. The heavy overrepresentation of African-Americans among those involuntarily committed to U.S. public mental institutions is well documented in the empirical literature, but there is an absence of data supporting any one explanation for this (Lindsay & Paul, 1989).

ENGAGEMENT WITH INVOLUNTARY
MENTAL HEALTH CLIENTS

Involuntary mental health clients may represent the truly involuntary: those who cannot give or withhold informed consent to participate in treatment. Involuntary clients enter the mental health system via private or public referral sources. Private referrals might include family, friends, or neighbors. Public referrals can come from schools, hospitals, law enforcement, or protective agencies. In many cases, the problems of the client will have come to the attention of many others; the point of actual referral may represent a social juncture indicating that available informal and formal resources have been exhausted. Often, the immediate need for medical attention may surpass the need for mental health care. Drug overdose, alcohol toxicity, dangerous dehydration or metabolic imbalance, and overexposure to heat or cold are examples of medical problems that require immediate attention found frequently among mentally disordered individuals.

Typical client responses to the possibility of involuntary mental health care are hostility, anger, and even physical resistance. This is particularly true if the client feels tricked into entering a care setting. Sometimes clients understand that their behavior has raised concern about their mental health status and may act enraged at mild exploratory questions that imply that they are not in control. It is not uncommon to have clients become verbally abusive, even threatening legal action against the practitioner and hospital, when involuntary treatment is proposed. Clients are often understandably anxious and scared, or may even be terrified about what will happen next. Practitioners should regard this behavior as expected and normal. It is important to remember that actions depriving others of their freedom and civil rights, however well-intentioned or judged as necessary, are coercive by nature.

Ironically, the practitioner should also be prepared for the opposite reaction. Seemingly involuntary clients may be relieved and grateful when someone else offers to assume temporary control and responsibility. Sometimes, if they feel they need to be hospitalized, clients themselves may embellish complaints that are more likely to result in admission (e.g., suicidality, threats against others) and may downplay factors that might decrease their chances of admission (e.g., possessing medication for symptoms, but not taking it). Due to the scarcity of publicly funded inpatient psychiatric beds in urban centers and decreased mental health funding, only patients presenting the most severe problems can be admitted, and numbers of individuals who need treatment are not admitted due to financial, space, or other systemic limitations. Patients who know this may attempt to increase the likelihood that their problems will receive what they judge as appropriate and adequate attention.

The practitioner attempting to assess such a client acts quickly. There are several methods of decreasing the client's and family's apprehension that will allow the worker to gather necessary information. Both the client and those accompanying them, family or professionals, need *reassurance* that the problem can be constructively addressed once assessment is underway and sufficient information is gathered. As described in Chapter 2, the clinic practitioner in this situation should be clear, direct, and honest. After introducing herself, she states the reason for concern. A *first-things-first approach* is often useful to clarify for both the patient and others what to expect during this time. The practitioner briefly outlines to the others what will happen, such as,

> First we need to find out whether (client) has been using any drugs or alcohol, then we need to talk with (client) and then with you to best determine what needs to happen next. Can you bear with us for a few minutes while we try to do this? I know this is hard, but if you can wait outside, we'll call you as soon as we finish talking with (client). We'll be able to tell you more in a few minutes.

The assessment process may be lengthy, however, so both family and client also need to understand that several hours may pass before important decisions can be made.

In addition to reassurance, the patient and family or others also need whatever *factual information* is available. Small, simple facts that might be available during this time include the sequence of events that will follow, how long the client and others may have to wait to see care providers, and what kinds of information different providers will be requesting. The practitioner may say such things as "We will be ready to talk with you in about 15 minutes" or "The nurse is going to give you an injection to help you calm down a little now while we talk to you."

While this may not always be possible and facts may not be known for several hours or even days, facts provide an anchor and can have a stabilizing effect.

The practitioner can also use *normalization* with the patient and family, pointing out and describing aspects of the current presenting problem that are common to the patient's ongoing disorder or to others with similar presenting problems. Depression, for example, has an unfortunately high rate of recurrence; telling a frightened patient this is not extremely unusual can sometimes be helpful. The same is true with some patients on antipsychotic medications: Thought disorder and hallucinations can occur even when the patient regularly takes prescribed doses of medication. Recurrence of symptoms does not necessarily indicate medication noncompliance. Explaining that this happens to many people and that it can usually be helped by adjusting or changing medication may be useful.

Keeping focus can be difficult as violence or conflict precipitates many involuntary patients' visits to service providers. The patient and family members may still be arguing and even attempting to involve the practitioner, thereby avoiding focus on the patient's mental state. The practitioner must quickly sort through which variables are directly related to the patient's mental status and which are related to the present conflictual interaction. Finally, the patient's *expectations* about what will happen over the next few hours should be addressed as clearly and sympathetically as possible. Maintaining this can be difficult when the practitioner is desperately searching for an available inpatient bed for an anxious and uncooperative involuntary client. Furthermore, the client's previous experiences in involuntary settings can create negative expectations that make communication more difficult. If the practitioner is aware of past negative experiences, they should be addressed to correct any misconceptions at this time. In many cases, however, a client's history is totally new to the practitioner. In working with severe and persistently disordered individuals it is generally safe to assume that they have uncomfortable or even extremely fearful feelings about receiving care. Again, being clear and concrete about the chain of events that will transpire is one of the most helpful ways a practitioner can address expectations. It also is wise to be aware that, under duress, information may not be accurately received. Repeating the same details several times may be helpful.

Do involuntary clients recant and become pliable and cooperative when practitioners follow the above-recommended actions or do they remain resistant and uncooperative? Most involuntary clients, whether mandated or nonmandated, do not accept the necessity for restrictive treatment simply because what the practitioner says makes sense. Many clients possess long histories of negative experiences with hospitalizations and medication trials. While a client's suspiciousness and reluctance to engage may be somewhat due to the disorder itself, it clearly also is due to past experiences with hospitalization, medication, and the social context of mental health service delivery.

The presence of involved family members during engagement with an involuntary client is an advantage. While it increases the number of individuals the practitioner must attend to, family members can serve as important allies in establishing a relationship with the client. During engagement and early assessment, family members can best assist by providing information about the chain of events that preceded the current crisis (antecedents). This information can help the practitioner communicate more easily with the client and proceed with assessment tasks.

Those accompanying an involuntary client are frequently also in crisis themselves. When families bring members for mental health care, it generally indicates they can no longer cope with trying to manage the problem disorder on their own; they turn to a mental health professional because they are unable to deal with the client's behavior. Unfortunately, family members and significant others may be least able to manage and respond appropriately to angry or acting-out behavior by the client. Family members may make things worse if they respond angrily or lose control at this crucial time. The practitioner should assess family members' current coping and acknowledge the difficulties in trying to care for a mentally disordered person. The worker should also ensure that if a family demonstrates difficulty maintaining control, an immediate, brief time-out and support in regaining composure are provided.

Families may also be concerned about the restrictiveness of involuntary mental health care and express the hope that involuntary hospitalization might be avoided. They may hope that bargaining with the client for improvements, seeking a just-discovered miracle drug, or simply talking with the practitioner will produce change. In rare cases, this may be true. Families may not be aware of the procedures and state laws governing mandated involuntary admission or that once in the hospital, the client's length of stay, discharge plans, and perhaps even treatment methods may be solely the decision of the hospital staff or the court.

Engagement with involuntary clients and their families means achieving a working agreement that allows assessment and treatment to move forward. Stabilization of the immediate crisis is a prerequisite for engagement. We have described a general process above and illustrate this process below by introducing a case example we will use throughout the remainder of this chapter.

Case Example

Matalie C., female, aged 42, African-American, uses a women's shelter as her address, but visits there only during mealtime and for required meetings, spending most nights in the bus station. Diagnosed as schizophrenic almost 18 years ago, she has been psychiatrically hospitalized more than 17 times. About 5 years ago, her diagnosis was changed to manic-depressive disorder. Matalie has not had contact with her husband or children, who live about 20 miles away in another town, in the past 4 years.

Matalie's history is sketchy and not reliable, gathered from available old medical and mental health records, and from Matalie's self-report. Matalie reports that for the past 20 years or so, she has had periods of depression alternating approximately every four to five months with periods of high activity. Her behavior during the periods of high activity became more and more bizarre over the years: She spent large amounts of money, "talked crazy about get-rich schemes," and associated with people who scandalized and scared her family. As a result of this behavior and her lengthy hospitalizations, she lost her job 15 years ago. Matalie's initial hospitalization 18 years ago was 5 weeks in length and apparently the result of deteriorating self-care over several months coupled with a very high, nonfocused activity level. Her husband cajoled her to a hospital mental health clinic by telling her he wanted her to accompany him to see a counselor because he just couldn't "keep up" with her any more. She states that his trickery and dishonesty are the reasons she does not live at home or have contact with family members any longer. All available evidence suggests the family coped with Matalie's disorder up until the last four years, when, following a series of particularly fast cycling moods with serious violence and risk to other family members, they did not feel she could be reasonably maintained at home any longer. They asked for help finding an intermediate care facility. Matalie lived in the halfway house for about two months and then moved out to the street, arriving at her current arrangement with the shelter about 2 years ago.

Initial Contact and Engagement

The shelter worker expressed concern about the discoloration of Matalie's ankles and said she would accompany Matalie to the walk-in clinic at the nearby hospital. The shelter social worker escorted Matalie to the walk-in clinic. Matalie's feet were unwrapped; they smelled indescribably foul and looked coldly white and shriveled. Observing that Matalie's feet were probably gangrenous, the caseworker and medical staff both realized that Matalie was obviously not providing adequate self-care. Despite crowded inpatient psychiatric conditions, it was felt that Matalie required highly restrictive psychiatric care at this time based on her dissociation from reality and inability to care for herself. A mental health practitioner joined the social worker after Matalie became verbally abusive to the social worker and medical staff.

The clinic mental health practitioner was clear, direct, and honest with Matalie. She introduced herself and stated the reason for concern, namely that Matalie's thinking was going so quickly that others were concerned about her safety and ability to care for herself. She explained that treating Matalie's feet would require several days of bed rest and acknowledged that the thought of several days in bed was probably uncomfortable right now. The practitioner's explanation was quite concrete and used frequent, simple reassurance. She frequently stopped her explanations to see whether Matalie was following, and asked Matalie simple questions to check for understanding. The practitioner told Matalie that she would need to stay in the hospital for about a week just for her feet, and then for a while longer until they were sure her thinking was at a pace that would help Matalie take care of herself at the shelter or on the street. Matalie was not happy about the prospect of going into the hospital, but the practitioner's calm voice explaining that there was something seriously wrong with her feet made sense. The shelter social worker clarified the consequences of taking or refusing care, explaining that Matalie could return to the shelter after hospitalization, but that because of her recently increasing conflicts and the medical seriousness of her feet, she could not now return and use the shelter in this condition.

Based on the severity of her psychiatric disorder, Matalie was admitted to the psychiatric unit of a general hospital on an involuntary 10-day hold for the purposes of evaluation and stabilization. After thorough cleaning, antibiotic treatment was begun for her feet. Medical staff indicated it would be 3–5 days before they would know the extent of nerve and tissue damage and whether amputation was necessary. The shelter caseworker stayed at the hospital until Matalie was taken to the psychiatric unit. While Matalie's feet were treated, the caseworker met with the clinic mental health practitioner.

ASSESSMENT WITH INVOLUNTARY
MENTAL HEALTH CLIENTS

The general purpose of assessment with involuntary mental health clients is twofold: (1) To understand the history, development and functional relationships of problem variables in the client's life; and (2) To evaluate the adequacy of the client's intrapersonal, interpersonal, and environmental resources to cope with the nature and sequelae of mental disorder. More concretely, this involves five steps:

1. Describing the history and development of the mental health problem.
2. Describing the client's development and background relevant to the mental health problem.
3. Describing the current problem by identifying the nature, extent, and relative level of the symptomatology or disorder.
4. Conducting a functional analysis of the problem(s) to identify likely factors precipitating this episode.
5. Designing an intervention plan to address immediate behavioral stabilization and to identify moderate- to long-term treatment objectives.

Below we focus first on general problems practitioners encounter in assessment with involuntary mental health clients. We then follow by describing the process of assessment with involuntary mental health clients. We return to the case of Matalie and her practitioner as they proceed through this phase of practice.

Problems in Assessing Involuntary Mental Health Clients

There are two related challenges in the assessment of involuntary mental health clients: the *availability* and the *reliability* of accurate assessment information. The availability of assessment data, that is, the amount of information accessible to the practitioner, is complicated by the fact that some clients are simply unable to provide accurate information. This inability, or cognitive dysfunction, may be independent or related to the mental disorder. The long-term effects of substance abuse or being drunk, high, frightened, or scared at the time of assessment are all examples of cognitive impairment caused by factors other than those directly related to a specific psychiatric disorder. Depression, anxiety, thought disorders, and other symptoms related to acute or persistent mental health dysfunction can also cause changes in one's ability to recall and process information.

Unfortunately, collateral sources of information may not be available at the time of initial assessment. Many involuntary clients are not surrounded by family or others willing or able to share the client's history and participate in treatment planning. The lives of numerous involuntary clients in urban centers are such that there may be no identifiable next of kin, the nearest family member resides distantly and has not had recent contact with the client, or the client is estranged from family and close others with neither side desiring reconciliation. In addition to lacking a stable personal network, many persistently disordered individuals may have sporadic relationships with medical and mental health providers. Trying to piece together this information can be like working on a two-sided jigsaw puzzle! Local clinics and hospitals are often too busy to quickly respond to requests for records; assessment, treatment, and discharge or termination may be completed before the information is even received. Problematic, time-delayed tracking or monitoring systems can plague individual cases and some records seem to simply have vanished. Records of hospitalizations in one county or region may wait months before entry into a central mental health information system. Even when obtained, the utility of these records in assessment and treatment planning varies widely; some contain only brief narrative reviews, the state code numbers for treatment services provided, diagnoses, and admission and discharge dates. Others may be a morass of individual progress notes written by each worker in contact with the patient, providing little summative data or assessment.

The reliability, or the consistency of the measurement used to obtain assessment information, is of high concern with mentally disordered individuals who use multiple care providers, may be homeless, and generally lead chaotic lives. Measures used with mental health clients include psychometric testing, DSM diagnosis, practitioner- or agency-recorded materials, and the reports of family or other collaterals about the client's behavior over time.

Psychometric and Neuropsychological Testing

Psychometric testing includes many different types of standardized instruments designed to measure psychological and internal processes of the brain. Usually conducted by psychologists, such testing can be used to assess intelligence, personality, and neurological functioning. Those most often used include the Minnesota Multiphasic Personality Inventory II (MMPI: Hathaway & McKinley, 1989), the Thematic Apperception Test (TAT; Murray, 1971), and the Wechsler Adult Intelligence Scale (WAIS) and Wechsler Intelligence Scale for Children (WISC; Wechsler, 1974; 1981). Neuropsychological testing, used to determine the location of brain dysfunction and the extent of cognitive impairment, is conducted following stabilization of acute symptoms with some cases. The most commonly used test batteries are the Halstead Reitan (Reitan & Wolfson, 1985) and the Luria Nebraska Neuropsychological Test Batteries (Golden, Hammake, & Purisch, 1980). Both psychometric and neurological tests are less frequently used in publicly funded clinics and inpatient facilities than in privately funded settings due to lengthy and high administration and interpretation costs. As results may be used to determine eligibility for services or special program participation, practitioners are encouraged to seek consultation if these tests are used with their clients for two reasons: (1) Compared to other tests, these often possess less psychometrically adequate norms; and (2) comparing an individual's performance to a normative sample does not provide much information about within-person variability, particularly in relation to impaired brain-behavior relations (Hynd & Semrud-Clikeman, 1990).

DSM Diagnosis

Effective treatment planning must involve the reliable and valid description of the problem areas that are the focus of intervention. The traditional way to describe problem areas is by an organized and agreed-upon diagnostic system. The current system is the DSM-IIIR. The DSM-IIIR is helpful because it is relatively objective and atheoretical in its description of symptom complexes. Whether treatment is focused on symptom complexes or more complicated conflict syndromes, however, the DSM-IIIR does not provide the necessary model of the thoughts, feelings, and behaviors that are the focus of assessment necessary to plan an organized, hierarchical intervention.

As noted in Chapter 2, this is the most widely used mental health diagnostic system. While it offers many providers a type of shorthand to communicate a set of symptoms or a syndrome, a client's past diagnosis of schizophrenia only tells us that in the view of one provider (individual or agency), during a period of service provision, the client appeared to meet the criteria for this diagnosis. The reliability of this measure is such that it is very likely another practitioner would make a different diagnosis, and that 6 months or a year later the same practitioner would make a different diagnosis (Kirk & Kutchins, 1992). Practitioners should not assume that a previous diagnosis is accurate and so, to the extent possible, assessment must proceed on a disconfirmatory basis, testing and challenging assumptions.

Individuals admitted to psychiatric inpatient facilities or units must have a DSM diagnosis. If one regards DSM as a collection of symptoms and behaviors that reflect the kinds of problems that patients bring to mental health practitioners, the criteria can be conceptually grouped into symptoms of mood (depression, anxiety), symptoms of thought (thought disorder), faulty interpersonal behaviors (e.g., assaultiveness), and habitual motoric behaviors that are disruptive (e.g., drug abuse, anorexia, bulimia, specific fears, and phobias). A helpful aspect of these general categories is that they provide information about the range of treatment foci a practitioner may encounter in dealing with a symptomatic complaint (Beutler & Clarkin, 1990). For example, McCrady (1985) has noted that the most successful treatment packages for dealing with alcohol abuse focus both on substance abuse and on improving the social support network of the patient.

Practitioners should be familiar with the implications various diagnoses have for their clients' lives. Underdiagnosis can result in inadequate care and lack of access to treatment or rehabilitation resources, while overdiagnosis may result in conservative treatment methods that take no chance the symptom will recur, perhaps involving too much medication. The worst consequence of overdiagnosis is that, due to the inferences made about a particular diagnosis, clients may be viewed as having poor prognoses for recovery, causing treatment providers and systems to respond, "What's the use of trying?" Despite the misleading claims of reliability attached to DSM-IIIR (Kirk & Kutchins, 1992), all practitioners working in mental health settings should be familiar with this system because it is the current system in use in the United States and other English-speaking countries and is frequently used by psychiatrists and third-party payors to determine the appropriate type and length of mental health treatment.

Recorded Materials

Practitioner- or agency-recorded materials can include the products of prior interviews and assessments, progress notes, and monitoring forms, as well as the results of standardized assessment measures. A chief problem in using unstandardized sources of data such as progress notes or termination summaries is that recorders of such data usually do not specify how, or under what conditions, measurement occurred. With careful reading, one can find notes and summaries that contain impressionistic or highly inferential information presented as objective or factual data. The reliability of practitioner materials, as well as client self-report data, may be compromised by a desire to affect the consequences of the assessment. Among practitioners, this may take the form of describing symptoms in a way that ensures admission to a particular unit in a hospital. Among clients, self-report information may also be modulated by intense affect such as anxiety or rage or by the shock that can follow trauma. This desire to achieve particular outcomes in their personal best interests evokes strong reactions from some clients. An example was a client who, when asked if thinking about hurting herself, replied, "Yes, and if you let me leave here I'm going to just go get it all over with! I can guarantee you that!" This threat, in fact, resulted in her hospitalization. Twelve hours later on the inpatient unit, the client was heard confiding in another patient that she was depressed over the loss of a recent love interest, but would never really hurt herself.

Collateral Reports

While family or close others who can provide information about past behavior over time can be very helpful, practitioners sometimes accept these reports as measures of client functioning without sufficient questioning. Practitioners can feel compelled to use this information widely because there may be no other source of direct observation of the client. Collateral reports, however, are usually gathered very unsystematically and are subject to all of the above caveats and potential biases. In some cases, such information may represent a sequence of impressions related to a common domain, for example, "For the past 3 weeks, he hasn't left the house except to go buy cat food" or "She seems to be feeling worse and worse about herself; all she ever does is put herself down." When hurried, the practitioner may not have time to query and evaluate the basis or method of these measures.

Improving Assessment Data

The first strategy we recommend to improve data gathering is to use all available sources of information. The client, others involved in the client's current life or care, records, and other agency or institutional information all hold useful data. Some sources possess only data for one period of time, while others have ongoing, regular measures of the client's problem and functioning. The practitioner's primary data source in most cases is the client. Studies show that information about psychological and psychiatric symptoms gathered via self-report from general populations, psychiatric inpatients, and prison inmates is no more likely to be inaccurate than information from other sources of data. Research suggests that social desirability, the tendency to respond in the most socially appropriate manner, may be lower among some psychiatric patients, particularly suicide attempters, than among less disordered individuals (Linehan & Neilsen, 1981; Ivanoff & Jang, 1991). Few studies of deception among involuntary mental health clients have been conducted. Our recommendation is that self-report data should be gathered first and discounted only after disconfirming evidence is found.

When client self-report information is severely limited or judged unreliable, the practitioner turns first to family and others near the client for assessment data. These collaterals can provide new or missing data and, very importantly, can corroborate, disconfirm, or challenge data from other sources. Whether the collaterals are family, agency staff, or strangers, to the extent the situation allows, the practitioner should attempt to gather whatever salient information these individuals have to offer. For example, while police officers may not have historical information about the client, they are trained reporters and can relate, in context, the events that transpired during their contact with the client.

When no current observers or family are accessible during assessment, the practitioner must necessarily rely more heavily on methods of gathering data using other sources of information. Naturally, the practitioner's interview and direct observation usually comprise the major portion of assessment data. Interview data include the client's responses to the practitioner's questions as well as the practitioner's observation of *how* the client responds to the questions. The practitioner's judgment of the client's reliability, honesty, and capacity to provide information are important. Observational data gathered by the practitioner include appearance, general motor behavior, and specific behavioral symptom manifestations. For example, flattened or blunted affect may indicate depression or thought disorder, while talking to unseen others may indicate auditory hallucinations, as might a distracted or agitated manner in the absence of external stimuli. Client verbalizations such as "I'm so angry at these stupid people I'm gonna get a gun and shoot them" or "I just want to be dead" and motor activity such as the involuntary movements of extrapyramidal symptoms caused by prolonged heavy antipsychotic use are valuable data.[1] This information is immediately useful in short-term treatment planning, and also in ongoing measurement of the same symptoms. To use these data in monitoring requires the practitioner to specify, from the beginning of assessment, the method of measurement and the circumstances under which the data are collected.

The second major strategy for improving assessment data is multiple methods of measuring the same problem. Multimethod assessment can begin with things as simple as asking a question differently or asking client, family, and others the same question. For example, when a delusional young man was asked by a practitioner, "Who are you?" he replied, "I am Jesus Christ." When asked, "What name do others call you?" he responded, "They call me Jeffrey Cross." Even in early assessment, multimethod assessment is often available. In assessing a client's drug use or medication compliance, for example, a practitioner might collect self-report data from the client and direct observation and impressionistic information from family or other collaterals, and request a urine specimen from the client for analysis. Thus, there are four possible sources of data: client self-report, practitioner, family and other collaterals, and urine. From these four sources, a total of three different types of measurement are obtained: self-report, observation, and biological markers.

Biological characteristics or markers such as blood, urine, and other chemical assays provide yet another form of standardized measurement often available in health and restrictive mental health settings. They may provide important corroborative or disconfirming data. Because they are not dependent on self-report or practitioner interpretation and are believed to be more objective, such measures are highly valued in rigorously designed clinical outcome studies of intervention effectiveness. As with all measurement, however, biological measures are only as good as the measurement methods underlying them. They are subject to the same errors in reliability as other measures, sometimes resulting in false negatives, or false positives. Although research into the role of biological markers in mental disorder suggests some preliminary findings, the use of complex diagnostic markers is not in wide clinical use. This is likely due to the fact that these markers provide little direction for treatment (Kalat, 1992). Neither have strategies for identifying genetic biologic markers yet produced a proven marker for mental disorders (Nurnberger & Gershon, 1988).

Many client problems, however, cannot be assessed with biological measures. Behavioral states and symptoms also require multimethod assessment. Below we have outlined a number of ways multimethod assessment data on common mental health problems could be collected from multiple sources.

Auditory Hallucinations

Self-report:	Have you been hearing any voices?
	Are these voices inside or outside your head?
	What are the voices saying to you?
Observation:	Client has difficulty listening or paying attention, distractibility.
	Client answering or talking back to unseen others.
Family/Collateral:	Client states behavior is determined by directions of voices.
	Client verbalizations about voices.
Self-rating:	Relative magnitude of interference voices cause, rated by "Compared to the last time you came to the hospital, how much are you hearing the voices?" or "If 5 (draw out line) is the loudest the voices have ever been and 0 means no voices at all, how loud would you say the voices are now?"

Mania or Manic Behavior

Self-report:	Do you always feel like this?
	Are your thoughts racing?
Practitioner:	Flight of ideas.
	Inflated self-esteem.
Observation:	Rapid, forced speech.
	Distractibility.
	Vocational impairment.

Family/Collateral: Overspending.
                       Excessive pleasurable behavior with high consequences.
                       Irritability.
                       Decreased need for sleep.
                       Impairment of normal interpersonal relationships.

Self-rating: Rating of distress/interference caused by racing thoughts.
                       Rating of euphoria, i.e., "the best you've ever felt." (On a
                       1–5 scale, manic clients may rate 7.)

Suicidality—Assessing Suicide Risk

Self-report: Have you recently experienced a loss or major disappoint-
                       ment?
                       Do you have thoughts of wanting to hurt yourself?
                       Have you ever done anything to intentionally hurt yourself
                       in the past?
                       Do you have plans of how you would hurt yourself this
                       time?

Practitioner: Depressed affect.
                       Scars or other signs of previous suicide attempts.
                       Presence of other known status risk factors such as single/
                       divorced, unemployed male.

Observation: Hoarding drugs.
                       Altered state, i.e., drunk or high.

Family/Collateral: Client verbalizations about suicide.
                       Preoccupation with death or with means such as playing
                       with a gun or a knife.
                       Making final plans such as a will or giving things away.

Self-rating: Intensity of hopelessness.
                       Urges to suicide.
                       Reasons for living.
                       Mood level.

Paranoid Delusions

Self-report: Tell me about the important situation going on with you
                       right now.

Observation: Suspicious, monitoring or tracking behavior around area of
                       delusion.

Family/Collateral: Verbalizations about delusions.

Self-rating: Times when most aware of delusion.
                       Times when delusion results in highest arousal, e.g.,
                       whether anxiety, excitement, fear, or anger. (This can be
                       difficult if the client has no insight into delusional possibil-
                       ities.)

The Assessment Process With Involuntary Mental Health Clients

Involuntary mental health treatment often takes the initial form of inpatient hospitalization. Crises that might precipitate involuntary admission generally include the inability to care for self or the indication of homicidal or suicidal intent. When decisions are made to hospitalize clients involuntarily, the responsible practitioner may make the decision with extremely abbreviated assessment data. In the most severe cases, the client is unable to offer any information and a decision to hospitalize is made based on observational data collected by the practitioner and others. In cases of chronic disorder, the interview may obtain a rudimentary self-reported history with focus on the time period since the last psychiatric hospitalization. This culminates with the incident or events that precipitated this referral for hospitalization or care. With clients who apparently have no history of mental disorder, the practitioner must proceed carefully and systematically. This involves using observation, available client self-report, and any collateral information to explore the development of the possible disorder as well as the intervening presence of substance use.

Accepting self-report information from an individual with an apparent thought disorder can be uncomfortable for the practitioner when the global parameters of the cognitive impairment are unknown. Often practitioners begin by asking, "Do you know why you're here?" The practitioner quickly moves into a more formal short mental status examination. A mental status examination is the mental health equivalent of the physical examination and reviews major areas of cognitive function. While there are many different versions of mental status examinations, all cover essentially the same material. In some clinical settings, shortened forms such as the Mini-Mental State Exam (MMSE; Folstein & Folstein, 1975) are often used. Topical areas covered by the MMSE are listed in Table 7.1. In emergent care situations, a starkly abbreviated version checking only for orientation asks: "Does the client know who she is, where she is, and what date it is?" Often this is written in charts as "oriented X3."

The next question the practitioner must answer is "Does this client pose an immediate threat to self or others?" That is, if this client leaves here untreated, in this affective/cognitive/behavioral state, and returns to the environment that precipitated this crisis, what is the likelihood of severe risk to self or others? At the same time, the practitioner must be evaluating the reliability of any self-reported information. Is the client attempting to minimize the severity of symptoms to avoid involuntary hospitalization? Does the client have reasons outside mental disorder to seek involuntary admission? This may sound odd, as we usually assume that if clients *want* treatment, they are then voluntary. There are, how-

Table 7.1.   Mini-Mental State Examination Questions

Orientation
   What is the (year) (season) (date) (day) (month)?
   Where are we: (state) (county) (town) (hospital) (floor)?

Registration
   Name 3 objects: 1 second to say each. Then ask the patient all 3 after you
            have said them.

Attention and Calculation
   Serial 7s:
   Alternatively spell *world* backwards.

Recall
   Ask for the 3 objects repeated above.

Language
   Name a pencil and watch.
   Repeat the following: No ifs, and, or buts.
   Follow a 3-stage command: Take the paper in your right hand, fold it in
      half, and put it on the floor.
Read and obey the following:
   Close your eyes.
   Write a sentence.
   Copy a design.

Source: Adapted from Folstein, M. F., & Folstein, S. E. (1975). "Mini Mental State." A practical method for grading the cognitive state of patients for the clinician. *Journal of Psychiatry Research, 12,* 189–198.

ever, many reasons why clients might prefer involuntary admission, including threats from family, friends, enemies, or the criminal justice system, homelessness, familiarity with staff in specific involuntary units, and knowledge of differential lengths of stay for voluntary and involuntary admissions.

Even when initially cooperative, as the client becomes aware that involuntary treatment is a possible consequence of interaction, cooperation may cease. If the client feels the interaction is adversarial, the reliability of information is also likely to drop significantly. As the client reacts negatively to the possibility of involuntary treatment, the practitioner's attitude should shift. It is important to keep in mind that a negative response is a healthy and normal response to proposed infringement on personal freedom. Further gains in rapport and engagement with a client under these circumstances should not be expected. The practitioner's goal is to move the client into treatment quickly. Almost as important as movement into treatment, however, is doing so in a manner that maximizes the likelihood that, once in treatment, the client will respond openly to overtures from those providing care. The relationship foundation laid through the practitioner's genuineness, honesty, and straightforward manner often assists in these difficult interactions.

Once on the inpatient unit, further assessment may have to be delayed from 6 to 24 hours if immediate medication is needed to stabilize the patient's behavior or mood. This is often regarded as improving the patient's accessibility to treatment. Statutes regarding involuntary medication vary from state to state, but all make some provision for involuntary medication when the patient's behavior seriously threatens self or others.

From this point on, assessment proceeds in more standard fashion. While practitioners on inpatient units may have greater access to clients than in outpatient facilities, the course of assessment is generally the same. A series of interviews with the client, family members, or significant others, contact with others involved in the client's care, and consultation from supervisors and others result in goals and a working plan for intervention and monitoring progress toward goals.

Case Example

Matalie was taken to the unit in a wheelchair. Once in her room, she stayed in the wheelchair, carefully sorting through her large bag of possessions. Talking quietly to herself she finally took out three items and indicated she wanted to keep them with her on the unit: a snapshot of her daughter, a book of African proverbs, and a small folding knife. Staff tried to explain that she was safe here and did not need the knife, but this resulted in Matalie yelling and threatening to hurt staff. Rather than reacting quickly and deciding to isolate, restrain, or medicate her, one persistent individual explained that no one here had knives and that if she were to keep hers on the unit, it might get stolen. This seemed to make more sense to Matalie, she tucked the knife back into her bag and handed it to the staff member, who promised to put it in a safe place. She then got up out of the wheelchair and examined the room thoroughly. Appearing somewhat more relaxed, she sat back down in the wheelchair and announced she wanted to see the rest of the unit. Matalie participated in unit orientation and community meeting; she became disruptive, yelling loudly during the meeting about how she was tricked into the hospital. She was returned to her room at that time. The practitioner continued the assessment the following morning.

The overall purpose of the practitioner's assessment of Matalie was threefold:

1. To describe the current problem state by identifying the extent of Matalie's thought disorder and the relative level of manic behavior.

2. To conduct a functional analysis of the problem(s) to identify likely factors responsible for this episode.
3. To design an intervention plan to address behavioral and medication stabilization.

Matalie's diagnosis at last hospitalization discharge was Bipolar Disorder, Mixed (296.6x). Despite hospital notes indicating good early adjustment, there was no evidence that her medication (Lithobid) continued effective after discharge. Five months ago, she spent one week as an inpatient on a general medical unit for pneumonia, but received no other regular medical care. Contacts with the shelter social worker during this time were minimal; Matalie refused to meet with the consulting psychiatrist, picked up her checks and occasionally ate at the shelter, and generally avoided most other contact.

Information about Matalie's moods, feelings, attitudes, and beliefs (Type II information) was gathered both from Matalie's self-report and standardized rating scales. Type III information concerning Matalie's current functioning was also obtained through standard measures. Despite her continuing suspiciousness and disordered thinking, Matalie was able to tell the practitioner her name, social security number, what hospital she was in, and what day of the week it was. She also identified her shelter social worker and the then-president of the United States (amidst vociferous profanity) by name. When asked why she was brought to the clinic, she said she was being locked up for fighting in the TV room at the shelter. When reminded of her gangrenous feet she admitted that, "Yes, it is probably good to have them looked at."

Matalie stated she had been more depressed than usual during the past year, beginning within 2 months after discharge and lasting 4–6 months, feeling sick most of the time. She reported that the medication she had been given at discharge was rotten; someone was putting garbage into it and it made her feel like throwing up so she stopped taking it within 2 weeks after discharge. Matalie and the practitioner developed and used a 10-point self-anchored scale to assess her current mood. On this visual scale, the practitioner labeled 1 as the most depressed Matalie had ever felt and asked her to tell her when that was. Ten on the scale was labeled as the best Matalie ever felt; Matalie identified this time as well. They continued by identifying where Matalie would presently locate herself along the scale, illustrated in Figure 7.1. This self-anchored mood scale was similar to one the shelter worker used with Matalie when she would pick up her monthly checks. Matalie agreed that she would rate her mood at the beginning of each talk with the practitioner.

Prior to this rehospitalization, few people were in positions to systematically observe Matalie's behavior in order to gather Type IV assess-

1— *the day my family betrayed me and locked me up*

2—

3—

④ ✓ *11/9 current rating*

5— *going to sleep at night in a place where I'm not scared*

6—

7—

8—

9—

10— *the day my daughter was born*

Figure 7.1. Matalie's mood rating scale from worst to best.

ment information. The shelter caseworker had documented the number of conflicts or anger outbursts that occurred when Matalie visited the shelter and found they were increasing over the past 3 months. This is extremely useful information, despite the fact it was gathered only when Matalie visited the shelter. The practitioner asked staff on the inpatient unit to monitor this as well. Matalie's lack of concern about her feet indicated her dissociation; therefore, appropriate expressions of concern related to personal physical well-being were also monitored. The monitoring form the practitioner inserted into the chart is depicted in Figure 7.2.

Matalie's cooperation varied widely during the assessment interviews and indeed, throughout her stay: Gathering the information above required patience and persistence on the part of the practitioner. Three brief meetings of approximately 15 minutes each were held to collect this information. It was the practitioner's assessment that more intense contact would increase Matalie's agitation. During her first night, staff documented and Matalie corroborated that she slept not at all, instead sitting up in bed and crying until staff moved her to her wheelchair so she could wheel herself around the unit. She complained three times during the night of her head being "too tight" and having "too much up there." Shortly before dawn, Matalie became very agitated, yelling that they had no right to keep her in the hospital. She wheeled herself to the locked unit doors and rattled and shook them. A staff member returned

Patient Name: _Matalie_

Monitoring Target #1: _Appropriate expressions of self-concern or care_

Day: _Friday_

Date: _11-9_   Frequency: _____ / _____

Precipitants/Resolution

Time: _4:05 p_   _acknowledged foot needed attention_

_____ _____

_____ _____

_____ _____

_____ _____

Day: _Saturday_

Date: _11-10_   Frequency: _____ / _____

Precipitants/Resolution

Time: _10:00 a_   _comment about good to have foot looked at—_

_____ _____

_____ _____

_____ _____

_____ _____

Figure 7.2.   Inpatient unit monitoring form.

her to her room. The next morning a new trial of Lithobid was begun; initially 300 mg, twice daily. Matalie initially accepted the medication willingly when told it was to help her head. Medically, Matalie was not yet stable and her feet, now swollen and red, were still in danger. The foul odor emanating from the sores on her feet demanded that the loose dressing be changed almost every 2 hours. Matalie tolerated this contact well. Medical staff noted Matalie's lack of pain complaints. Such reduced pain awareness is not uncommon among individuals suffering from psychotic disorders.

Patient Name: *Matalie*

Monitoring Target #2: *Receptivity to alternate living situations*

Day: *Saturday*

Date: *11–10*   Frequency: *//*

                        med group   Precipitants/Resolution

Time: *11:00 a* ⌈ *medication group—how life structure helps one remember*
                    to take medication
       11:10 a ⌊ *too much trouble to mess with all those people*

Day: *Sunday*

Date: *11–11*   Frequency: */   /*

                        Precipitants/Resolution

Time: *1:20 p* ⊕ *guess I'll have to find someplace to stay*
       4:20 p ⊖ *I ain't going nowhere they tell me to — it's a trap*

Day: *Monday*

Date: *11–12*   Frequency:

                        Precipitants/Resolution

Time: *10:00 a* ⊕ *indicated wants help remembering meds*
       1:15 p   ⊕ *asked if she could stay in hospital until better*
       1:45 p   ⊕ *nodded approval of another pt's. group home choice*

Figure 7.2.   Continued.

SELECTING RESEARCH-BASED INTERVENTIONS FOR INVOLUNTARY MENTAL HEALTH CLIENTS

Treatment outcomes in mental health are generally of two types: those designed to result in a change in symptoms or in a resolution of internal conflicts. The differences between them can be most clearly observed if one contrasts the effects of broadly focused psychological mental health therapeutic approaches such as interpersonal, experiential, and psychodynamic, with the effects of more narrowly focused therapies such as somatic (pharmacotherapy), behavioral, and cognitive (Beutler & Clarkin, 1990). Therapy models that emphasize symptom change do not ordinarily devote time and attention to the genesis of symptoms or the presence of unconscious motivations, while those that emphasize conflictual change do not devote a great deal of time and energy to discussing symptom intensity or consequence. Here, as in other forms of practice with involuntary clients, the outcome goals defined have a direct bearing on what will be addressed and serve as the focus of the treatment.

General support exists for beginning with symptomatic focused treatments unless there is clear evidence for the conflictual basis of the problems. This support is based in the observation that while the use of a conflict-focused treatment, that is, a broadband approach, to treat a simple problem may be inefficient, the reverse is not true. There is no indication that the application of a symptom-focused treatment, i.e., a narrow-band approach to a complex problem, creates negative results. While symptom patterns may recur when narrowly focused treatments are applied alone to complex problems (Beutler et al., 1987; Coyne, 1989) mixing treatments of varying breadths actually may allay this recurrence. The mandates for work with involuntary clients center strongly on symptomatic focused treatment.

Using the guidelines suggested in Chapter 3 to select an intervention in mental health is a complex task for several reasons. First, the mental health literature is enormous; staying current on new developments is an onerous task. Second, the mental health literature is, for the largest part, driven by decisions of theoretical orientation or discipline politics. This means that if a practitioner has access to and reads primarily psychiatric, pharmaceutical-company-sponsored, or psychoanalytic materials, this practitioner would likely have a markedly different approach to practice than would a practitioner who reads social work, philosophical, or cognitive-behavioral materials. Third, because the mental health field is so diverse and evolving, today's miracle intervention is quickly replaced. Fourth, these issues taken together tend to create a sense of futility among practitioners, a "What's the use in even *trying* to stay current?" attitude, which encourages more reliance on personal experience and less on using the work of others to develop practice knowledge.

It is unreasonable to expect each practitioner to be intimately acquainted with all new mental health knowledge. This said, we also believe that practitioners have an ethical, as well as a practical, responsibility to continue to learn new and different kinds of treatment methods, especially those with empirical support. Accepting "But this is the way we've always handled this problem" is no better for clients than it is for organizations or a government.

Practitioners in mental health share several areas of knowledge responsibility necessary in treatment selection. These include (1) the laws governing involuntary commitment in this state and all geographically proximal states; (2) the array of local and regional agencies providing services to involuntary mental health clients; (3) general knowledge about major mental disorders and about suicidal behavior such that the practitioner can carry out competent assessment and treatment planning. For affective or mood disorders, bipolar (manic-depressive) disorder, and schizophrenic disorders, mental health practitioners should have a working knowledge of (a) common presenting manifestations, (b) assessment issues, and (c) empirically based interventions. In involuntary mental health settings, intervention selection is guided by the mandate for treatment, with long-term needs sometimes receiving inadequate attention. Immediate needs clearly take precedence over longer-term needs in involuntary settings. Intervention priorities must be clear for the practitioner to work most effectively.

Psychotropic Medications

The use of psychotropic medications is a controversial issue. Particularly in work with involuntary clients, the possibility of coercive control and the unintended adverse consequences of psychotropic medications is frightening to clients, their families, and advocates of the mentally ill. Unfortunately, there is some evidence that damage and seriously adverse side effects are caused by these drugs (Breggin, 1991) and that such control has been a social reality with disenfranchised individuals, the poor, ethnic-racial minorities, and women (Frank, 1978). The rights of psychiatric patients to refuse medication have been compellingly debated from a social work perspective by Bentley (1993) and Rosenson (1993). There is also a body of evidence suggesting that psychotropic medications can help clients regain personal control over destructive or personally frightening states. The literature on treating unipolar depression in adult outpatients suggests that a combination of cognitive-behavioral therapy and psychopharmacological treatment is the most effective method (Hollon et al., 1991); among some schizophrenic individuals there is evidence that Clozapine, while unfortunately very expensive, may be effective at decreasing both positive and negative symptoms of the disorder without many of the side effects of earlier antipsychotic drugs (Kane, 1988). Psychoeducational family aftercare interventions combined with neuroleptic medications for schizophrenia have demonstrated significant decreases in relapse rates (Strachan, 1986) and psychoeducation, medication, and social skill training were found effective even at 2-year follow-up (Hogarty, 1993). Practitioners must learn and stay current with information about the medications available, the benefits and risks attributed to their use, those most commonly prescribed in their agency, and the common side effects patients report from these medications.

Medications are often prescribed on the basis of the medical practitioner's hypothesis about the symptoms or disorder affecting the patient. If the symptoms subside after the medication has been taken for a reasonable trial, the practitioner then often indirectly assumes the hypothesized disorder was correct, and further, that the medication is appropriate for the patient's problem. An example of this is the patient with manic symptoms who is given lithium; the lithium appears to have some modulating effects on mood. Assuming that this patient suffers from bipolar disorder based solely on these data is erroneous. Knowledge of a client's medication should not be directly interpreted as knowledge of the client's particular disorder.

As noted in Chapter 3, all practice prescriptions, whether psychosocial, psychological, environmental, or pharmacological in nature, should be offered under one of two conditions: (1) when there is evidence supporting the intervention's effectiveness and relevance to this case; or (2) when the prescription is understood and offered as a hypothesis for clinical testing. It is important to recall that many, if not the majority, of psychotropic and psychological mental health interventions fall under the second condition.

DEVELOPING GOALS AND CONTRACTING

The purposes of both programmatic and individually determined goals are to guide treatment and to monitor progress. The final goals of most mental health interventions are similar: to alleviate the symptoms or problems that brought the patient for help. Instrumental or intermediate goals, the steps necessary to reach final goals, are determined by the practitioner's orientation to practice and to a lesser extent, by the patient's problem. For example, in working with a suicidally depressed individual, the final goal of treatment is generally clear. The steps necessary to accomplish this goal, however, may be quite different depending on the focus placed on individual characteristics, environmental characteristics, and the patient's previous success at coping with similar problems. Before setting goals with a client or client's family, the practitioner must understand agency or institutional mandates that may limit or otherwise influence goal setting. Aftercare planning, referrals to outside agencies, and pursuit of client goals at odds with agency philosophy are all examples of goal areas that may be directly affected by agency mandate.

When involuntary mental health clients enter inpatient or programmatic treatment settings such as day treatment or psychosocial community settings, there are usually standard final program goals that apply to each client, independent of instrumental or intermediate individual goals or needs of the client. Examples of standard goals on an inpatient unit include adjustment to unit, development of a treatment plan, and development of a discharge plan. Operationally, adjustment to unit may mean attending and participating in community meetings, as well as socially appropriate interaction with other residents and staff. Goals in day treatment programs often include regular attendance, participation in group meetings, involvement in recreational activities, social and life skills development, as well as appropriate interaction with other clients and staff. Because these goals apply to all clients in the program they are broad; this leaves defining instrumental goals that mark progress toward these final goals to the practitioner, client, and collaterals. A list of instrumental goals often tied to specific mental health problems are listed in Table 7.2. These actual case examples illustrate that interrelated goals may exist on multiple levels.

The mandated purpose of treatment is usually never far from the practitioner's mind in generating intervention hypotheses. As in other practice domains, the treatment mandate in mental health often provides the initial focus for goal setting. In mental health, however, once the involuntary nature of treatment is established, there is often less disagreement about a mandated goal, such as suicide prevention or adequate self-care.

In any technically well-executed mental health intervention, the focus consists of a chain of hypothesized relationships among precipitating events and the final objectives of change, the specific symptoms or conflict patterns. Throughout assessment, the practitioner develops intervention hypotheses, which provide the basis for goal setting and contracting. The hypotheses may be either global, addressing final goals, or specific, focusing on instrumental or intermediate steps. As identified in Chapter 2, the four steps in developing intervention hypotheses apply directly to work in mental health: (1) Identify the treatment (goals); (2) specify the dependent variable; (3) identify any predicted intervening variables; and (4) predict the expected effect of the independent variable. Table 7.3 gives some examples of global and specific intervention hypotheses made by practitioners working with involuntary mental health clients. Note that not all hypotheses contain intervening variables.

Table 7.2.   Final Goals, Instrumental Goals, and Subgoals

Problem: Suicide Attempt	Instrumental Goals:
Final Goal: Eliminate suicidality	Eliminate medication stash
	Resolve interpersonal conflict with sister
	Increase reasons for living
	Increase physical activity level
	Work on improving problem-solving skills
	Find new living situation
	Work on changing patterns of hopeless thinking
Problem: Acute Schizophrenic Episode	Instrumental Goals:
	Begin/restart/modify medication regimen
Final Goal: Maximize life functioning	Decrease positive symptoms such as hallucinations, delusions
Immediate Goal: Stabilize mood, reduce symptomatology	Decrease environmental stress
	Subgoals:
	Obtain disability (SSI)
	Find permanent housing
	Improve relationship with family
	Subgoals:
	Make contact with mother
	Call sister and ask to come visit
	Teach medication management and compliance
Problem: Depression	Instrumental Goals:
Final Goals: Improve mood, resume regular life activities	Increase physical activity level
	Increase positive activities
	Improve social skills
	Identify role conflict

Frequently the client and family members have been involved in developing intervention hypotheses, identifying what has been tried, successfully, and unsuccessfully, in the past. This discussion, when conducted as a collaborative exchange, can further engagement. To establish a collaborative, helping relationship, it is critically important that the goals of therapy selected by the practitioner can be accepted by the patient. Irrespective of the worker's theoretical perspective, the patient's presenting complaints must be incorporated into the criteria by which the success of treatment is judged. In work with involuntary patients, while the mandated treatment goal must remain primary, it may be possible to further involve patient and family in prioritizing goals. In some cases, the practitioner guides the discussion of goals temporally, naturally proceeding forward into time and outlining the instrumental goals. Nonetheless, there may be unusual patient or family characteris-

Table 7.3. Sample Intervention Hypotheses

A few days in a supportive hospital milieu positively affects and stabilizes
  mood.
To decrease auditory hallucinations, increase antipsychotic medication.
Involvement in day treatment programming increases social interaction.
Daily contact (with practitioner) increases client work on agreed-upon tasks
  if the relationship with the practitioner is supportive.
Discharge planning initiated soon after admission keeps patient focus on
  returning to life outside the hospital.
Attendance in inpatient community meetings can decrease isolation if the
  patient can verbally participate.
Supportive practitioner attitude and behavior are positively associated with
  client improvement in mood.
Increasing positive activity level can improve mood level unless anxiety is
  too high.
Following a suicide attempt, suicidal ideation will decrease during a brief
  hospitalization and mood level often improves.
Family involvement during hospitalization can increase later follow-through
  on discharge plans.
Patient education about medication side effects and their management can
  increase compliance and patient perception of control.

---

tics, circumstances, or stressors that make such a plan infeasible. To the
extent possible, such plans or outlines should be reviewed to check for
these exceptions. Realistically, it may not be possible or desirable to
actively engage all family members of involuntary clients and their families. However, once involuntary status is established and the final mandated goal is clear to those involved, other final and instrumental goals
of perhaps even more importance to the patient or family can be discussed.

Treatment goals must be translated into measurable terms, so
progress toward the goals can be monitored. Using our list of instrumental goals from Table 7.2, we provide examples from practice of ways
in which these goals have been broken down and translated into measurable terms in Table 7.4. These examples are not intended as exhaus-
tive and provide only one possible form of measurement.

Contracting is the active process of agreeing on the goals for work, on
who (client, practitioner, family, or other collaterals) will do what to
accomplish the goals, and on what criteria will be used to measure
progress toward the goals. In Chapter 3 we discussed the possibilities
and problems in contracting with involuntary clients. Mental disorders
differentially affect patients' ability to contract. Practitioners generally
find that making contracts more immediate, of shorter duration, and as
operationally concrete as possible facilitates their use with emotionally
distressed or cognitively limited individuals. Contracts between practitioner and suicidal patients to avoid suicide attempts or suicide, such as

Table 7.4.   Measuring Instrumental Goals.

Improve reasons for living: Increase number of reasons client identifies as keeping her going, e.g., hopefulness about future, children, optimism about personal ability to solve problems, friends, etc.

Involvement in positive activities: Frequency of goal-oriented activities.

Decreasing hopelessness: Decrease in the magnitude of hopelessness as measured by client-centered rating scale used at beginning of each contact with practitioner.

Decreasing suicidal ideation: A decrease in the number of times client is aware she is thinking about suicide.

Improving problem-solving: Practitioner monitoring of an increased number of alternatives client is able to generate a problem situations.

Eliminate medication stash: (presence or absence) Removal of box of pills kept under bed (must be thrown out in presence of reliable witness or given to the practitioner).

Resolve interpersonal conflict with sister: Meet or talk with sister calmly about resolving differences. Enter into negotiation about how to resolve differences.

Increase physical activity level: Increase in amount of time spent walking, e.g., trips around unit, around recreation yard, number of repetitions with weights. Increase in the number of hours spent out of bed.

Find new living situation: (presence-absence) Sign rental agreement or lease.

Work on changing patterns of hopeless thinking: Practitioner monitors in-session frequency of hopeful statements about self, future, events.

Begin/restart/modify medication regimen: Patient accepts and takes medication each time it is administered by staff.

Decrease positive symptoms such as hallucinations, delusions: Decrease in number of times unit staff notices (document) symptoms such as talking to unseen others, distractedness, inability to participate in conversations due to listening to other voices, verbalizations about delusions, behavior congruent with delusions.

Decrease environmental stress: Move out of parents' home and into group home.

Improve relationship with family: Reduction in incidence of angry or irritable behavior during interaction with parents.

Teach medication management and compliance: Practitioner orally asks patient questions to test knowledge of medication compliance.

Improve social skills: Patient does not interrupt others during group meeting.

Identify role conflict: Client can verbalize feelings of being unsure where she fits in.

"If I am feeling suicidal, I agree to call before I do anything to hurt myself," can be simple, but effective interventions in themselves. By agreeing to contact the practitioner before taking any action, work begins sooner to avoid the spiraling, narrowing thinking that leads to suicidal behavior. When patients agree verbally, or in writing, to these contracts, there is evidence they generally keep them (Motto, 1976).

Case Example

Matalie was admitted involuntarily because she was unable to care for herself to the extent this posed a serious risk to her well-being. In addition to conducting her own assessment, the practitioner, who had been working on the inpatient unit for 3 years, carefully reviewed the reports of Matalie's symptoms and sketchy past medication history, consulted a recent book on bipolar disorder (looking for information on manic episode variations), and spoke with the attending psychiatrist before agreeing with the diagnosis.

Standard goals on the inpatient unit included: orient to unit; contract/ develop individual goal plan; participate (to extent possible) in unit activities; and participate (to extent possible) in discharge planning activities. Following the 3 meetings of approximately 15 minutes each with Matalie, the practitioner developed several intervention hypotheses. The monitoring begun during Matalie's initial contacts with the practitioner also reflected these hypotheses. Generation of these hypotheses was guided by the symptoms and condition Matalie presented, the inpatient unit's orientation to practice and hierarchy of treatment needs, and the practitioner's assessment of the antecedent, precipitant, and intervening psychosocial variables that affect Matalie's case. There were three main goals or treatment objectives:

1. Stabilize psychotropic medication.
2. Stabilize medically.
3. Discharge to a more stable living environment.

Instrumental goals included teaching Matalie how to monitor her medication and side effects, increasing attention to self-care, and involving family in helping find a more stable living situation. The practitioner hypothesized that Matalie's mood and thought disorder required modulation before any treatment objective could be attained. Further, she hypothesized that Matalie's physical self-care and ability to maintain herself in a stable housing environment would not improve until she received medication for her manic-depressive disorder. Other intervention hypotheses included the use of education to increase medication compliance and successful management of side effects, and the positive impact a more stable living situation would have on medication self-management.

As in most involuntary mental health treatment, the practitioner in this case clearly focused on symptomatic treatment. Her treatment selection took into account available resources on the inpatient unit, e.g., a medication group, family therapy, discharge planning contacts (individual and group), and the psychiatric expertise to begin and stabilize a medication regimen. The practitioner also was prepared to work with a rehabilitation specialist pending the prognosis on Matalie's feet.

The practitioner's knowledge of bipolar disorder included the following empirically based practice tenets:

1. Medications such as lithium can help control the severe mood swings associated with bipolar disorder. When the mood level evens out, dissociation and thought disorder that may accompany bipolar disorder often remit as well.
2. Even when medication is taken consistently, a patient may still experience symptom breakthrough.
3. Episodes of mania and depression are variable in occurrence and duration.
4. Psychosocial assistance and a stable, not overly stressful living situation can help mitigate recurrence and the severity of recurrence.

Measuring progress toward the treatment objectives was accomplished in a variety of ways. The mood monitoring depicted in Figure 7.1 was continued to obtain self-report data on the effects of the medication. The monitoring of appropriate self-concern comments conducted by staff was also continued to track dissociation or thought disorder distraction (see Figure 7.2). Matalie's attendance at medication group was monitored by unit staff, and the practitioner asked Matalie questions about her understanding of the content presented in the group. Matalie expressed minimal interest and concern about finding a permanent place to live. As the practitioner felt that progress toward this goal would be slow, she began by keeping track of Matalie's in-session receptivity to alternative living possibilities. Any strongly positive or negative comments were also recorded verbatim. Receptivity could be either verbal (a positive comment or sound) or nonverbal (nods or other behavior indicating approval or agreement).

IMPLEMENTING INTERVENTIONS

The task of implementing interventions with involuntary mental health clients is equally complex, sometimes requiring the choreography of a ballet or a well-practiced rugby team. The questions of *accurate implementation, problems in implementation,* and *assessing progress* are especially salient in work with mental health clients. In some cases, the patient may appear at the center of a large whirlwind of intervention activity involving the practitioner, other professionals and agencies, family or significant others and, of course, the unseen participant, the state or local sanction providing the original treatment mandate. As in contracting, depending on the severity of the patient's disorder, these others may be the primary actors in implementation. During implementation, however, the rationale for involving the patient to the fullest extent possible becomes clear: If the patient is extremely uncooperative or noncompliant, even the best-laid intervention plans may be for naught. For example, after a practitioner worked many hours to find a placement for a 22-year-old schizophrenic young man who also had AIDS, on the day of planned discharge and move, the patient decided that the placement was completely unsatisfactory and refused to go. Involving the patient in contracting to whatever extent functionally possible is in the best interests of treatment implementation.

Once the intervention is applied and the implementation phase has begun, monitoring focus broadens. Monitoring both implementation of the intervention and progress toward treatment objectives becomes important. Monitoring intervention implementation with involuntary mental health clients is particularly important because multiple mental health service providers may be involved in time-limited service, such as during 3-, 10-, or 14-day inpatient stays. Team approaches to patient management often help ensure that the interventions are in place and that the most expert individuals are monitoring implementation in each domain. The team as a whole monitors implementation systematically during unit staff meetings when all involved practitioners take turns reporting what has occurred since the previous meeting. Working with an involuntary inpatient, for example, interventions may involve psychotropic medication, one to one (individual) contact, group interventions, attention to existing medical conditions, family conferences, involvement in discharge planning, and/or community reentry activities. This approach works well when all members understand the priorities and the time frame for work, and operate in synchrony. Potential problems with the team approach include assuming that all individuals on the team define specific intervention activities in the same way, and inadequately coordinating the pacing of intervention activities. Both of these suggest greater specification and more careful monitoring of activities may be necessary.

Procedural specification is particularly important in mental health treatment, as numerous theoretical jargons and buzz words are used. Working in teams, there is also an urgency to accept what is taking place as the intended intervention. Implementation variability takes many forms in mental health practice. The following examples illustrate common situations, using the list of sources of variability from Chapter 3.

Lack of knowledge or understanding: A substitute practitioner conducts medication education for several days and because she does not have a copy of the regular protocol, makes up what she thinks is supposed to happen as she goes along.

Inaccurate implementation: Discharge planning alternatives are discussed at a time when the patient is feeling extremely threatened and as a result the patient feels railroaded into accepting an initial alternative and subsequently withdraws from the process.

Interpersonal obstacle: A practitioner finds herself enraged with a particularly difficult client whom the practitioner has gone far out of her way to help.

Non-implementation: Although the intervention plan includes involving the family of the patient, the practitioner has difficulty reaching the family and then experiences further problems attempting to schedule an appointment. The practitioner does not persist in her efforts.

Unreliable client-system involvement: A delusional patient believes that the food served at the treatment center is poisoned. She takes samples (stuffs quantities in her bag) to send for testing. She agrees that depriving other clients of food is a problem (sort of . . . after all, it *is* poisoned) and agrees to work with staff to allow others to eat what they choose. Her behavior does not change and she adamantly refuses to discuss it further.

Monitoring progress toward goals is usually done by the practitioner and team. Reports and updates on progress should also be regularly discussed with the patient and any involved family members. Many practitioners who work in these settings automatically reassess progress toward goals at the beginning of each contact. Positive progress in functioning and psychological states may be either rapid or very slow. Due to the strong presence and effect of environmental influences on mental health variables, practitioners should examine results carefully for the presence of intervening variables that may be responsible for results. If positive progress is made toward goals, the practitioner attempts to carefully discern what factors were responsible for the change. As an example, many mentally distressed and more severely disordered individuals experience abrupt symptom abatement shortly after entering the hospital: Does this mean the medication is working? that the practitioner's reassurances were effective? or perhaps simply that admission to the hospital, i.e., a safer, more controlled environment, results in decreased stress?

Case Summary

Matalie began to sleep at night on night 2, following initiation of the Lithobid trial. Her medical condition extended the length of her hospital stay to at least 3 weeks, making it possible for all facets of intervention implementation to occur in planned fashion. The practitioner met regularly with Matalie, once or twice daily on weekdays, for about 15–20 minutes, although this time period lengthened as the practitioner assessed that Matalie was able to benefit from more contact. By day 2, Matalie was competent with her wheelchair, able to proficiently navigate almost all self-care. As some feeling began to return to her feet, she found herself in severe pain and was given 800 mg Ibuprofen, four times daily.

Matalie was enrolled in and attended a medication group each weekday for 45 minutes beginning on day 3 of her stay. While she was unable to tolerate staying for the entire period the first 3 days she attended, her continued efforts to attend were interpreted positively by the practitioner as an indication that she was taking some interest in self-care. When the practitioner mentioned this, commenting positively that Matalie might be feeling better about herself, Matalie became embarrassed and said she guessed it wouldn't hurt anything to learn about this "stuff." As she was able to stay in the group for longer periods of time, she was able to report more of the group content to the practitioner. This reporting was conducted in an informal, almost chatty fashion, with the practitioner inviting Matalie to tell her what she'd learned in the group that day. As Matalie's involvement in the group continued, she was able to identify side effects she had previously experienced that occasioned her noncompliance. She also gained a rudimentary understanding of how the noncompliance may have occasioned her relapse. The monitoring form the practitioner used is found in Figure 7.3.

On day 7, medical staff announced that Matalie would, miraculously, not lose either of her feet. She would, however, need to remain in the wheelchair for approximately another month, and require ongoing physical rehabilitation and therapy for up to 6 months to regain the use of her feet. This necessitated placement in a group home or facility with access to rehabilitation facilities.

The practitioner contacted Matalie's family on day 2 of Matalie's stay, unfortunately without telling Matalie she was doing so. She spoke to Matalie's sister and later to her husband. While the family was relieved to know that she was safe and receiving care, they were somewhat perplexed by the practitioner's call. Matalie had made it clear to them that she wanted no further contact and would not welcome any overtures on their part. The practitioner spoke with Matalie about this. Although this was day 4, and staff had already documented how much less angry and irritable Matalie was acting, she became agitated, and angry, cursing at the practitioner,

Attendance	Understanding (as indicated by responses to questions	
11–12	*1*	0 = none
11–13	*2*	1 = slight
		2 = some
11–14	*1*	3 = good
		4 = excellent
11–15	*2*	
11–16	*3*	
11–17	*3*	
11–18	*3*	

Figure 7.3.   Medication group attendance understanding.

You fuckin' chiquita! Who the hell you think you are, messin' with me?!
I told you what these people did to me and all you want to do is bring 'em
back in here—for what? So they can locks me up for good this time? You'd
like that wouldn't you? Then you wouldn't have to deal with me no more!

Although it took considerable time and an apology from the practitioner, 2 days later Matalie returned to mostly cooperative interpersonal
interactions. She refused however, to talk with or meet with her family,
telling the practitioner that she must work only with her. She asked the
practitioner not to contact the family further. The practitioner was forced
to change her plans concerning family involvement and pursued living
arrangements for Matalie in a group residence in an area of the city
adjacent to the shelter.

11–9:	*2*	*11–16:*	*1*
11–10:	*3*	*11–17:*	*2*
11–11:	*2*	*11–18:*	*6*
11–12:	*5*	*11–19:*	*5*
11–13:	*6*	*11–20:*	*5*
11–14:	*4*	*11–21:*	*6*
11–15:	*1*	*11–22:*	*5*

Figure 7.4.   Matalie's mood rating during hospitalization.

Matalie's progress toward the treatment objectives is reflected in the progress illustrated on her graphs and monitoring forms, shown on Figures 7.4, 7.5, and 7.6. Matalie was quite depressed when informed she would be in the wheelchair for another month and then require therapy, but stated that perhaps it would help keep her "straight" on her medication. She stated, "Sometimes my thinking about these pills just goes crazy."

Patient Name: *Matalie*

Monitoring Target #1: *Appropriate expressions of self-concern or care*

Day: *Monday*

Date: *11-20* Frequency: *THT*

Precipitants/Resolution

Time:
7:15 a "Today I'm going to take all my medication"
9:00 a Med group—questions about side effects
10:48 a I'll be here until my feet get better
12:15 p It's important to eat well to get better
3:50 p I need to take care of myself

Day: *Tuesday*

Date: *11-21* Frequency: *THT I*

Precipitants/Resolution

Time:
7:20 a "Today I'm going to take all my medication"
9:15 a "I need to take care of myself"
1:10 p "I need to take care of myself"
5:00 p made effort with appearance/dress
6:50 p "I like going to PT; it helps me"
8:10 p joined prayer group—prayed for feet to heal

Figure 7.5. Inpatient unit monitoring form II.

Patient Name: *Matalie*

Monitoring Target #2: *Receptivity to alternate living situations*

Day: *Monday*

Date: *11-20*   Frequency: *///*

Activity/Verbalization

Time: *10:00 a*   *1:1 session—5 comments*

11:30 a   *called re: services adjacent to halfway house*

1:00 p   *overheard talking about possible placement*

Day: *Tuesday*

Date: *11-21*   Frequency: *///*

Activity/Verbalization

Time: *7:00 a*   *"Today I visit where I may go to live"*

8:15 a   *Community mtg: offered that she will*
be leaving soon for "someplace better"

2:00 p   *Asked SW assistant for help with SFI in case*
she is accepted into group home

Day: *Wednesday*

Date: *11-22*   Frequency: *////*

Activity/Verbalization

Time: *7:00 a*   *Asked to call group home re: application decision*

7:35 a   *excited to call group home re: application decision*

11:00 a   *told therapist "really wants" to go to group home*

2:40 p   *listed advantages to group vs. living alone*

Figure 7.5. (Continued.)

Attendance	Understanding (as indicated by responses to questions	
11–19	*3*	0 = none
11–23	*4*	1 = slight
		2 = some
11–24	*4*	3 = good
		4 = excellent
11–28	*3*	
11–30	*4*	

Figure 7.6. Medication group attendance and understanding.

TERMINATION AND FOLLOW-UP

There are four main tasks of termination and follow-up planning: to ensure that the patient has supportive informal and formal social support systems available after treatment, to anticipate potential problems, to prepare plans for handling future stress, and to plan for particular follow-up contacts with the practitioner. Accomplishing these tasks with involuntary mental health clients may be extremely difficult. The reality is that in many urban and rural settings, limited formal and informal support systems may exist for these clients. Knowledge of the primary agencies serving such clients is an important prerequisite to planning termination and follow-up.

Termination ideally represents the mutually agreed-upon end of formal interventive contact. With involuntary clients, premature termination or intervention abortion happens frequently in inpatient and in outpatient settings. Clients may leave a hospital or not attend required community treatment sessions. The pressure on inpatient settings to discharge patients quickly also may result in termination of contact before the practitioner judges the client prepared to function with the outside environment. Knowledge of agency appeal processes can be useful in advocating for clients and avoiding premature termination. Planning for termination should begin at admission, when an estimated length of stay or treatment is determined. At this time the practitioner should begin developing contingency or alternative termination and follow-up plans, in addition to an optimal plan. In one of the author's cases, a 29-year-old man admitted on a 14-day involuntary hold had an opportunity for placement in a small group home rather than a large shelter. His behavior and medication compliance, however, were not stable enough at the end of his hospitalization to meet admission criteria for the group home. As services in the shelter were less available and generally of lesser quality, more time and effort were required arranging follow-up services and care.

Medication compliance after termination is a complex issue with mentally disordered individuals. While psychotropic medication cannot be forced on individuals once released to the community, some intensive case management efforts suggest that encouragement and assistance with side effects can increase compliance significantly (Rubin, 1992).

The practitioner's role may be necessarily quite active in arranging termination and follow-up with mentally disordered clients. Creating a clear, supportive bridge for the client between the practitioner-agency (or hospital) and new worker, agency setting, etc., can occur if there is time to have the client meet the new worker and visit the agency well before termination. Such meetings can reduce confusion about what is to follow, can mitigate feelings of rejection or abandonment by the current practitioner, and may positively influence the client's view about the new worker and setting. Upon return to the familiar working relationship, these meetings can provide the opportunity for the client to ask questions and may save time moving to the new agency. They may have both specific and general positive effects on the effectiveness of termination and follow-up.

Follow-up meetings with clients following involuntary mental health care are, in reality, voluntary, as few sanctions (other than arrest when warranted by specific behavior) are available to enforce adherence to follow-up plans. Therefore, the purpose and expected consequences of follow-up meetings must be extremely clear to the client prior to termination. Even when this has been accomplished, mentally disordered clients are likely to forget scheduled meetings and appointments, particularly during periods when symptoms increase. A written schedule of follow-up appointments, including an identified purpose for the meeting (e.g., check on my application to group home; see if my medication is working right; see if I can get more counseling) is a useful idea. These can be made in wallet or wall size, or both. Mailed reminders of meetings (again, with purpose stated), telephone calls when possible, and contact through staff in residential or other agencies the client regularly visits, may be not only courteous, but necessary to ensure the client is reminded and makes a conscious decision to attend or not attend.

Case Study

Matalie and the worker reviewed the progress Matalie had made since coming in to the hospital. The data from the unit chart and the infor-

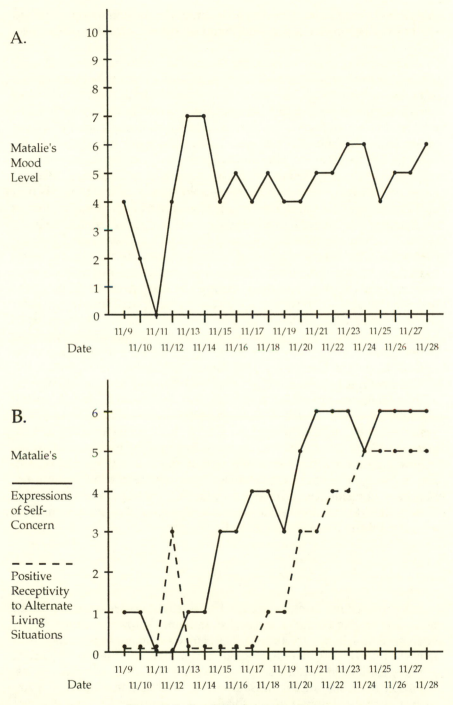

Figure 7.7. Pending client permission.

mation the practitioner collected were graphed and Matalie was able to see the change in her mood and behavior over the past 3 weeks (See Figure 7.7ab).

Matalie asked if she could stay in the hospital until her feet were healed, and the worker explained that it was not possible due to other inpatients who needed 24-hour care. This moved the session to exploring Matalie's concerns and fears about being discharged from the hospital and then to discussing her temporary placement in the nearby group home. Matalie was pleased she would receive rehabilitation services at the hospital, despite the fact that her case would be officially transferred to the rehabilitation department. A meeting was scheduled for Matalie and the practitioner to meet with the worker from this unit and discuss Matalie's problems and goals for the future, i.e., staying on medication, placement in group home in her old neighborhood near the shelter. Matalie was not happy about the transfer, "Just after I got you trained up to be normal," and the worker admitted that she had enjoyed working with Matalie. They planned a schedule of monthly follow-up meetings for the next 3 months during the period while Matalie was receiving rehabilitation services. There were two purposes identified for these meetings: to help Matalie keep focused on goals she developed while on the unit and to proceed with plans to move to the group home in her old neighborhood (e.g., initiating other services in area, exploring options for ongoing mental health care).

The meetings were helpful in keeping Matalie focused on the future; when Matalie stopped taking her medication one week before an appointment, the worker was able to successfully intervene to re-enlist her adherence and avoid acute symptom recurrence. At the end of her medical rehabilitation, Matalie was able to move into the group home in the neighborhood near the shelter and was involved in a twice-weekly women's group program as well as twice-monthly medication monitoring. Maintaining residence in the group home was contingent on medication adherence; Matalie seemed to understand this and indicated that she would continue to take the medication.

CONCLUSION

Practice with involuntary mental health clients represents one of the most challenging clinical and service domains. While the progress and goals accomplished with some of these clients who are persistently mentally disordered may be of a different magnitude, we believe they are as worthwhile and important to improving life quality as the goals of less disordered populations. Because it was not possible to discuss all forms of service to this population we focused our examples on inpatient psychiatric and, to a lesser extent, outpatient care. Although our case examples illustrate only a small amount of the complexity involved in working with these clients, our approach to practice has been on methods and procedures that possess empirical validation. In cases where this is lacking, we have relied on procedures we and others have found clinically useful in work with our clients. Both present pictures of real practice with acknowledgedly ideal intent, meant to illustrate the possibilities in practice, not minimize attention to the complexity of our client's problems.

We began this chapter by defining the parameters of involuntary mental health treatment and proceeded through each phase of practice, identifying and illustrating potential problems related to work with this population. We describe strategies for strengthening engagement, assessment, intervention, and follow-up, both directly and through our case example. When Matalie read this chapter she made several comments and changed some dialogue (!) from what had been in the author-written case records. Among the numerous marginalia she wrote on the chapter itself, she noted two things that summarize our approach to this work: (During the good times) she felt like a therapist, with the author, in making things change, and that she remembered how good it felt when she saw, *with her own eyes*, how she had changed, "from watching the lines move across those papers" (the graphs).

NOTE

1. The extrapyramidal system, one of two major systems in the cerebral cortex that control the motor neurons of the spinal cord and the medulla, is responsible for postures, general body movements, and muscles close to the center of the body.

References

Abadinsky, H. (1987). *Probation & parole: Theory and practice* (3rd ed.). Englewood Cliffs, NJ: Prentice-Hall.

Achenbach, T. M., & Edelbrock, C. (1983). *Manual for the Child Behavior Checklist and Revised Child Behavior Profile*. Burlington: University of Vermont Press.

Alcabes, A., & Jones, J. A. (1985). Structured determinants of clienthood. *Social Work, 30,* 49–53.

American Psychiatric Association. (1987). *Diagnostic and statistical manual of mental disorders* (rev. 3rd ed.). Washington, DC: Author.

Andrews, D. A., Zinger, I., Hoge, R. D., Bonta, J., Gendreau, P., & Cullen, F. T. (1990). Does correctional treatment work? A clinically relevant and psychologically informed meta-analysis. *Criminology, 28,* 369–404.

Asher, R. (1972). *Richard Asher talking sense*. London: University Park Press.

Bandura, A. (1986). *Social foundations of thought and action: A social cognitive theory*. Englewood Cliffs, NJ: Prentice-Hall.

Beck, A. T., Ward, C., Mendelson, M., Mock, J., & Erbaugh, J. (1961). An inventory for measuring depression. *Archives of General Psychiatry, 4,* 561–571.

Behavioral Sciences Institute. (1990). *Homebuilders evaluation summary*. Federal Way, WA: Author.

Bentley, K. J. (1993). The right of psychiatric patients to refuse medication: Where should social workers stand? *Social Work, 38,* 101–106.

Berlin, S. B. (1978). *An investigation of the effects of cognitive behavior modification treatments on problems of inappropriate self criticism among women*. Unpublished doctoral dissertation, University of Washington, Seattle.

Berlin, S. B. (1985). Maintaining reduced levels of self-criticism through relapse prevention treatment. *Social Work Research & Abstracts, 21,* 21–33.

Berlin, S. B., & Marsh, J. C. (1993). *Informing practice decisions*. New York: Macmillan.

Beutler, L. E. (1979). Toward specific psychological therapies for specific conditions. *Journal of Consulting and Clinical Psychology, 47,* 882–897.

Beutler, L. E., & Clarkin, J. F. (1990). *Systematic treatment selection: Toward targeted therapeutic interventions*. New York: Brunner/Mazel.

Beutler, L. E., Mahoney, M. J., Norcross, J. C., Prochaska, J. O., Sollod, R. M., & Robertson, M. (1987). Training integrative/eclectic psychotherapists II. *Journal of Integrative and Eclectic Psychotherapy, 6,* 296–332.

Blackburn, R. (1980). *Still not working? A look at recent outcomes in offender rehabilitation*. Paper presented at the Scottish Branch of the British Psychological Society Conference on Deviance, University of Stirling, Scotland, February.

Bloom, M., & Fischer, J. (1982). *Evaluating practice: Guidelines for the accountable professional*. Englewood Cliffs, NJ: Prentice-Hall.

Blythe, B. J. (1983). Social support networks in health care and health promotion. In J. K. Whittaker & J. Garbarino (Eds.), *Social support networks: Informal helping in the human services* (pp. 107–131). Hawthorne, NY: Aldine de Gruyter.

Blythe, B. J., Jiordano, M. J., & Kelly, S. A. (1991). Family preservation with substance abusing families: Help that works. *Child, Youth, and Family Services Quarterly, 14*(3), 12–13.

Blythe, B. J., & Tripodi, T. (1989). *Measurement in direct social work practice*. Newbury Park, CA: Sage.

Blythe, B. J., Tripodi, T., & Briar, S. (in press). *Direct practice research in human service agencies*. New York: Columbia University Press.

Breggin, P. R. (1991). *Toxic psychiatry*. New York: St. Martin's Press.

Brehm, S. S., & Smith, T. W. (1986). Social psychological approaches to psychotherapy and behavior change. In S. L. Garfield & Bergin (Eds.), *Handbook of psychotherapy and behavior change* (3rd ed., pp. 69–115). New York: Wiley.

Bronson, D. E., & Blythe, B. J. (1987). Computer support for single-case evaluation of practice. *Social Work Research & Abstracts, 23*, 10–14.

Bureau of Justice Statistics (1989). *Prisoners in 1988*. Washington, DC: United States Government Printing Office.

Bush, J. M. (1991). Counseling the criminal client. *Counselor, 9*, 12–16.

Camp, B. W., & Bash, M. A. S. (1981). *Think aloud: Increasing social and cognitive skills—A problem solving program for children*. Champaign, IL: Research Press.

Cartledge, G., & Milburn, J. F. (1986). *Teaching social skills to children: Innovative approaches* (2nd ed.). New York: Pergamon.

Cheers, B. (1987). The social support network map as an educational tool. *Australian Social Work, 40*, 18–24.

Cingolani, J. (1984). Social conflict perspective on work with involuntary clients. *Social Work, 29*, 442–446.

Compton, B. R., & Galaway, B. (1989). *Social work processes* (4th ed.). Belmont, CA: Wadsworth.

Corcoran, K., & Fischer, J. (1987). *Measures for clinical practice: A sourcebook*. New York: Free Press.

Cox, J. F., Landsberg, G., & Paravati, P. M. (1989). The essential components of a crisis intervention program for local jails: The New York local forensic suicide prevention crisis service model. *Psychiatric Quarterly, 60*, 103–117.

Cox, J. F., & Morchauser, P. (1993). Community forensic initiatives in New York State. *Innovations in Research in Clinical Service, Community Support, and Rehabilitation, 2*, 29–38.

Cox, V. C., Paulus, P. B., & McCain, G. (1984). Prison crowding research. *American Psychologist, 39*, 1148–1160.

Coyne, J. C. (1989). Thinking post-cognitively about depression. In A. Freeman, H. Arkowitz, L. E. Beutler, & C. Simon (Eds.), *Comprehensive handbook of cognitive therapy*. New York: Plenum.

Cromwell, P. F., Jr., Killinger, G. C., Kerper, H. B., & Walker, C. (1985). *Probation and parole in the criminal justice system*. St. Paul, MN: West.

Dell'Apa, F., Adams, W. T., Jorgenson, J. D., & Sigardson, H. R. (1976). Advocacy, brokerage, community: The ABC's of probation and parole. *Federal Probation, 30,* 37–44.

DeVoge, J. T., & Beck, S. (1978). The therapist-client relationship in behavior therapy. *Progress in Behavior Modification, 6,* 203–248.

Diorio, W. D. (1992). Parental perceptions of the authority of public child welfare caseworkers. *Families in Society, 73,* 222–235.

Dixon, S. L. (1987). *Working with people in crisis* (2nd ed.). Columbus, OH: Merrill.

Edelman, E., & Goldstein, A. P. (1984). Prescriptive relationship levels for juvenile delinquents in a psychotherapy analog. *Aggressive Behavior, 10,* 269–298.

Edelson, J. L. (1985). Rapid assessment instruments for evaluating practice with children and youth. *Journal of Social Service Research, 8,* 17–32.

Eisikovitz, Z. C. & Edleson, J. D. (1989). Intervening with men who batter: A critical review of the literature. *Social Service Review, 63,* 384–414.

Epstein, L. (1985). *Talking and listening: A guide to the helping interview.* St. Louis: Times Mirror/Mosby.

Eysenck, H. J., & Gudjonsson, G. H. (1989). *The causes and cures of criminality.* New York: Plenum.

Fabiano, E. A., Porporino, F. J., & Robinson, D. (1991). Canada's cognitive skills program corrects offenders' faulty thinking. *Corrections Today, 53,* 102–108.

Federal Bureau of Investigation. (1992). *Crime in the United States 1991.* Washington, DC: United States Department of Justice.

Feldman, R. A., Caplinger, T. E., & Wodarski, J. S. (1983). *The St. Louis conundrum: The effective treatment of antisocial youths.* Englewood Cliffs, NJ: Prentice-Hall.

Fischer, J. (1973). Is casework effective? A review. *Social Work, 19,* 19–32.

Fischer, J. (1978). *Effective casework practice: An eclectic approach.* New York: McGraw–Hill.

Flanagan, T. J., & Jamieson, K. M. (1988). *Sourcebook of criminal justice statistics.* Washington, DC: Bureau of Justice Statistics, U. S. Department of Justice.

Flanagan, T. J., & Maguire, K. (1992). *Sourcebook of criminal justice statistics.* Washington, DC: Bureau of Justice Statistics, U. S. Department of Justice.

Fleischman, M. J., Horne, A. M., & Arthur, J. L. (1983). *Troubled families: A treatment program.* Champaign, IL: Research Press.

Folstein, M. F., & Folstein, S. E. (1975). Mini Mental State. A practical method for grading the cognitive state of patients for the clinician. *Journal of Psychiatry Research, 12,* 189–198.

Forehand, R., & McMahon, R. J. (1981). *Helping the noncompliant child: A clinician's guide to parent training.* New York: Guilford.

Frank, L. R. (1978). *The history of shock treatment.* San Francisco: Frank.

Gambrill, E. D. (1977). *Behavior modification: Handbook of assessment, intervention, and evaluation.* San Francisco: Jossey-Bass.

Gambrill, E. D. (1983). *Casework: A competency-based approach.* Englewood Cliffs, NJ:Prentice-Hall.

Gameson, W. A. (1968). *Power and discontent.* Homewood, IL: Dorsey Press.

Garrett, C. J. (1984, November). Efficacy of treatment for adjudicated delinquents: Meta-analysis. Paper presented at the annual meeting of the American Society of Criminology, Cincinnati, OH.

Garrett, C. J. (1985). Effects of residential treatment for adjudicated delinquents: A meta-analysis. *Journal of Research and Crime and Delinquency, 22,* 287–308.

Garvin, C. D., & Seabury, B. A. (1984). *Interpersonal practice in social work: Processes and procedures.* Englewood Cliffs, NJ: Prentice-Hall.

Gendreau, P., & Andrews, D. A. (1990). Tertiary prevention: What the meta-analysis of the offender treatment literature tells us about "what works." *Canadian Journal of Criminology, 32,* 173–184.

Gitterman, A. (Ed.) (1991). *Handbook of social work practice with vulnerable populations.* New York: Columbia University Press.

Golden, C. J., Hammake, T. A., & Purisch, A. D. (1980). *The Luria Nebraska Neuropsychological Battery.* Los Angeles: Western Psychological Services.

Goldstein, A. P., Heller, K., & Sechrest, L. B. (1966). *Psychotherapy and the psychology of behavior change.* New York: Wiley.

Goldstein, A. P., & Higginbotham, H. N. (1991). Relationship-enhancement methods. In F. H. Kanfer & A. P. Goldstein (Eds.), *Helping people change: A textbook of methods* (4th ed.). New York: Pergamon.

Goldstein, A. P., Keller, H., & Erné, D. (1985). *Changing the abusive parent.* Champaign, IL: Research Press.

Gottfredson, M. R., & Hirschi, T. (1990). *A general theory of crime.* Stanford, CA: Stanford University Press.

Gottlieb, B. H. (Ed.). (1981). *Social networks and social support.* Beverly Hills, CA: Sage.

Gottschalk, R., Davidson, W. S., Gensheimer, L. K., II, & Mayer, J. P. (1987). Community based interventions. In H. C. Quay (Ed.), *Handbook of juvenile delinquency* (pp. 266–289). New York: Wiley.

Grier, P. E. (1988). Cognitive problem solving skills in antisocial rapists. *Criminal Justice and Behavior, 15,* 501–504.

Grodd, B., & Simon, B. (1991). Imprisonment. In A. Gitterman (Ed.), *Handbook of social work practice with vulnerable populations* (pp. 677–709). New York: Columbia University Press.

Grotevant, H. D., & Carlson, C. I. (1989). *Family assessment: A guide to methods and measures.* New York: Guilford.

Handler, E. (1975). Social work and correction: Comments on an uneasy partnership. *Criminology, 13,* 240–254.

Hare, R. D. (1991). *The Hare Psychopathy Checklist-Revised.* Toronto: Multi-Health Systems.

Hare, R. D., Hart, S. D., & Harpur, T. J. (1991). Psychopathy and the DSM-IV criteria for antisocial personality disorder. *Journal of Abnormal Psychology, 100,* 39–398.

Hartman, A. (1978). Diagrammatic assessment of family relationships. *Social Casework, 59,* 465–476.

Hartman, A. (1979). *Finding families: An ecological approach to family assessment in adoption.* Beverly Hills, CA: Sage.

Hartman, A. (1982). *Post adoptive services to children and families.* Paper presented at the NASW Clinical Practice Conference, Washington, DC.

Hathaway, S. R., & McKinley, J. C. (1989). *MMPI-2: Minnesota Multiphasic Per-*

sonality Inventory-2: Manual for administration and scoring. Minneapolis: University of Minnesota Press.

Hawkins, R. P., Almeida, M. C., Fabry, B., & Reitz, A. L. (1992). A scale to measure restrictiveness of living environments for troubled children and youths. *Hospital and Community Psychiatry, 43*, 54–58.

Heitler, J. B. (1973). Preparation of lower-class patients for expressive group psychotherapy. *Journal of Consulting and Clinical Psychology, 41*, 251–260.

Heitler, J. B. (1976). Preparatory techniques in initiating expressive psychotherapy with lower class, unsophisticated clients. *Psychological Bulletin, 83*, 339–352.

Henggeler, S. W. (1991). *Treating conduct problems in children and adolescents: An overview of the multisystemic approach with guidelines for intervention design and implementation*. Columbia: South Carolina Department of Mental Health.

Henggeler, S. W., Melton, G. B., & Smith, L. A. (1992). Family preservation using multisystemic therapy: An effective alternative to incarcerating serious juvenile offenders. *Journal of Consulting and Clinical Psychology, 60*, 953–961.

Hepworth, D. H., & Larsen, J. A. (1993). *Direct social work practice: Theory and skills* (4th ed.). Belmont, CA: Wadsworth.

Hill, R. (1972). *The strengths of black families*. New York: Emerson-Hall.

Hodges, V. G., & Blythe, B. J. (1992). Improvising service delivery to high-risk families: Home-based practice. *Families in Society, 73*, 259–265.

Hogarty, G. E. (1993). Prevention of relapse in chronic schizophrenic patients. *Journal of Clinical Psychiatry, 54* (suppl.), 18–23.

Holder, W. M., & Corey, M. (1986). *Child protective services risk management: A decision making handbook*. Charlotte, NC: Action for Child Protection.

Hollon, S. D., Shelton, R. C., & Loosen, P. T. (1991). Cognitive therapy and pharmacotherapy for depression. *Journal of Consulting and Clinical Psychology, 59*, 88–99.

Hosch, D. (1973). *Use of the contract approach in public social services*. Los Angeles: Regional Research Institute in Child Welfare, University of Southern CA.

Hudson, W. W. (1982). *The Clinical Measurement Package: A field manual*. Homewood, IL: Dorsey Press.

Hudson, W. W., Nurius, P., & Reisman, S. (1988). Computerized assessment instruments: Their promise and problems. *Computers in Human Services, 3*, 51–70.

Husband, S. D., & Platt, J. J. (1993). The cognitive skills component in substance abuse treatment in correctional settings: A brief review. *Journal of Drug Issues, 23*, 31–42.

Hutchinson, E. D. (1987). Use of authority in direct social work practice with mandated clients. *Social Service Review, 61*, 581–598.

Hynd, G. W., & Semrud-Clikeman, M. (1990). Neuropsychological assessment. In A. S. Kaufman (Ed.), *Assessing adult and adolescent intelligence* (pp. 638–695). Boston: Allyn and Bacon.

Ingram, J. C., Dixon, D. N., & Glover, J. A. (1983). Problem-solving as a function of race and incarceration. *Journal of Social Psychology, 120*, 83–90.

Intagliata, J. (1978). Increasing the interpersonal problem-solving skills of an alcoholic population. *Journal of Consulting and Clinical Psychology, 46*, 489–498.

Ivanoff, A., Blythe, B. J., & Briar, S. B. (1987). The empirical clinical practice debate. *Social Casework, 68,* 290–298.

Ivanoff, A., Robinson, E. A. R., & Blythe, B. J. (1987). Empirical clinical practice from a feminist perspective. *Social Work, 32,* 417–423.

Ivanoff, A., & Jang, S. J. (1991). The role of hopelessness and social desirability in predicting suicidal behavior: A study of prison inmates. *Journal of Consulting and Clinical Psychology, 59,* 394–399.

Ivanoff, A., Jang, S. J., Smyth, N. J., & Linehan, M. M. (in press). Fewer reasons for living when you're thinking about killing yourself: The Brief Reasons for Living Inventory. *Psychopathology and Behavioral Assessment.*

Ivanoff, A., Smyth, N. J., Grochowski, S., Jang, S. J., & Klein, K. (1992). Problem solving and suicidality among prison inmates: Another look at state versus trait. *Journal of Consulting and Clinical Psychology, 60,* 970–973.

Izzo, R. L., & Ross, R. R. (1990). Meta-analysis of rehabilitation programs for juvenile delinquents: A brief report. *Criminal Justice and Behavior, 17,* 134–142.

Jacobsen, N. S., Follette, W. C., & Revenstorf, D. (1984). Psychotherapy outcome research: Methods for reporting variability and evaluating clinical significance. *Behavior Therapy, 15,* 336–352.

Jayaratne, S. (1978). Analytic procedures for single-subject designs. *Social Work Research & Abstracts, 14*(3), 30–40.

Johnson, A. B. (1990). *Out of Bedlam: The truth about deinstitutionalization.* New York: Basic Books.

Johnson, D. W. (1980). Attitude modification methods. In F. H. Kanfer & A. P. Goldstein (Eds.), *Helping people change* (2nd ed., pp. 58–97). Elmsford, NY: Pergamon.

Kadushin, A. (1983). *The social work interview* (2nd ed.). New York: Columbia University Press.

Kadushin, A., & Martin, J. A. (1988). *Child welfare services.* (4th ed.). New York: Macmillan.

Kalat, J. W. (1992). *Biological psychology* (4th ed.). Belmont, CA: Wadsworth Publishing Company.

Kane, J. M. (1988). Clozapine in treatment of resistant schizophrenia. *Archives of General Psychiatry, 45,* 789–796.

Kinney, J., Haapala, D., & Booth, C. (1991). *Keeping families together: The Homebuilders model.* Hawthorne, NY: Aldine de Gruyter.

Kirk, S. A., & Kutchins, H. (1992). *The selling of DSM: The rhetoric of science in psychiatry.* Hawthorne, NY: Aldine de Gruyter.

Koehler, R. J., & Lindner, C. (1992). Alternative incarceration: An inevitable response to institutional overcrowding. *Federal Probation, 56,* 12–18.

Kramer, J. J., & Conoley, J. C. (Eds.) (1992). *The eleventh mental measurements yearbook.* Lincoln: The University of Nebraska Press.

Larson, C. Y. (1983). *Persuasion: Reception and responsibility* (3rd ed.). Belmont, CA: Wadsworth.

Lee, M., & Prentice, N. M. (1988). Interrelations of empathy, cognition, and moral reasoning with dimensions of juvenile delinquency. *Journal of Abnormal Psychology, 16,* 127–139.

Leukefeld, C. G., & Tims, F. M. (1992). *National Institute on Drug Abuse: Treatment in prisons and jails (118)*. Rockville, MD: U. S. Department of Health and Human Services.

Levitt, J., & Reid, W. R. (1981). Rapid assessment instruments for practice. *Social Work Research and Abstracts, 17,* 13–19.

Levy, R. L. (1977). Relationship of an overt commitment to task compliance in behavior therapy. *Journal of Behavior Therapy and Experimental Psychiatry, 8,* 25–29.

Lindquist, C. A., Smusz, T. D., & Doerner, W. (1985). Causes and conformity: An application of control theory to adult misdemeanant probationers. *International Journal of Offender Therapy and Comparative Criminology, 29,* 1–14.

Lindsay, K. P., & Paul, G. L. (1989). Involuntary commitments to public mental institutions: Issues involving the overrepresentation of blacks and assessment of relevant functioning. *Psychological Bulletin, 106,* 171–183.

Linehan, M. M., & Neilsen, S. L. (1981). Assessment of suicide ideation and parasuicide: Hopelessness and social desirability. *Journal of Consulting and Clinical Psychology, 49,* 773–775.

Lipton, D., Martinson, R., & Wilks, J. (1975). *The effectiveness of correctional treatment: A survey of treatment evaluation studies.* New York: Praeger.

Lorion, R. P. (1974). Patient and therapist variables in the treatment of low-income patients. *Psychological Bulletin, 81,* 344–354.

Lorion, R. P., & Felner, R. P. (1986). Research on psychotherapy with the disadvantaged. In S. L. Garfield & A. E. Bergin (Eds.), *Handbook of psychotherapy and behavior change* (3rd ed.). New York: Wiley.

Lorion, R. P., & Parron, D. L. (1985). Countering the countertransference: A strategy for treating the untreatable. In P. Pederson (Ed.), *Handbook in cross-cultural counseling and therapy* (pp. 79–86). New York: Greenwood Press.

Luborsky, L. (1984). *Principles of psychoanalytic psychotherapy.* New York: Basic Books.

Lundman, R. J. (1984). *Prevention and control of juvenile delinquency.* Oxford: Oxford University Press.

Magazino, C. J. (1983). Services to children and families at risk of separation. In B. G. McGowan & W. Meezan (Eds.), *Child welfare: Current dilemmas, future directions.* Itasca, IL: F. E. Peacock.

Magura, S., & Moses, B. S. (1986). *Outcome measures for child welfare services: Theory and application.* Washington, DC: Child Welfare League of America.

Mangrum, C. T. (1976). Corrections' tarnished halo. *Federal Probation, 40,* 9–14.

Marlatt, G. A., & Gordon, J. R. (1985). *Relapse prevention.* New York: Guilford.

Martin, S. E., Sechrest, L. B., & Redner, R. (1981). *New directions in the rehabilitation of criminal offenders.* Washington, DC: National Academy Press.

Martinez, L. (1989). *The Family Assessment Factor Worksheet.* Springfield, IL: Illinois Department of Children and Family Services.

Martinson, R. (1974). What works? Questions and answers about prison reform. *Public Interest, 35,* 22–54.

Martinson, R., & Wilks, J. (1977). Save parole probation. *Federal Probation, 41*(3), 23–27.

Mattaini, M. A. (1993). *More than a thousand words: Graphics for clinical practice.* Washington, DC: NASW Press.

McCrady, B. S. (1985). Alcoholism. In D. H. Barlow (Ed.), *Clinical handbook of psychological disorders* (pp. 245–298). New York: Guilford.

McGoldrick, M. (1985). *Genograms in family assessment.* New York: Norton.

McGuire, J., & Priestly, P. (1985). *Offending behaviour: Skills and stratagems for going straight.* London: Batsford, Academic & Educational.

McMahon, P. M. (1987). Shifts in intervention procedures: A problem in evaluating human service interventions. *Social Work Research & Abstracts, 23,* 13–16.

Megargee, E. I. (1993). Aggression and violence. In P. B. Sutker & H. E. Adams (Eds.), *Handbook of psychopathology* (pp. 617–644). New York: Plenum.

Menninger, K. A. (1935). Psychology of a certain type of malingering. *Archives of Neurology and Psychiatry, 33,* 507–515.

Merriam Webster, Inc. (1990) *Webster's ninth new collegiate dictionary.* Springfield, MA: Author.

Miller, J. S., Williams, K. M., English, D. J., & Olmstead, J. (1987). *Risk assessment in child protection: A review of the literature.* Washington, D. C.: American Public Welfare Association.

Moncher, F. J., & Prinz, R. J. (1991). Treatment fidelity in outcome studies. *Clinical Psychology Review, 11,* 247–266.

Motto, J. A. (1976). Suicide prevention for high risk persons who refuse treatment. *Suicide and Life Threatening Behavior, 6,* 223–230.

Munjack, D., & Oziel, J. L. (1978). Resistance in the behavioral treatment of sexual dysfunctions. *Journal of Sex and Marital Therapy, 42,* 122–138.

Murdach, A. D. (1980). Bargaining and persuasion with non-voluntary clients. *Social Work, 25,* 458–461.

Murray, H. A. (1971). *The Thematic Apperception Test manual.* Boston, MA: Harvard University Press.

National Commission on Child Welfare and Family Preservation (1991). *A commitment to change.* Washington, DC: American Public Welfare Association.

Nelsen, J. C. (1983). *Family treatment: An integrative approach.* Englewood Cliffs, NJ: Prentice-Hall.

Netherland, W. (1987). Corrections system: Adult. In A. Minahan (Ed.), *Encyclopedia of Social Work: Vol. 1* (18th ed., pp. 351–360). Silver Spring, MD: NASW Press.

Nezu, A. M., & Nezu, C. M. (Eds.). (1989). *Clinical decision making in behavior therapy: A problem solving perspective.* Champaign, IL: Research Press.

Nietzel, M. T. (1979). *Crime and its modification: A social learning perspective.* New York: Pergamon.

Nurius, P. S., & Hudson, W. W. (1988). Computer based practice: Future dream or current technology. *Social Work, 33,* 357–362.

Nurnberger, J. I., Gershon, E. S. (1988). Genetic factors and genetic counseling for families with affective disorders. In E. D. Hibbs (Ed.), *Children and families: Studies in prevention and intervention* (pp. 417–442). Madison, CT: International Universities Press.

Pallone, N. J., & Hennessy, J. J. (1992). *Criminal behavior: A process psychology analysis.* New Brunswick, NJ: Transaction.

Patterson, G. R. (1977). *Living with children* (rev. ed.). Champaign, IL: Research Press.

Pecora, P. J., Whittaker, J. K., & Maluccio, A. N. (1992). *The child welfare challenge: Policy, practice, and research*. Hawthorne, NY: Aldine de Gruyter.

Pepper, S. C. (1942). *World hypotheses*. Berkeley: University of California Press.

Peterson, L., Homer, A. L., & Wonderlich, S. A. (1982). The integrity of independent variables in behavior analysis. *Journal of Applied Behavior Analysis, 15*, 477–492.

Platt, J. J., Scura, W., & Hannon, J. (1973). Problem solving thinking of incarcerated heroin addicts. *Journal of Community Psychology, 1*, 278–281.

Pressley Ridge Schools. (1993). PRYDE log of early events. Pittsburgh, PA: author.

Quay, H. C., & Parsons, L. (1970). *The differential behavioral classification of the juvenile offender*. Washington, DC: Bureau of Prisons, U. S. Department of Justice.

Rachin, R. L., Inciardi, J., & Martin, S. (Ed.). (1993). *Journal of Drug Issues [Special Issue], 23*.

Ransohoff, P., Zachary, R. A., Gaynor, J., & Hargreaves, W. A. (1982). Measuring restrictiveness of psychiatric care. *Hospital and Community Psychiatry, 33*, 361–366.

Raynor, P. (1978). Compulsory persuasion: A problem for correctional social work. *British Journal of Social Work, 8*, 411–424.

Reid, W. J. (1978). *The task centered system*. New York: Columbia University Press.

Reid, W. J., & Davis, I. P. (1987). Qualitative research methods in single-case research. In N. Gottlieb, H. A. Ishisaka, J. Kopp, C. A. Richey, & E. R. Tolson (Eds.), *Perspectives in direct practice evaluation* (pp. 56–74). Seattle: University of Washington Center for Social Welfare Research.

Reid, W. J., & Hanrahan, P. (1982). Recent evaluations of social work: Grounds for optimism. *Social Work, 27*, 328–340.

Reitan, R. M., & Wolfson, D. (1985). *The Halstead-Reitan Neuropsychological Test Battery: Theory and clinical interpretation*. Tuscon, AZ: Neuropsychology Press.

Risley, T. R. (1970). Behavior modification: An experimental- therapeutic endeavor. In L. A. Hamerlynck, P. O. Davidson, & L. E. Acker (Eds.), *Behavior modification and ideal mental health services*. Calgary, Alberta: University of Calgary Press.

Rogers, R. (1987). The assessment of malingering within a forensic context. In D. N. Weisstaub (Ed.), *Law and psychiatry: International perspectives: Vol. 3* (pp. 216–219). New York: Plenum.

Rogers, R. (Ed.) (1988). *Clinical assessment of malingering and deception*. New York: Guilford.

Romig, D. A. (1978). *Justice for our children*. Lexington, MA: Heath.

Rooney, R. H. (1988). Socialization strategies for involuntary clients. *Social Casework, 69*, 131–140.

Rooney, R. H. (1992). *Strategies for work with involuntary clients*. New York: Columbia University Press.

Rosenson, M. K. (1993). Social work and the right of psychiatric patients to refuse medication: A family advocate's response. *Social Work, 38*, 107–112.

Ross, R. R., & Fabiano, E. A. (1985). *Time to think: A cognitive model of delinquency prevention and offender rehabilitation*. Johnson City, NJ: Institute of Social Sciences and Arts.

Rubin, A. (1985). Practice effectiveness: More grounds for optimism. *Social Work,* *30,* 474–477.

Rubin, A. (1992). Is case management effective for people with serious mental illness? A research review. *Health and Social Work, 17,* 138–150.

Salend, S. J. (1984). Therapy outcome research: Threats to treatment integrity. *Behavior Modification, 8,* 211–222.

Seabury, B. A. (1976). The contract: Uses, abuses and limitations. *Social Work, 21,* 16–21.

Sechrest L., & Redner, R. (1979) Strength and integrity in treatment in evaluation studies, (pp. 19–62). *Evaluation Reports Annual.* Washington, DC: National Criminal Justice Reference Service.

Sechrest, L., White, S. O., & Brown, E. D. (1979). *The rehabilitation of criminal offenders: Problems and prospects.* Washington, DC: Naval Academy of Sciences.

Seligman, L. (1990). *Selecting effective treatments.* San Francisco: Jossey-Bass.

Siegel, D. H. (1984). Defining empirically based practice. *Social Work, 29,* 325–331.

Simons, R. L. (1982). Strategies for exercising influence. *Social Work, 27,* 268–274.

Smith, A. B., & Berlin, L. (1988). *Treating the criminal offender* (3rd ed.). New York: Plenum.

Snowden, L. R., & Cheung, F. K. (1990). Use of inpatient mental health services by members of ethnic minority groups. *American Psychologist, 45,* 347–355.

State of New York, Department of Correctional Services, Division of Parole (1993). *The fifth annual SHOCK legislative report.* Albany: State of New York Department of Correctional Services, Division of Parole.

Stein, T. J. (1981). *Social work practice in child welfare.* Englewood Cliffs, NJ: Prentice-Hall.

Stein, T. J., Gambrill, E. A., & Wiltse, K. T. (1978). *Children in foster homes: Achieving continuity of care.* New York: Praeger.

Stein, T. J., Gambrill, E. A., & Wiltse, K. T. (1979). Foster care: The use of contracts. *Public Welfare, 32,* 20–25.

Stone, E. M. (1988). *American psychiatric glossary.* Washington, DC: American Psychiatric Press.

Strachan, A. M. (1986). Family intervention for the rehabilitation of schizophrenia: Toward protection and coping. *Schizophrenia Bulletin, 12,* 678–698.

Strasburger, L. H. (1986). The treatment of antisocial syndromes: The therapist's feelings. In W. H. Reid, D. Dorr, J. I. Walker, & J. W. Bonner (Eds), *Unmasking the psychopath: Antisocial personality and related syndromes* (pp. 191–208). New York: Norton.

Stumphauzer, J. S. (1986). *Helping delinquents change: A treatment manual of social learning approaches.* New York: Haworth.

Sue, S., McKinney, H., Allen, D., & Hall, J. (1974). Delivery of community mental health services to black and white clients. *Journal of Consulting and Clinical Psychology, 42,* 794–801.

Sussman, A., & Cohen, S. (1975). *Reporting child abuse and neglect: Guidelines for legislation.* Cambridge, MA: Ballinger.

Sutker, P. B., Bugg, F., & West, J. A. (1993). Antisocial Personality Disorder. In P. B. Sutker & H. E. Adams (Eds.), *Handbook of psychopathology* (pp. 337–369). New York: Plenum.

Szasz, T. S. (1974). *The myth of mental illness: Foundations of a theory of personal conduct.* New York: Pergamon.

Tartara, T. (1990). *Characteristics of children in substitute and adoptive care: A summary of the VCIS National Child Welfare Data Base.* Washington, DC: American Public Welfare Association.

Teplin, L. A. (1990). The prevalence of severe mental disorder among male urban jail detainees: Comparison with the epidemiologic catchment area program. *American Journal of Public Health, 80,* 663–668.

Teplin, L. A. (1991). *The criminalization hypothesis: Myth, misnomer or management strategy.* In S A. Shah and B. D. Sales (Eds.), *Law and mental health: Major developments and research needs.* Rockville, MD: National Institute of Mental Health.

Thomas, E. J. (1984). *Designing interventions for the helping professions.* Beverly Hills, CA:Sage.

Thomas, E. J., Bastien, J., Stuebe, D. R., Bronson, D. E., & Jaffe, J. (1987). Assessing procedural descriptiveness: Rationale and illustrative study. *Behavioral Assessment, 9,* 43–56.

Thyer, B. A. (1987). *Treating anxiety disorders.* Newbury Park, CA: Sage.

Toch, H. (1992). *Mosaic of despair: Human breakdowns in prison.* Washington, DC: American Psychological Association.

Toch, H., Adams, K., & Grant, J. D. (1989). *Coping: Maladaptation in prisons.* New Brunswick, NJ: Transaction.

Tolman, R. A., & Bhosely, X. X. (1991). The outcome of participation in a shelter-sponsored program for men who batter. In D. D. Knudsen & J. L. Miller (Eds.), *Abused and battered.* Hawthorne, NY: Aldine de Gruyter.

Toseland, R. W., Rossiter, C. M., & Labrecque, M. S. (1989). The effectiveness of three group intervention strategies to support family caregivers. *American Journal of Orthopsychiatry, 59,* 420–429.

Tripodi, T. (1974). *Uses and abuses of social research in social work.* New York: Columbia University Press.

Tripodi, T., Fellin, P., & Meyer, H. J. (1983). *The assessment of social research* (2nd Ed.). Itasca, IL: F. E. Peacock.

Turner, S., & Armstrong, S. (1981). Cross-racial psychotherapy: What the therapists say. *Psychotherapy: Theory, Research, and Practice, 18,* 375–378.

U. S. Department of Justice (1983). *Report to the nation on crime and justice* (NCO-87068). Washington, DC: U. S. Government Printing Office.

Videka-Sherman, L. (1985). *Harriett M. Bartlett Practice Effectiveness Project: Report to NASW board of directors.* Washington, DC: NASW.

Videka-Sherman, L. (1988). Metaanalysis of research on social work practice in mental health. *Social Work, 33,* 325–338.

Von Cleve, E., Jemelka, R., & Trupin, E. (1991). Reliability of psychological test scores for offenders entering a state prison system. *Criminal Justice and Behavior, 18,* 159–165.

Vriend, J., & Dyer, W. (1973). Counseling the reluctant client. *Journal of Counseling Psychology, 20,* 240.

Wasik, B. H., Bryant, D. M., & Lyons, C. M. (1990). *Home visiting: Procedures for helping families.* Newbury Park, CA: Sage.

Weary, G. (1987). Natural bridges: The interface of social and clinical psychology. *Journal of Social and Clinical Psychology, 5,* 160–167.

Wechsler, D. (1974). *Manual for the Wechsler Intelligence Scale for Children-Revised (WISC-R),* San Antonio, TX: Psychological Corporation.

Wechsler, D. (1981). *Manual for the Wechsler Adult Intelligence Scale-Revised (WAIS-R).* San Antonio, TX: Psychological Corporation.

Wedenoja, M., Nurius, P. S., & Tripodi, T. (1988). Enhancing mindfulness in practice prescriptive thinking. *Social Casework, 69,* 427–433.

Weiss, H. B., & Jacobs, F. H. (Eds.). (1988). *Evaluating family programs.* Hawthorne, NY: Aldine de Gruyter.

Wells, K., & Biegel, D. E. (1992). Intensive family preservation services research. Current status and future agenda. *Social Work Research & Abstracts, 28,* 21–27.

Wexler, H. R., Falkin, G. P., & Lipton, D. S. (1990). Outcome evaluation of a prison therapeutic community for substance abuse treatment. *Criminal Justice and Behavior, 17,* 71–92.

Whittaker, J. K., & Garbarino, J. (Eds.). (1983). *Social support networks: Informal helping in the human services.* Hawthorne, NY: Aldine de Gruyter.

Whittaker, J. K., & Tracy, E. M. (1989). *Social treatment: An introduction to interpersonal helping in social work practice* (2nd ed.). Hawthorne, NY: Aldine de Gruyter.

Wilson, P. H. (Ed.). (1992). *Principles and practice of relapse prevention.* New York: Guilford.

Witkin, S. L. (1991). Empirical clinical practice: A critical analysis. *Social Work, 36,* 158–165.

Wolberg, L. R. (1967). *The techniques of psychotherapy* (2nd ed.) New York: Grune & Stratton.

Wolfe, D., Kaufman, K., Aragona, J., & Sandler, J. (1981). *The child management program for abusive parents: Procedures for developing a child abuse intervention program.* Winter Park, FL: Anna.

Wood, K. M. (1978). Casework effectiveness: A new look at the research evidence. *Social Work, 23,* 438–451.

Index